Amanda Coffey
Paul Atkinson

MAKING SENSE OF QUALITATIVE DATA

Complementary
Research
Strategies

SAGE Publications
International Educational and Professional Publisher
Thousand Oaks   London   New Delhi

For information address:

 SAGE Publications, Inc.
2455 Teller Road
Thousand Oaks, California 91320
E-mail: order@sagepub.com

SAGE Publications Ltd.
6 Bonhill Street
London EC2A 4PU
United Kingdom

SAGE Publications India Pvt. Ltd.
M-32 Market
Greater Kailash I
New Delhi 110 048 India

Printed in the United States of America

Library of Congress Cataloging-in-Publication Data

Coffey, Amanda, 1967-
    Making sense of qualitative data: Complimentary research
    strategies / authors, Amanda Coffey, Paul Atkinson.
        p.   cm.
    Includes bibliographical references and index.
    ISBN 0-8039-7052-8 (cloth).—ISBN 0-8039-7053-6 (pbk.)
    1. Social sciences—Research—Methodology.   2. Social sciences—
    Research—Data processing.   I. Atkinson, Paul, 1947- .
    II. Title.
    HM48.C6   1996
    300′.723—dc20   95-41813

This book is printed on acid-free paper.

96   97   98   99   00   01   10   9   8   7   6   5   4   3

Sage Production Editor: Gillian Dickens
Sage Typesetter: Andrea D. Swanson

Contents

Preface and Acknowledgments

The outline proposal for this book was sketched by the pool in the courtyard of a small hotel in New Orleans. We had been discussing the idea of the book for a while and decided to put our ideas on paper while we were attending the American Educational Research Association annual conference. After writing our draft proposal, we bore it across the French Quarter to the carousel bar of the Hotel Monteleone, where Mitch Allen, then at Sage and now at Altamira, encouraged us to develop our tentative ideas into this book. We would like to thank him for his initial enthusiasm and for being so supportive throughout the course of the book's preparation.

The ideas we discuss in the chapters that follow owe much to the discussions and interactions we have had individually and collectively with students. Indeed, we conceived and wrote the book very much with our graduate students in mind. We have "sounded out" many of our ideas in the classes we jointly teach and have benefited from a lively response. The book's progress also has been aided by a considerable amount of support from colleagues and friends. We owe a particular debt of gratitude to Sara Delamont, who gave the manuscript her critical gaze and gave us enormous encouragement. Bob Burgess inquired about our progress with a resilient interest, for which we are grateful. Harry Wolcott and Matthew Miles provided us with useful comments on our initial proposal. Miles's comments on the first draft of the book were invaluable in its final preparation. Despite all that help and encouragement, responsibility for the book and its inevitable flaws rests with us alone.

The book is illustrated with data from a single data set. We are grateful to Sara Delamont and Odette Parry for sharing the data with us. The research from which those data are drawn was supported by the Economic and Social Research Council (ESRC). The interpretations offered in this book, however, are our own: They do not reflect ESRC policy.

A number of people have helped with the production of the book, and we thank them. The data were transcribed originally by Angela Jones. Early drafts of the book chapters were word processed by Sharen Bechares. Jackie Swift word processed most of the first draft, and Karen Chivers word processed some of the final manuscript. We appreciate their gallant efforts with our handwriting and our redrafting. We are, as always, grateful to Julian Pitt and Sara Delamont for companionship and colleagueship.

Amanda Coffey
Paul Atkinson

1

Varieties of Data and Varieties of Analysis

Setting the Scene

It is seven o'clock on a winter evening in Buriton, a British university town. Anne Catterick and Philip Fairlie, both doctoral students in sociology, are sitting despondently over the remains of an Indian take-away meal in the kitchen of the flat Anne shares with Eleanor Fosco (a student teacher) and Sarah Hartright (training to be a clinical psychologist). Anne and Philip have been to a graduate seminar at which a nervous fellow student, Felix Glyde, had presented a sparkling analysis of why the second-generation Vietnamese in the city (the children of refugees of the 1970s) were doing so much better in the education system than were any other ethnic minority in Buriton. This brilliant performance has cast Anne and Philip into gloom.

Eleanor and Sarah have gone out cheerfully to aerobics, and Anne and Philip are slumped in despair. Gradually they confess to each other that although their data collection has gone well—better than they had dared hope—they are now stuck. Anne has several hundred pages of fieldnotes, word processed and proofread, that she can hardly bring herself to touch.

Philip has done focus group interviews, taped them, and transcribed the tapes, but now is stuck. Both know that they must face analyzing their data, and both know that their own graduate seminar presentations are nearing. Both have supervisors who want to see some "results," some early draft chapters of the thesis. Abandoning the meal to go to the pub is tempting. Working on their data is not.

Anne and Philip are British, but we can imagine their counterparts in a college town anywhere in the United States, Canada, Australia, New Zealand, or Continental Europe. There is something daunting about the end of fieldwork, when there is nothing more to do than analyze and write up the data. Data analysis does not have to pose such glum prospects. We could write an equally fictitious scenario in which graduate students in anthropology or sociology breeze through the analysis and write-up of their materials, are never prey to self-doubt, and experience no problems. In our experience, however, the first scenario, or some variant of it, is more common. The analysis of qualitative data can prove to be a daunting task for students and even for the experienced field-worker. It is not necessary for this to be so, but it must be acknowledged that many graduate students and others have difficulty at some stage in the analysis of qualitative materials.

In an ideal world, Anne and Philip would not be in this predicament. We should never collect data without substantial analysis going on simultaneously. Letting data accumulate without preliminary analysis along the way is a recipe for unhappiness, if not total disaster. We must recognize that it can happen, and however diligent we are, we will face major tasks of data management and analysis at some stage in a research career. Paralysis and despair can easily occur.

It is equally paralyzing to think that the analysis, when tackled, has to be exactly right and must conform precisely to one or another orthodoxy. The search for one perfect method of data analysis is fruitless. It is easy to get so wrapped up in one's data (often gathered at considerable personal cost of time and effort) that one cannot see the forest for the trees and cannot get analytic purchase on the data collected. Too many people are so much in love with their data that they cannot bear to disturb their pristine beauty by interfering with them in any way. Both attitudes are sterile. There is no single right way to analyze qualitative data; equally, it is essential to find ways of using the data to think with. We have to find productive ways to organize and inspect our materials.

In the course of this book, we hope to provide some practical advice on ways of analyzing qualitative data. We illustrate many of the things we have to say with examples from our own analyses of qualitative data. The subject matter of the data we analyze—doctoral students and faculty members in social anthropology—is not a million miles away from the scenario we just introduced.

Our first message is a simple one: There are many ways of analyzing qualitative data. Indeed, there are many more approaches than we can deal with and illustrate in this book. In describing and exemplifying some of them, we want to urge our colleagues and students to enjoy and explore that diversity. Although we do not preach license to do as you please, we do want to counsel against the premature adoption of one or other analytic strategy to the exclusion of others. We certainly want to discourage our readers from uncritically adopting particular approaches to analysis without making principled decisions from among the available alternatives.

This introductory chapter serves three main purposes. First, we use this chapter to remind readers of the variety of qualitative data types and of the variety of approaches that researchers may adopt in order to analyze them. We stress at the outset that there are multiple practices, methods, and possibilities of analysis that qualitative researchers may employ. What links all the approaches is a central concern with transforming and interpreting qualitative data—in a rigorous and scholarly way—in order to capture the complexities of the social worlds we seek to understand. Our second task in this introductory chapter is to explain why we came to write this book and why we chose to write it in the way we did. In doing so, we try to stress the pragmatic approach we have adopted and our more intellectual interests that have influenced it. The third purpose of this chapter is to introduce the data that we draw on throughout the book to illustrate our ideas, suggestions, and arguments. These illustrative materials are drawn from a research project that used ethnographic interviews to collect data from PhD students and PhD supervisors in a number of social science disciplines. For this book, we have selected our exemplars from interviews with social anthropologists.

It is not our intent in this introductory chapter to provide a comprehensive review of the literature on qualitative research methods. A systematic and thorough discussion of the entire range of perspectives and procedures would need a volume of the length and scope of a handbook or encyclopedia (such as Denzin & Lincoln, 1994). Nor is it our intent to provide a textbook on "how to do" qualitative research in all of its aspects. Good introductions to this topic include Bogdan and Taylor (1975), Burgess (1982, 1984), Hammersley and Atkinson (1995), LeCompte and Preissle (1993), Lofland and Lofland (1984), and Silverman (1993).

In this chapter, and indeed throughout the book, we indicate the significance of analytical diversity and point out the variety of analytical strategies. Our overall aim is to introduce readers to a variety of approaches to qualitative data analysis. Some of the strategies we discuss will be familiar, others perhaps less so. Our central argument is that analysis implies, and indeed requires, principled choice. We also wish to stress that qualitative data analysis can be enjoyable and fun. Inevitably, there are other kinds of data and other analytic strategies that we do not cover in this book. Other introductory texts that focus on those additional approaches include Psathas (1994) on conversation analysis, Ball and Smith (1992) on visual data, Plummer (1983) on life histories, Hill (1993) on documentary materials, Thomas (1993) on critical ethnography, and van Manen (1990) on phenomenological methods.

Varieties of Perspective

Denzin and Lincoln's (1994) description of the qualitative researcher as *bricoleur* suggests that qualitative researchers employ a variety of strategies and methods to collect and analyze a variety of empirical materials. It is our intent in this book to explore only some elements of that complexity. We focus on a number of approaches to the analysis of qualitative data. As we shall try to justify throughout the book, we believe that it is important for qualitative researchers to explore their data from a variety of perspectives, or at least be able to make informed decisions about the analytic strategy adopted for a particular project.

Qualitative data occur in a variety of forms: There is not a single type. Data can take the form of fieldnotes, interview transcripts, transcribed recordings of naturally occurring interaction, documents, pictures, and other graphic representations. There is no single way of approaching those materials. Tesch (1990), for example, identifies no less than 26 analytic strategies, all of which can be applied to qualitative data. These exclude many aspects of visual and audio data, as she concentrates on textual data. In terms of a common thread linking all data types and analytic approaches, we stress that qualitative data analysis deals with meaningful talk and action. Even this, however, is too simplistic an approach. So too is the distinction that qualitative data are derived from a new paradigmatic, post-positivistic approach, while in contrast quantitative data are derived from a traditional, positivistic paradigm. As Tesch (1990) points out, positivists use words as data, and qualitative researchers use numbers as they search for patterns in human activity. Qualitative data therefore are not easily distinguished from quantitative: The distinction is more arbitrary than a reflection of major, inherent differences. This recognition, however, should not necessarily be viewed as a negative aspect of the qualitative research endeavor, as it does not imply that qualitative research is undistinguished and fuzzy. It does imply that a variety of perspectives is inherent in the qualitative approach in general. As Strauss (1987, p. 7) argues, qualitative researchers "have quite different investigatory styles, let alone different talents and gifts, so that a standardization of methods . . . would only constrain and even stifle social researchers' best efforts."

Variety stems not only from the range of researchers' commitments and talents; the diversity of social settings and attendant contingencies also have an impact on the collection of qualitative data, as does the aim of the research. The types of data that can be collected in various field settings also affect the possibilities for data analysis, as do the analytical aims of the researcher. This diversity associated with data leads us to a wide variety of analytic strategies for qualitative data collection and analysis. All is not confusion, however. Through all those different types of data and different analytic strategies, there emerge recurrent preoccupations. For example, Silverman (1993, p. 19) maintains that from the strength of diversity comes a distinctive form of analysis that "is centrally concerned with avoiding a 'social problem' perspective by asking how principals attach meanings to their activities and 'problems.' " In dealing with qualitative materials, then, analysts *make* problems, grounding them in the everyday realities and meanings of social worlds and social actors, rather than *taking* problems from policymakers, general theorists, or others.

In the following chapters, we consider a range of strategies for the analysis of qualitative data. Our overall aim is to "give permission" to experiment and play with analysis. In doing so, we might be accused of divorcing analysis from the collection of data and other aspects of the research enterprise. Insofar as that is the case, we do so for the purposes of clarity and also as a response to the common experiences of graduate students, colleagues, and occasionally ourselves in having collected data and then being at a loss as to what to do with them. It is worthwhile to reaffirm that such a divorce of collection from analysis is an artificial and not altogether desirable separation. The process of analysis should not be seen as a distinct stage of research; rather, it is a reflexive activity that should inform data collection, writing, further data collection, and so forth. Analysis is not, then, the last phase of the research process. It should be seen as part of the research design and of the data collection. The research process, of which analysis is one aspect, is a cyclical one.

We would also not wish to suggest that there is a single right or most appropriate way to analyze qualitative data. It is abundantly clear not only that there are many ways to undertake the analysis of qualitative data but also that analysis in general means different things to different people. A few years ago, Paul Atkinson met a fellow social scientist who also writes about qualitative methods. In the course of a general conversation, the methodologist complained that none of the existing textbooks on ethnographic methods—including Hammersley and Atkinson (1983)—had sustained treatments of analysis. Worried by that assertion, Atkinson looked again at that first edition of his book with Martyn Hammersley. Puzzled but relieved, he found a chapter on the recording and organization of data and a chapter on analyzing data. Clearly, the critic had meant that none of the texts discussed what *she* meant by qualitative data analysis. There is not, therefore, consensus about what the term *analysis* means in this context, let alone about the specific and precise formulation of strategies and techniques.

For some authors, analysis refers primarily to the tasks of coding, indexing, sorting, retrieving, or otherwise manipulating data (such as interview transcripts or fieldnotes). From such a perspective, the task of analysis can be conceived primarily in terms of data handling. Whether it is done by hand or by computer software, data analysis at this level is relatively independent of speculation and interpretation: *Procedures* of organization and retrieval are paramount. For others in the field, analysis refers primarily to the imaginative work of interpretation, and the more procedural, categorizing tasks are relegated to the preliminary work of ordering and sorting the data. For such authors, perhaps, analysis is essentially imaginative and speculative. Some perspectives emphasize the systematic display and representation with canons of rigor that reflect (though they do not slavishly follow) those of more standardized quantitative or formal methods. Others, by contrast, rely on the interpretation of data through the imaginative reconstruction of social worlds and often emphasize the unique rather than regularities of incidence or pattern.

It is not our purpose to review and justify or criticize all the current usages of the term *analysis* and their implications. We mention some alternative perspectives to emphasize that the general subject matter of this book itself is subject to various interpretations by researchers and methodological commentators. Such interpretations of analysis themselves are inescapably grounded in more general styles and work preferences. One therefore can discern stark differences in the work of a few prominent authors and their recent contributions to the methodological literature.

Take, for example, the definition of data analysis applied by Huberman and Miles (1994). They define data analysis as three linked subprocesses: data reduction, data display, and conclusion drawing and verification. They describe data reduction in terms of data selection and condensation. Data are reduced in anticipatory ways as conceptual frameworks are chosen and as instruments, cases, and questions are refined. Data here are summarized, coded, and broken down into themes, clusters, and categories. Data display, the second subprocess, describes the ways in which reduced data are displayed in diagrammatic, pictorial, or visual forms in order to show what those data imply. As Huberman and Miles (1994, p. 429) describe it, data display should be viewed as an "organized, compressed assembly of information that permits conclusion drawing and/or action taking." Huberman and Miles's third analytical subprocess is conclusion drawing and verification. This is where the displayed data are interpreted and where meaning is drawn. Again they suggest that this can be done by employing a variety of different tactics, for example, looking for comparative and contrasting cases; noting and exploring themes, patterns, and regularities; and using metaphors.

Huberman and Miles offer a systematic approach to the process of qualitative data analysis, but they are not overprescriptive. They observe that in order to describe and explain qualitative data, it is necessary to work toward a set of analytic categories that are conceptually specified. They acknowledge, however, that these categories can be arrived at and explored deductively or inductively, and they suggest that both methods can be valid and potentially useful. Huberman and Miles offer a variety of ways of reducing, displaying, and verifying qualitative data, and they stress that all three subprocesses offer a multitude of possibilities.

Dey (1993) offers a not dissimilar view of qualitative data analysis, describing it primarily in terms of identifying and linking analytic categories. Thought of in this way, analysis is a process of resolving data into its constituent components to reveal their characteristic themes and patterns. Dey also breaks qualitative data analysis into three related processes: describing, classifying, and connecting. According to this model, the analysis must first offer thorough and comprehensive descriptions that include (where appropriate) the context of action, the intentions of the social actor, and the processes in which the social action is embedded. Second, Dey suggests that data should be classified in order to "give meaning." Dey here means the categorization of data and the assigning of data bits to themes and codes. Third, Dey suggests that categorized or coded data can be analyzed in terms of the patterns and connections that emerge. This is where the pieces are put back together again. In Dey's terms (1993, p. 47), "Connecting concepts is the analytic equivalent of putting mortar between the building blocks." Dey's strategic approach to the conduct of qualitative analysis is to some extent driven by his interest in and use of computers in the analytic process. He is the author of a software package for analyzing data. Like Huberman and Miles, Dey defines the analysis of qualitative data in terms of clear, distinct, and identifiable subprocesses. Analysis according to these perspectives is, at least in principle, systematic and developmental.

Wolcott's (1994) description of what analysis means presents a rather different way of thinking about how we explore and interpret qualitative data. Wolcott uses the term *transformation* to describe a variety of strategies. He restricts the term *analysis* to a more specialized meaning. Wolcott (1994) argues that qualitative data can be transformed in different ways and to different ends. He also breaks up these methods into three types: description, analysis, and interpretation. Description follows from an underlying assumption that data should speak for themselves. The analytical account of the data should stay close to the data as they are originally recorded. Wolcott suggests that the question here is

"What is going on?" He does recognize that there is no such thing as pure description, as it takes a human observer to accomplish description. Nevertheless, the goal of description in Wolcott's terms is to tell the story of the data in as descriptive a way as possible.

Analysis, in Wolcott's terms, refers to a rather specialized way of transforming data, rather than being an all-encompassing term. Analysis in this context is the process by which the researcher expands and extends data beyond a descriptive account. A careful and systematic attention to the data here identifies key factors and key relationships. Analysis, then, is both cautious and controlled. It is also, according to Wolcott, structured, formal, bounded, systematic, grounded, methodical, particular, carefully documented, and impassive. The emphasis is on the search for themes and patterns from the data. Analysis involves systematic procedures to identify essential features and relationships. What Wolcott is describing here appears to be the work of data management as much as anything.

Wolcott describes his third way of transforming qualitative data as interpretation. This is where the researcher attempts to offer his or her own interpretation of what is going on. It is here that understanding and explanation are sought, according to Wolcott, "beyond the limits of what can be explained with the degree of certainty usually associated with analysis." In contrast to "analysis" in Wolcott's terms, interpretation is freewheeling, casual, unbounded, aesthetically satisfying, idealistic, generative, and impassioned. Wolcott (1994, p. 36) heralds interpretation as the threshold in thinking and writing, "at which the researcher transcends factual data and cautious analysis and begins to probe into what is to be made of them."

Wolcott's triad of approaches to the analysis or transformation of qualitative data at first glance appears similar to the sets of procedures offered by Huberman and Miles and by Dey. Unlike those authors, however, Wolcott does not envisage that description, analysis, and interpretation necessarily will be part of one overall schema, to be applied in its totality in all cases. He also does not see description, analysis, and interpretation as being mutually exclusive. The transformation of qualitative data can be done at any of the three levels, or in some combination of them. Wolcott argues that description, analysis, and interpretation are the three primary ingredients of qualitative research, from which different balances can be struck.

What "analysis" actually means is complex and is contested by qualitative researchers. Tesch (1990) identifies several key characteristics of qualitative data analysis that can be viewed as commonalities of the analytical process. She cautions that no characteristics are common to all types of qualitative analysis but suggests that there are a number of regular features. These include some characteristics already mentioned: Analysis is a cyclical process and a reflexive activity; the analytic process should be comprehensive and systematic but not rigid; data are segmented and divided into meaningful units, but connection to the whole is maintained; and data are organized according to a system derived from the data themselves. Analysis is, on the whole, an inductive, data-led activity. Tesch also points to the flexibility of analysis and to the absence of rules of how it should best be done. Analysis implies being artful (Guba & Lincoln, 1981) and playful (Goetz & LeCompte, 1984). Tesch maintains that this does not mean that analysis is a structureless process, nor that it should be done inattentively and sloppily. Qualitative data analysis requires methodological knowledge and intellectual competence. Analysis is not about adhering to any one correct approach or set of right techniques; it is imaginative, artful, flexible, and reflexive. It should also be methodical, scholarly, and intellectually rigorous.

Why We Wrote This Book

We approached this book with a very pragmatic interest. As we suggested at the beginning, all too often we encounter novice researchers—students and others—and sometimes more experienced researchers who need advice. They often start from the position of "I've collected all this data, now what should I do?" Others start from an equally problematic position of "I've collected all my data, now I'm going to analyze it and write it up." Both positions imply a woeful lack of appreciation of what is and what can be meant by analysis.

In recent years, qualitative data collection and analysis have become widespread throughout the social sciences. They are not the preserve of social and cultural anthropologists and some sociologists. Qualitative research, in many guises, is pursued by researchers in education, psychology, media studies, cultural studies, urban studies, human geography, and nursing, to name only some of the disciplines. This book, therefore, is for students and researchers in all those disciplines who face the challenge of making sense of data derived from qualitative methods. Our own orientation is sociological, and the data are about anthropologists. The general messages, however, apply much more widely beyond those two fields.

The diffusion and popularity of qualitative research methods are gratifying and serve as testimony to their value in the exploration and documentation of diverse social worlds and social practices. The diffusion of the research approaches has spawned a huge demand for methodological training and advice, including a stream of methods textbooks such as this one. On the other hand, there still seem to be too many students and practitioners who believe implicitly that qualitative research can be done in a spirit of careless rapture, with no principled or disciplined thought whatsoever. They collect data with little thought for research problems and research design, and they think that they will know what to do with the data once those data are collected. When they find that things are not quite so simple, they wail "I've got all these data. . . ." It is tempting to advise them to throw the data away and to start again; that if they do not know what to do with the data, then they probably do not know why they are doing the research in the first place. Such an attitude is uncharitable, and it is usually better in the long run to try to be helpful.

In an ideal world, nobody would ever get into such a predicament with their data. Researchers would realize that analysis is not a separate set of procedures applied to an inert body of data. Whatever research strategy is being followed, research problems, research design, data collection methods, and analytic approaches should all be part of an overall methodological approach and should all imply one another. Indeed, for most kinds of qualitative research, they should not even be thought of as different stages in the research process. What is conventionally referred to as analysis is a pervasive activity throughout the life of a research project. Analysis is not simply one of the later stages of the research, to be followed by an equally separate phase of "writing up results."

This book is meant to apply to those who have thought about their research strategy, not only to those who have reached an impasse as to what to do with their research material. On the contrary, we hope above all that our examples and advice will help readers to formulate sensible, well-informed plans and proposals for their research. An awareness of the possibilities for analysis should inform the entire research process. Well-informed research design and data collection always should be conducted with an understanding of what the analytic strategies are likely to be.

In recent years, there has seemed to be a slightly different danger emerging. It is not a problem of people not knowing what to do with their data. On the contrary, they seem to think they know how to analyze, because for them analysis has come to mean a very restricted set of procedures. The advent of computer-assisted qualitative data analysis (CAQDAS) has meant that qualitative data analysis may now be treated as being synonymous with the sort of procedures most commonly facilitated by such computing software. Some researchers make the assumption that computer-assisted analysis is the only way to proceed; the assumptions and limitations built into the software applications will be incorporated unthinkingly into the process of analysis. Most of these computer-based procedures rest on some form of coding of data, and there is a clear danger that coding and analysis will become treated as synonymous. Coding and analysis are not synonymous, and in any case many of the uses of computer software are most properly thought of in terms of the storage and retrieval of data, not their analysis, strictly speaking.

We also recognize that the research literature is replete with characterizations of the diversity of approaches to qualitative research in general, and various authors have attempted to provide lists or even typologies of them. Some commentators go even further by suggesting that qualitative research can be characterized in terms of a number of paradigms, that is, more or less incommensurable packages of assumptions, subject matter, and techniques. Most, if not all, of those paradigmatic statements are muddled and try to erect barriers and oppositions where none exist, or try to make differences of emphasis into insurmountable epistemological clashes. We recognize that there are differences, and we would not wish to convey the impression that qualitative methods are all of a piece.

We are even less enamored of the view that qualitative research constitutes a paradigm in its own right. Although the issue is not the focus of our book, we do not adhere to distinctions between qualitative and quantitative approaches, for example, and in addressing some issues in qualitative research we do not intend to imply any privileged status for those methods above all others. Indeed, we think that approaches that elevate all or some qualitative methods to the status of a paradigm have dangers. In particular, it is all too easy to fall into rigidly stereotyped thinking. If you believe in distinct paradigms, then you may be tempted to think that there is one and only one way to approach a given problem or research project. Research problems and research methods thus may become compartmentalized, to the detriment of creativity and genuine variety. It is, we think, far better to exploit a variety of approaches.

Eclecticism is not, and should never be, an excuse for sloppy, indiscriminate work. As we hope we make clear, it is always necessary for research methods to be used in a disciplined manner. Here we deliberately seek to benefit from the dual connotations of *discipline.* On one hand, it may be taken to refer to academic domains and subjects, and it should always be kept in mind that methods per se do not substitute for thorough disciplinary knowledge. It takes more than a particular style of data collection to make an anthropology, a symbolic interactionism, an ethnomethodology, or a phenomenology. Research—whatever its methods of data collection and analysis—needs a broader intellectual framework than those methods alone. On the other hand, discipline has connotations of rigor and care. We will reiterate throughout this book that data collection and analysis should always be conducted in accordance with standards or canons of rigor. We will not go into the niceties of validity and reliability here but will content ourselves that the conduct of research should be methodical. The analyst must exercise due care as to the consistency and comprehensiveness of analytic procedures, whatever they are.

We should acknowledge that the connotations of "discipline" also can be rather glum. Discipline and rigor have overtones of punishment, without the particular observations of Michel Foucault. Although the hard slog of detailed analysis, after months or years of data collection, does often feel like punishment, we want to emphasize the element of enjoyment. The variety of approaches to social research in general, and to qualitative data analysis more particularly, can be a source of fun. It can be a source of creativity as well. There is much to be gained from trying out different analytic angles on one's data. New insights can be generated, and one can sometimes escape from analytic perspectives that have become stereotyped and stale. We therefore want to encourage a (modestly) playful approach to the diversity of research approaches.

Throughout this book, then, we emphasize—and to some extent we celebrate—the variety of analytic strategies open to qualitative researchers in the social sciences. We do not cover all the available approaches and techniques, instead concentrating on a restricted set of them. We discuss a variety of approaches not in order to promote a randomly eclectic approach to research: There is variety in techniques because there are different questions to be addressed and different versions of social reality that can be elaborated. There are good reasons, in other words, for the existence of complementary or contrasting analytic strategies. A lazy reliance on one approach is unlikely to result in the most principled of analyses. A thoughtless resort to a large number of approaches, on the other hand, will not guarantee a better result. We address the variety of analytic strategies, therefore, in order not to advocate a simplistic idea of methodological triangulation.

Crude understandings of triangulation often imply that data from different sources, or derived from different methods, can be aggregated in some way in order to produce a fully rounded, more authentic, portrayal of the social world. Such a view would imply that the different data types, or different analytic strategies, would allow one to approximate with increasing fidelity a single, valid representation of the social world. That is not our view. We do not believe that the alternative perspectives that are generated by different methods and techniques can be summed. They do not aggregate toward a complete and rounded picture. (For an excellent discussion of the linkage of different data types, see Fielding & Fielding, 1986.) We can use different analytic strategies in order to explore different facets of our data, explore different kinds of order in them, and construct different versions of the social world. That kind of variety does not imply that one simply can take the results from different analyses and stick them together like children's building blocks in order to create a single edifice.

Equally important, the combination or juxtaposition of different research techniques does not reduce the complexity of our understanding. The more we examine our data from different viewpoints, the more we may reveal—or indeed construct—their complexity. We encourage the exploration of alternative strategies precisely in order to encourage the recognition and exploration of such complexity. We thus reject what might be called vulgar triangulation while endorsing a sensitive appreciation of complexity and variety.

When we approach our data, we do not try to impose a single methodological framework, nor do we try to boil the data down to a single version. We are familiar with the characteristic novice response to a field research project: "It all comes down to" power, patriarchy, bureaucracy, or whatever, or "It's just a question of. . . ." Such reductive arguments are always distressing, given the variety and complex organization of social worlds. They reflect mentalities that cannot cope with the uncertainties and ambiguities of social research. It is important to find and to contrive generic analytic themes in our research, but such intellectual work is not best served by denying the diversity of social phenomena and their exploration. We believe, therefore, that even with only one restricted data set, such as the one we use to illustrate this book, it is possible to make a more elaborated series of analyses than would be possible from a reliance on only one approach. Those analytic procedures and their outcomes do not necessarily converge on one single conclusion. They do not necessarily contradict one another either, but they are not simply additive. They may help to reveal different facets of the data.

The data that we use, like any data, are incomplete or partial versions. Again, we make it clear that we do not mean to imply that they are imperfect representations of an independent social reality that is itself perfectly coherent and integrated. On the contrary, we recognize that we produce versions of the social world through our data collection and our processes of analysis. We do not subscribe to the vulgar and extreme version of constructivism that implies that there is nothing referential about research because there is no reality independent of our constructions of it. Our knowledge is the outcome, we believe, of transactions with the social world, shaped by our methods of inquiry, and of transactions with the data we produce, shaped in turn by our ideas and our analytic procedures.

In the course of this book, therefore, we will explore and exemplify different ways in which order and pattern can be made from the same set of data. In doing so, we hope to persuade readers to do likewise: to treat data in different ways in order to produce rich and variegated analyses. For the purposes of this book, it makes little difference whether you believe that the different layers of form and content are inherent in the data or are imposed on them. As we have suggested, we believe both to be true to some extent, in that analyses emerge out of repeated interactions with conceptual frameworks and the data. More productive is recognition of the value of multiple investigations of the data.

The notion of "thick description" (Geertz, 1973) often is used to characterize the goal of qualitative, ethnographic research. That term itself is open to a variety of interpretations. One fruitful way of thinking about the production of "thick" analysis is to recognize the value of multiple analytic strategies. In examining our own data, for example, it will make sense to think not only in terms of the thematic content of our interviews but also in terms of their narrative forms. We will also examine aspects of their semantic and metaphorical content. We will go on to think about how we can write about and represent our ideas. We will stress the generation of ideas in order to draw attention to the fact that analysis must always go well beyond any specific analytic procedures and techniques. The manipulation and management of data are not ends in themselves; they are aspects of the broader task of theorizing and contributing to the disciplinary knowledge of the social sciences.

About Our Data

We have illustrated many of the themes in this book by examining extracts from the same set of data. We think it is important to keep stressing that there are always different analytic strategies available: One can often look at the same research and the same set of data from contrasting angles. It is useful, therefore, to keep coming back to the same data with fresh analytic perspectives. The aims of this book are methodological. It does not contain an empirical monograph. It is, however, possible to glimpse the fragments of a yet-to-be-written monograph. We try to share with readers some of the processes of thought and reflection, together with some of the strategies that inform the process of analysis and interpretation.

The data that we use derive from a series of interviews with graduate students in social anthropology in several academic departments in the United Kingdom, as well as interviews with the students' supervisors. We have chosen to present the data on anthropologists as the recurrent illustrative material for several reasons. First, the data constitute a relatively small corpus of materials. Second, we hope that the data may be of intrinsic interest to many of our readers. This is a book about qualitative data analysis, and many of our informants talked about the conduct and supervision of fieldwork. It seemed to us, therefore, that the data might well have some intrinsic interest for our readers: Many of our informants had things to say about ethnographic research. A methodological discussion based on data about fieldwork is not intended to launch a precious exercise of self-reference.

We are conscious of the fact that repeated analytic observations based on the same set of data can prove to be extremely tedious. Even imaginative solutions—such as Dey's use of Woody Allen scripts—can pall after several readings (Dey, 1993). We were eager, therefore, to draw on data that might sustain the interest of readers committed to the exploration of qualitative data. The materials derived from our fieldwork among anthropologists contain information and perspectives on more than fieldwork itself. Our anthropology students and academics talked about many aspects of the PhD experience, and several themes and problems are touched on as we use the data to illustrate our argument.

Our choice of illustrative data means that it is necessary to give some sense of the research from which it comes. We must also make explicit the limitations our choice of data impose. There are some things that can be illustrated rather well—in our opinion, at any rate—from the anthropology data. One must recognize that there will be other analytic possibilities that are not well addressed from such an angle.

The data form part of a much larger set, derived from a research project funded by the Training Board of the United Kingdom's Economic and Social Research Council (ESRC), which was in turn part of a wider research program of several projects on the social science PhD in the United Kingdom. A representative collection of papers (Burgess, 1994) gives an overview of the range of projects. There were three complementary projects following similar strategies of qualitative inquiry. The team at Cardiff (Odette Parry, Sara Delamont, and Paul Atkinson) undertook an investigation of PhD students and their supervisors (i.e., their academic advisers) in several social science disciplines that shared some family resemblances: social anthropology, development and regional studies, human geography, and town planning. Graduate students and academics in several departments of each discipline were studied. Parallel projects were pursued by teams at Warwick University (who focused on sociology, economics, and business) and at Bristol University (who concentrated on education and psychology).

The teams worked independently and with their own foreshadowed research problems. The Cardiff team members were particularly interested in processes of socialization into the particular cultures or subcultures of academic disciplines and departments.

Because the requirements of the research called for fairly extensive coverage of research sites, we were not able to undertake in-depth fieldwork at a small number of sites (our preferred research strategy). As a consequence, most of the data that were collected were in the form of ethnographic interviews, in which a fairly broad agenda of research questions was explored in a fairly open-ended way. Interviews were conducted with 24 graduate students and with 25 academic staff in social anthropology. These were collected in several different anthropology departments in British universities. For reasons of confidentiality, we have not divulged precisely how many research sites were visited in each of the disciplines we studied. (In small academic communities, it is extremely difficult to maintain discretion and confidentiality.) For the original research project, all but a few of those interviews were tape-recorded and transcribed; the remaining ones were recorded by means of extended notes.

Of the 24 graduate students we interviewed, 16 were men and 8 were women. Eight students were from overseas, and 16 were British nationals. Seven of the students had a first degree in social anthropology, and the remaining 17 had completed conversion courses such as a taught master's degree.

In using the data in this book, we are not attempting to reproduce a comprehensive analysis and write-up of those data. Some analyses have been published, and further publications will deal with specific issues. Many issues will be covered in work that combines the research in the social sciences with a second research project undertaken by the same team at Cardiff on selected departments and disciplines in the natural sciences. What we will do in the context of this book is use pertinent extracts from the data on anthropologists to outline and illustrate potentially useful analytic strategies and perspectives. The emphasis will be on how we would set about an analysis and what we might do with it, rather than on presenting the final results. We use selected extracts from our interview transcripts to illustrate our chosen analytic strategies. We have not attempted to analyze repeatedly precisely the same fragments of data, by subjecting them to different treatments. There is nothing in principle, or inherent in the data, that would prevent that. We do not mean to convey the impression that some data are analyzed one way, while other data are necessarily analyzed differently. Given that we can present only a few fragments of the data anyway, we decided to try to convey some flavor of the research, and its findings generally, by presenting a range of data fragments. We concentrate here on data derived from our interviews with students and academics. We collected some observational data as well, although that set of data is smaller than that from the interviews, and we do not use them in this book.

Many qualitative researchers use interview materials of different sorts and for different analytic purposes, and our treatment will follow some of those strategies. We are conscious of the fact that qualitative research takes many forms and generates many types of data. Those different data in turn may imply different approaches to analysis. In using the data we have chosen, therefore, we must acknowledge their limitations. Interview data do not give us direct access to the details of naturally occurring interaction. They certainly do not give us access to how people actually perform a wide variety of daily activities.

By concentrating on our interview data, for example, we cannot document directly, for example, how research seminars are conducted in anthropology departments or how students and supervisors actually talk to one another as they discuss the progress of students' research and the writing of a doctoral thesis. There are limitations on our evidence about anthropology departments (though we have some participant-observation data about seminars and other activities in the departments). The data place limits on our use of them to illustrate analytic strategies. We wish to emphasize that we are not by implication advocating the use of interview data as the preferred approach. Indeed, we are skeptical observers of the current fashion for life-history and ethnographic interviewing. We cannot use the interview data to illustrate, for example, conversation analysis. (It is possible to analyze interview data from that perspective, but we believe that it would be stretching our analytic strategies a bit thin.) In an ideal world, it would have been perfectly reasonable for us to have collected such data, perhaps by recording and transcribing social encounters such as research student seminars and meetings between students and supervisors. There are good introductory sources that deal with such approaches, however, and we are content to refer the reader to them (see, e.g., Psathas, 1994).

Our data do not include visual materials. The Cardiff research team's project did not include the collection of photographs or the video-recording of seminars and meetings, nor did we systematically collect visual materials of other sorts. We could have collected such data, and in retrospect it is a pity that they were not collected, but the research had specific purposes and was not intended originally as an extended methodological exemplar. We do not want to overemphasize the limits of our chosen data. It will be seen that they can be approached by means of a number of analytic techniques, and a number of complementary analyses thus can be projected. Those approaches are not confined solely to the kind of interview data that we have. Many can be used to make sense of fieldnotes constructed on the basis of participant or nonparticipant observation; some certainly can be used with transcripts of social encounters other than interviews. We will from time to time draw attention to the scope of our chosen types of analysis.

By using the data from a real project to illustrate a diversity of analytic approaches, we are thereby constrained by the design and conduct of the original research itself. Moreover, such a strategy means that the data themselves are a bit restricted in scope. On the other hand, it gives greater cogency to our overall message. That is, it is possible to approach the same data from different perspectives. It is always possible to demonstrate diverse strategies by selecting different kinds of data from different sources so as to ensure a goodness of fit between examples and strategies. Textbooks such as Silverman's (1993) provide excellent overviews of different approaches. Unlike this book, however, Silverman's is structured in terms of different kinds of data (interview data, transcripts of recorded interaction, texts). Although Silverman himself would not be guilty of such an oversimplification, the unwary could fall into the trap of assuming that each type of data—defined in terms of its method of data collection, such as interviewing or transcribing—implies its own distinctive style of analysis. In practice, there is not such one-to-one correspondence. We believe, therefore, that in contrast to the limitations of our data is the strength of helping us to concentrate on using multiple strategies. We stress throughout the book that, analytically speaking, there is more than one way to skin a cat.

Some of the analyses we suggest here are part of the Cardiff research team's approach to the wider project and its publication; others are not. We stress that in this book—the point of which is methodological—we are not using the data to recapitulate "the" analysis of the research or of academic socialization in general. We will not present complete treatments of our analytic themes, and this is not a surrogate research monograph. We will indicate how a mode of analysis could and would be initiated and developed. We do not do this for the entire research process. It is worth pointing out, however, that the Cardiff team's treatment of its own data already has followed more than one approach. The interview data were all transcribed. They were then all coded using *The Ethnograph* software for storage and retrieval of textual data. They have been analyzed partially and written up from a thematic perspective. This first pass at the data, therefore, has been undertaken in very straightforward, conventional ways.

In addition, the data have been examined selectively for narrative performances. In particular, supervisors' narratives have been identified. They have intrinsic interest, and they suggest some insights into wider issues of academic folklore. The exploration of supervisors' accounts is related to another analytic theme currently being explored: the expression and legitimation of knowledge and expertise. We are able to explore how academics and students talk about the core competencies, problems, and research methods that are held to characterize their own academic discipline and its distinctive research culture.

In working with our academic colleagues, and hence in reproducing data gathered from them, we have been acutely conscious of the need to preserve the confidentiality of information. In a small world like that of academic anthropology in the United Kingdom, it is extremely difficult to preserve the anonymity of individual informants and to disguise the research sites (i.e., the academic departments) in which the research was conducted. In order to try to maintain the anonymity that we promised to students and academic staff, we have changed many proper names. Each university has been given an entirely fictitious name, as has each informant. We also have falsified details about individual careers and research projects; for example, we have changed the locations of anthropological fieldwork.

It will be seen that we have from time to time included reference to real anthropologists and real departments. Some such reference is inevitable. The culture of anthropology is based on key characters and the distinctive subcultures of university departments. A wholesale substitution with entirely fictitious names and locations could render the anthropologists' accounts nonsensical. We have done our best, however, to change the self-referential elements of our informants' accounts. If a real anthropologist is referred to, therefore, we may have changed names and locations, or if we have not done that, then we have altered other aspects of the account in order to muddy the waters.

About the Book

The chapters that follow elaborate and expand upon many of the themes and ideas touched on in this introductory chapter. We identify a number of analytic strategies and exemplify them with reference to our own data, as well as giving relevant examples from published research. At the end of each chapter we also offer more specific suggestions for further reading. These suggestions are very much our own and do not necessarily represent "the best" of all possible examples. They are not intended to provide a definitive list of sources; rather, they are there to provide guidance on where one might go for a more thorough exploration of a particular strategy or analytic approach. We have chosen what we regard as particularly apt, accessible, useful, or interesting examples of analytic strategies and their uses.

Each chapter deals with a particular set of analytic strategies. For each strategy, we provide a systematic introduction that highlights its rationale and approach. In each chapter, we use the anthropology data as a means of illustrating, in an empirical fashion, how one might set about using the different analytical approaches. It is important to stress that we do not provide a prescriptive set of techniques that should be followed in order to achieve a particular kind of analysis. Rather, we hope to provide a "hands-on" feel to the book, permitting the reader insight as to how qualitative data can be thought about, manipulated, and explored. We would argue that it is impossible to break down the task of analysis, using any strategy or combination of strategies, into a fail-safe procedure. As we hope to demonstrate throughout the following chapters, analysis is as much about ideas as it is about particular techniques.

We begin with a discussion of how qualitative data can be categorized and conceptualized. We address a number of closely related strategies that are dependent on coding the data and using the codes to retrieve analytically significant segments of data. We begin here because this is a common starting point for researchers. The identification of analytic themes and the fragmentation of the data in accordance with an emergent conceptual scheme are widespread among researchers and in the relevant literature. For many purposes, this is an important way to organize data and to develop analytic ideas. It is not the whole story, however, and in the chapters that follow we explore a number of alternative approaches.

We recognize that the fragmentation of data implied in the coding strategy often leads researchers to overlook the form of their data. We therefore turn to a parallel consideration of narrative. Interview data such as ours lend themselves especially well to narrative analysis. From this point of view, we are interested not only in what people say and do but in how they express themselves. We can examine the forms and the functions of narratives.

We then go on to look at some other aspects of language and meaning. We can often learn much from paying close attention to how informants and others express themselves. We exemplify this kind of approach by writing about the investigation of metaphor. We also examine how we can develop semantic analyses of actors' cultural categories, specifically through domain analysis.

We also want to insist that analysis is inseparable from writing and strategies of representation. We choose how to analyze our data, and we must also exercise choice as to how we reconstruct social realities through our textual practices. Writing up research is not a mechanistic activity, and there is not one way of constructing academic texts. The decisions we make about representation essentially are part of the analyses we undertake.

We recognize equally that analysis is inseparable from processes of theorizing. We therefore devote a chapter to the interaction between analysis and ideas. This is not a separate phase in the research process. Dialogue between data and theory should be a recurrent, pervasive feature of all qualitative research.

Finally, we deal with the issue of computer-aided qualitative data analysis. We present our various approaches before the introduction of computing because we wish to establish that contemporary computer software can be used to facilitate a variety of analytic approaches. Computer software does not provide a single perspective on the data, although each program may inscribe a specific set of assumptions, and it is unwise to adopt one or another program without a principled choice of research strategy and goals.

Each chapter is written to be reasonably self-contained, so that a reader can dip into one chapter at a time in order to pursue a particular area of interest. On the other hand, we have thought carefully about the structure of the book and the placing of each chapter. The book is intended to be coherent in its entirety. The strategies we explore should not be thought of as mutually exclusive. In advocating awareness of the diversity of available strategies, we are especially keen to urge readers not to become fixated on any one analytic approach. We hope that in the chapters that follow, readers will see the value of a variety of approaches and that qualitative research should draw strength from the diversity of analytic strategies that are available. We take as our general inspiration an observation by Denzin and Lincoln (1994, p. 2): "The multiple methodologies of qualitative research may be viewed as a bricolage and the researcher as *bricoleur.*" The bricoleur is someone who is skilled at using and adapting diverse materials and tools: It is a handy metaphor for the qualitative researcher.

Suggestions for Further Reading

Delamont, S. (1992). *Fieldwork in educational settings: Methods, pitfalls and perspectives.* London: Falmer.

> *An especially accessible introduction to qualitative research, useful beyond the confines of educational research, including discussions of analyzing and theorizing as well as of data and texts.*

Hammersley, M., & Atkinson, P. (1995). *Ethnography: Principles in practice* (2nd ed.). London: Routledge and Kegan Paul.

> *A general introduction to ethnography and qualitative methods more generally. Includes chapters on data organization, analysis, and writing.*

Lofland, J., & Lofland, L. H. (1984). *Analyzing social settings* (2nd ed.). Belmont, CA: Wadsworth.

> *A classic exegesis of fieldwork methods that is especially good on the development of ideas. Well referenced.*

Silverman, D. (1993). *Interpreting qualitative data: Methods for analysing talk, text and interaction.* London: Sage.

> *An especially well-illustrated introduction to a range of qualitative data types and analytic approaches: observations, interviews, texts, and transcripts. Includes practical exercises.*

Strauss, A. L. (1987). *Qualitative analysis for social scientists*. Cambridge, UK: Cambridge University Press.

A thorough review, densely illustrated, of Strauss's characteristic approach to data analysis. Includes transcripts of collective exercises that convey something of the flavor of Strauss's graduate seminars.

Wolcott, H. (1994). *Transforming qualitative data: Description, analysis, and interpretation*. Thousand Oaks, CA: Sage.

An engaging series of reflections on making sense of ethnographic work. Illustrated with empirical examples of Wolcott's own anthropological research.

2

Concepts and Coding

Linking Concepts and Data

Many analyses of qualitative data begin with the identification of key themes and patterns. This, in turn, often depends on processes of coding data. The segmenting and coding of data are often taken-for-granted parts of the qualitative research process. All researchers need to be able to organize, manage, and retrieve the most meaningful bits of our data. The usual way of going about this is by assigning tags or labels to the data, based on our concepts. Essentially, what we are doing in these instances is condensing the bulk of our data sets into analyzable units by creating categories with and from our data. This process is usually referred to as coding, although that can imply a rather mechanistic process. We prefer to think in terms of generating concepts from and with our data, using coding as a means of achieving this.

We stress here that although coding may be part of the process of analysis, it should not be thought of as the analysis in itself. In other words, coding should not be seen as a substitute for analysis. It would be as much a mistake to think that coding is an activity that is universally understood across the qualitative (or indeed quantitative) research spectrum. Rather, the term *coding* encompasses a variety of approaches to and ways of organizing qualitative data. As parts of an analytical process, however, attaching codes to data and generating concepts have important functions in enabling us rigorously to review what our data are saying.

The analytic procedures that underpin coding procedures establish links of various sorts. First, codings link different segments or instances in the data. We bring those fragments of data together to create categories of data that we define as having some common property or element. We define them as being about or relating to some particular topic or theme. The coding thus links all those data fragments to a particular idea or concept. As we will see, such concepts are in turn related to one another. Codes, data categories, and concepts are thus related closely to one another. The important analytic work lies in establishing and thinking about such linkages, not in the mundane processes of coding. The importance of the work lies in how we use the codings and concepts, not in whether we use computer software to record them or rely on manual ways of marking and manipulating the data.

Important analytic work also lies in the identification of relevant concepts. We use the data to think with, in order to generate ideas that are thoroughly and precisely related to our data. Coding can be thought about as a way of relating our data to our ideas about those data. Because codes are thus links between locations in the data and sets of concepts or ideas, they are in that sense heuristic devices. Coding reflects our analytic ideas, but one should not confuse coding itself with the analytic work of developing conceptual schemes. As Seidel and Kelle (1995, p. 52) note, "codes represent the decisive link between the original 'raw data,' that is, the textual material such as interview transcripts or fieldnotes, on the one hand and the researcher's theoretical concepts on the other."

In practice, coding can be thought of as a range of approaches that aid the organization, retrieval, and interpretation of data. Miles and Huberman (1994) suggest that coding constitutes the "stuff of analysis" (p. 56), allowing one to "differentiate and combine the data you have retrieved and the reflections you make about this information" (p. 56). They argue that coding is a process that enables the researcher to identify meaningful data and set the stage for interpreting and drawing conclusions. They describe codes as tags or labels for assigning units of meaning to the descriptive or inferential information compiled during a study. Codes usually are attached to "chunks" of varying size—words, phrases, sentences or whole paragraphs, connected or unconnected to a specific setting. They can take the form of a straightforward category label or a more complex one (e.g. metaphor). (Miles & Huberman, 1994, p. 56)

They go on to say how they see codes being used to retrieve and organize data:

The organizing part will entail some system for categorizing the various chunks, so the researcher can quickly find, pull out and cluster the segments relating to a particular research question, hypothesis, construct or theme. (Miles & Huberman, 1994, p. 57)

Later in this chapter, we provide some examples, drawn from the data on anthropology students and their mentors, illustrating how codes can be assigned to chunks of data and how we can then use these codes to generate concepts and themes. Before we do so, however, it might be useful to review some of the different ways in which coding can be approached.

On the one hand, coding can be thought about in terms of data simplification or reduction. If the codes are kept to a general level and their number relatively small, then the data are reduced to their bare bones, stripped down to a simple general form. This coding approach can be compared directly to simple forms of content analysis (Krippendorf, 1980). The addition of simple, broad analytic categories or codes can thus be used to reduce the data to manageable proportions. Here the analyst is concerned primarily with the identification of a simple conceptual schema. The main goal of such coding is to facilitate the retrieval of data segments categorized under the same codes. Coding in this context is essentially a process of indexing the data texts, whether they be fieldnotes, interview transcripts, or other documents. Data are reduced to equivalence classes and categories. The qualitative analyst will thus be able to retrieve chunks or segments of textual data that share a common code. Such code-and-retrieve procedures can be used to treat the data in quasi-quantitative ways by, for example, aggregating instances, mapping their incidence, and measuring the relative incidence of different codes. Such coding and retrieving can be implemented in a

variety of manual styles. Texts can be marked up physically with marginal keywords or code words, different colors can be used to mark or
highlight the texts, and index cards can be used to cross-reference
instances to numbered pages or paragraphs in the data.

Such a code-and-retrieve procedure also has been implemented using
a number of computer software packages. There are now a number of
applications designed specifically for the analysis of qualitative data,
some of which we introduce in more detail in Chapter 7. Many of the
contemporary programs incorporate code-and-retrieve functions. Such
data-handling procedures also can be accomplished to varying degrees
by the general cut-and-paste functions of word-processing software (see
Stanley & Temple, in press).

Coding and retrieving is the procedure most often associated with
coding as an analytic strategy. The role of coding in such a conceptualization is to undertake three kinds of operations, according to Seidel and
Kelle (1995, pp. 55-56): (a) noticing relevant phenomena, (b) collecting
examples of those phenomena, and (c) analyzing those phenomena in
order to find commonalities, differences, patterns, and structures. Seidel
and Kelle are clear that even when coding is used to reduce data, codes
are heuristic devices. In this sense, coding qualitative data differs from
quantitative analysis, for we are not merely counting. Rather, we are
attaching codes as a way of identifying and reordering data, allowing the
data to be thought about in new and different ways. Coding is the
mechanics of a more subtle process of having ideas and using concepts
about the data. It can be viewed as

> nothing more than a preparation for this process which is based on a careful
> inspection and analysis of raw data (that is segments of text) and on their
> comparison for the sake of identifying patterns and structure. (Seidel & Kelle,
> 1995, p. 58)

As well as data simplification and reduction, coding can be conceptualized as data complication. Coding need not be viewed simply as
reducing data to some general, common denominators. Rather, it can
be used to expand, transform, and reconceptualize data, opening up
more diverse analytical possibilities. We go on to say more about this
later in the chapter, but it is important to recognize at the outset that in
the hands of commentators such as Anselm Strauss, coding can refer to

a different kind of orientation toward one's data from that implied by
data reduction. The general analytic approach here is not to simplify the
data but to open them up in order to interrogate them further, to try to
identify and speculate about further features. Such data complication is
not used to retrieve and to aggregate instances to a restricted number of
categories; rather, it is intended to expand the conceptual frameworks
and dimensions for analysis. Coding here is actually about going beyond
the data, thinking creatively with the data, asking the data questions, and
generating theories and frameworks.

In practice, coding usually is a mixture of data reduction and data
complication. Coding generally is used to break up and segment the data
into simpler, general categories *and* is used to expand and tease out the
data, in order to formulate new questions and levels of interpretation.
One should try to ensure that coding does not lose more than is gained.
It is especially important to avoid the use of coding merely to apply
simple and deterministic labels to the data. Data reduction or simplification of that sort is not the main analytic purpose of qualitative coding.
Coding should be thought of as essentially heuristic, providing ways of
interacting with and thinking about the data. Those processes of reflection are more important ultimately than the precise procedures and
representations that are employed.

Seidel and Kelle (1995, p. 58) capture this by saying that "codes do
not serve primarily as denominators of certain phenomena but as *heuristic devices* for discovery." This is apparent whichever model or approach to coding is adopted. Take, for example, the approach of Tesch
(1990). Tesch describes qualitative analysis in terms of decontextualization and recontextualization. Decontextualizing data involves segmenting portions of data and slicing up the data set. Tesch defines segmenting
as dividing data into portions that are comprehensible by themselves and
large enough to be meaningful. Decontextualization means separating
data extracts from their original context while retaining meaning. Segmented data are then organized and sorted as part of a process of
recontextualization. Tesch (1990) suggests that the first step of sorting

> consists of tagging text segments with information about the category of the
> organizing system into which it belongs (or several categories if the segment
> is relevant to more than one). Many researchers call this process "coding."
> (p. 121)

Tesch (1990) suggests that once data segments have been coded, they are still not ready for interpretation. Drawing on the work of Marton (1986), who argues that each quotation has two contexts—the one from which it was taken and the "pool of meaning" to which it belongs—Tesch suggests that an organizing system for data is based on developing pools of meaning. Concepts are identified or constructed from prior material, theoretical frameworks, research questions, or the data themselves. The segmented data are coded according to those organizing categories and then re-sorted, again according to those categories. Data segments are reassembled or recontextualized. Coding as part of this process aids the recontextualization of data, giving a new context for data segments. In this way, Tesch regards coding as a means of providing new contexts for viewing and analyzing data. Decontextualizing and recontextualizing help to reduce and then expand the data in new forms and with new organizing principles. To put it another way, segmenting and coding data enable the researcher to think about and with the data.

Strauss (1987) provides perhaps the best example of using coding to complicate and expand qualitative data. We discuss the work of Strauss and his collaborators in more detail later in this chapter. For now, it is important to note that Strauss advocates coding as an essential analytical procedure. He argues that qualitative researchers must learn to code well and easily. Strauss also is keen to stress that coding is often misunderstood to be a simple and unproblematic procedure. The argument here is that coding is much more than simply giving categories to data; it is also about conceptualizing the data, raising questions, providing provisional answers about the relationships among and within the data, and discovering the data. Strauss argues that coding should be used to open up the inquiry and move toward interpretation. Coding is thus about breaking the data apart in analytically relevant ways in order to lead toward further questions about the data. To paraphrase Strauss (1987), coding can be viewed as a way toward the excitement and inevitable payoff of grounded conceptualization.

We can get ideas for coding from a variety of sources that are not mutually exclusive. We can start with a simple framework for coding based on what we as researchers are interested in. Reading through data extracts, one might discover particular events, key words, processes, or characters that capture the essence of the piece. Alternatively, one might code the data extracts using a code list created prior to reading the data. Miles and Huberman (1994) suggest that this method, of creating a "start list" of codes prior to reading the data or even prior to the fieldwork, is a useful way of beginning to code. These codes or categories can come from a variety of sources. For example, we can start from our theoretical or conceptual frameworks—coding data according to key concepts and theoretical ideas. We might have hypotheses that could be used to select code words to identify segments of the data, in order to test or modify those ideas. Equally, we could start with preselected codes taken from our reading in the general area, or a comparative area, or previous studies. Key variables and concepts can be derived from the research literature.

Another way of beginning to code is to start from the foreshadowed research question that inspired the research project. One might begin with the data and categorize them in a more inductive fashion, starting with the local categories of the actors or informants themselves. We can thus categorize the data more in accordance with the indigenous terms and categories of the culture or the individual informants. We will try to illustrate such thought processes when we explore some of our own data later in this chapter.

It is worth stressing here that codes are organizing principles that are not set in stone. They are our own creations, in that we identify and select them ourselves. They are tools to think with. They can be expanded, changed, or scrapped altogether as our ideas develop through repeated interactions with the data. Starting to create categories is a way of beginning to read and think about the data in a systematic and organized way.

What to code, or what categories to create, will always partly depend on the intent of your data analysis. Strauss (1987) makes the distinction between sociologically constructed codes and in vivo codes. The latter refer to codes that derive from the terms and the language used by social actors in the field, or in the course of interviews. The systematic use of in vivo codes can be used to develop a "bottom up" approach to the derivation of categories from the content of the data. Initial coding, then, should help us to identify themes, patterns, events, and actions that are of interest to the researcher and that provide a means of organizing data sets. Coding can be more or less complex, depending on the level of analysis.

The Coding Process

The segmenting of data using codes or categories, as we have indicated, can be achieved in a variety of ways, through the application of a variety of analytical strategies. For the purposes of illustration, we have taken an extract from an interview with an established academic in anthropology. The interview extract focuses on the question of what makes a good doctorate. Set out below is the interview extract, to which we have attached a number of coding categories.

Extract From Interview With Dr. Fitton (Kingford University)

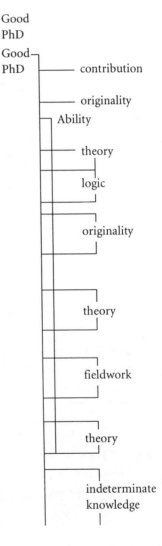

Odette Parry: What do you think makes a good PhD? — Good PhD

Dr. Fitton: I think PhDs should show a substantial contribution to research, but I don't think that necessarily means innovation for innovation's sake. — Good PhD — contribution — originality

I personally would want to favour a PhD which showed a very sound knowledge of theoretical positions, an ability to sort out those positions and put forward something in a logical, coherent, structured fashion. I'd favour someone who was able to do that over someone who has studied something that no one had thought of studying before, and you're encouraging something that is peripheral, marginal, not necessarily of significance. So I think that what I would look for is a very sound acquaintance with theoretical work, an ability to sort it out, and take it further—have a sufficient substantial commentary on that work, combined in the case of anthropology with fieldwork, and showing that the fieldwork had been done in a way which shows empathy with the people you'd studied, and that the fieldwork and the theoretical part had been merged together. — Ability — theory — logic — originality — theory — fieldwork — theory

Quite a tall order. I'd look for a "feel" about the work, I wouldn't have a list of guiding points, because I don't think you can do that—they are too different. It has — indeterminate knowledge been said that the strength of anthropology is its eclecticism, it relies on qualitative analysis rather than quantitative.

Odette Parry: This is really a general question. Why do you think people do anthropology PhDs?

Dr. Fitton: In some cases it's the obvious reason that doing a PhD will hopefully lead to the first rung of the academic track. My own motivation was not that clear. I was surprised when I did get a job at the end of it, but to further an interest I wanted to take as far as I could. I expect most people doing a PhD are doing it to further an interest they have. There seems to be a trend towards PhDs written to do with development, so you could say that a concern for other societies is another factor. So it's not just a selfish endeavour. I can think of one student I've had, the interest in doing a PhD wasn't there, there was an external push, she was expected to get high qualifications. And because her heart wasn't in it, she didn't have the necessary enthusiasm and drive for it.

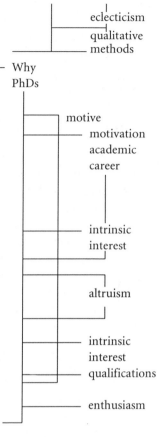

As shown here, with a relatively simple approach to the process of coding, different levels of complexity can be explored. What we have done here, in fact, is summarize a series of successive decisions about the data and its categorization. When they are superimposed in one display, it easily can look as if they were all derived simultaneously, from the same set of interests and concerns. That is not the case, and here we try to indicate some of the decisions that have gone into such a coding outcome.

At the simplest level, the data can be reduced to two possible generic categories: "a good PhD" and "why people do a PhD." These reflect directly the questions that Odette Parry asked and reflect two of the substantive problems that the research team brought to the data-collection exercise. The research was intended to examine some of the personal and institutional factors that influence the PhD process, including views on the PhD itself as a means of academic socialization. Clearly, coding the data according to those themes adds nothing initially to our understanding of the data. It is essentially a data-reduction task. Segmenting and coding the data in that particular way would at least allow us to characterize what each stretch of the interview was about in terms of general thematic content, in this instance relating directly to the topics of the interview elicitations and responses. Such wide, generic categories would facilitate the retrieval of different segments of data that deal with descriptions of good PhDs and academics' speculations as to doctoral candidates' motivations.

The application of these and equivalent codes, reflecting substantive research questions, would be one basic way of organizing the data. Such procedures have considerable practical value. The nature of qualitative data means that data relating to one particular topic are not found neatly bundled together at exactly the same spot in each interview (and field-notes usually have even less predictable organization). The ability to locate stretches of data that, at least ostensibly, are "about" the same thing is a valuable aspect of data management. Such coding, therefore, can be a useful preliminary to more detailed analysis. We could proceed a little further in the same vein. Another way of thinking about this particular data extract would be to "code" in terms of specific abilities or competencies identified by the informant. That is, as we have indicated, the first half of the interview extract definitely describes a number of abilities or attributes linked to the production of a good PhD. Coded as "ability," this data segment could be used to search for and compare other aspects of the data set where graduate students' abilities are referred to. For example, PhD supervisors might in other contexts refer to the abilities required for supervising doctoral work or for being a successful academic more generally. Likewise, doctoral students in interviews might also describe their experience in terms of the abilities they brought to their studies, developed over the course of their research, failed to develop, and so forth. Each category of actor might refer to their own competence and that of other actors. As is clear, these very general categories promote the reordering of the data in accordance with preliminary ideas or concepts. They are not necessarily the final ways in which the data can be examined and explored. This first approach to the data, however, does little or nothing toward complicating the questions we can ask about them. If we are going to use coding to generate more interesting and complex ideas about our materials, then we need to do something more. Most fundamentally, we need to think more about how we interact with the data.

Coding at such a very general level is a first step toward organizing the data into meaningful categories. It can be seen as the first level of coding. As we demonstrate in the data extract above, coding also can be thought about in a more complex way. Using a *good PhD,* or *ability,* or *why a PhD* as initial codes or categories, a number of subcategories can be generated and used to segment the data. In this extract, we have identified a number of such categories and attached codes accordingly. Some of those more detailed codes come more or less directly from the informant's words, such as *enthusiasm.* Others are our summary glosses of what the informant seems to be referring to or describing at a particular point in the text. For example, we have glossed one of the motivating factors as *altruism,* not the actual word used by the informant but used by us to capture descriptions of motivation based on or ascribed to the desire to help others or a commitment to another culture. Other codes reflect more directly *our* conceptual interests. For example, we have categorized one segment as referring to *indeterminate knowledge.* Dr. Fitton is talking about evaluating a PhD with reference to its "feel" and talks about a lack of specific guidelines. Our identification of the segment in this way, and our decision to code as we have, reflects our own interest in pursuing how anthropologists talk about their own knowledge and the knowledge of other anthropologists, past and present. Here, therefore, we note an appeal to an apparently indeterminate criterion in evaluating doctoral students' work. In coding it as we have, we can collate all the instances where similar appeals to indeterminate knowledge have been made, talked about, or denied. We can inspect those instances further to examine the varieties of indeterminate knowledge and their sources, how indeterminate knowledge is evaluated, how it is learned, and so on.

These more detailed subcategories can be represented by a single code attached to a discrete segment of the data. Subcategories also can overlap one another. Codes and their segments can be nested or embedded within one another, can overlap, and can intersect. The same subcategory can be applied several times in a single unit of data (such as an interview), and the same segment can have more than one code attached to it. In the data extract above, the dense nesting and overlapping of the more detailed codings can be seen. These dense patternings are quite characteristic of code maps of qualitative data. After all, ordinary social action, including conversational talk, does not present itself to us in neatly bounded packages. When we segment the data by attaching codes, we often reflect how topics run into one another and how there may be multiple issues to concern ourselves with simultaneously.

Coding is never a mechanistic activity. Because of our selection of a data extract, we hope that the outcomes are fairly transparent, but they are by no means automatic. We need to *decide,* for example, not only what aspects of the data to tag with codes but also what levels of generality or detail to go into. As we have indicated in the extract above, we have identified and defined three levels of generality. The most general categories are two: what makes a good PhD and the motivation to undertake a PhD. In this instance—and by no means is this always true—the categories correspond with the thrust of questioning in the interviews and were part of the agenda followed in the semistructured interviews themselves. We have here identified an intermediate category, having to do with the abilities or competencies required for the successful completion of a PhD. The third and most specific level of category breaks down those more general themes into more specific and detailed codes. As can be seen from how we have marked those codes on the extract, they also relate to stretches of the interview of different lengths. The more detailed, specific codes are embedded within the longer, more general ones. This is a feature of dense, detailed coding that becomes especially important in the computer-assisted handling of qualitative data, which we discuss in Chapter 7. The identification of codes and decisions about levels of detail are far from straightforward. As Weaver and Atkinson (1994, p. 32) put it:

> [I]f we decide to delineate a number a number of general, inclusive categories, much of the text will be coded with a single code (or conjunction of codes). The advantage of this strategy is that it should maximize the usefulness of the codes; they are likely to be applied to enough segments to justify the purpose of recontextualization. However, it may also have several disadvantages. First, since so much text will be coded with the same category, there might be difficulty in locating particular episodes significant to analysis; a likely scenario is that the researcher will have to siphon through reams of

irrelevant data, despite recontextualization. Second, coding may be too crude, and this might make the analysis seem rather vague, lacking detail, or the exploratory avenues of analysis being superficially restricted.

On the other hand, coding schemes that are too detailed can be equally problematic:

> [I]f we decide to define a large number of categories, with fairly exclusive meaning, the problems are reversed. Coding will be more detailed and intricate, and there will be a greater differentiation of segments accordingly. However, if the segmentation of text is too intricate, in that specific categories are attached to very small segments of text, important contextual information may be lost, and thereby some of the segments' meanings. (Weaver & Atkinson, 1994, p. 32)

As a consequence, Weaver and Atkinson made an explicit decision to include codes of different degrees of generality so that data retrieval could be undertaken at different levels.

We can develop and illustrate decision-making processes, as well as the significance of different levels of coding, with another extract from the interview data. As will be seen, it deals with a set of issues similar to those identified from our first extract.

Extract From Interview With Dr. Throstle (Southersham University)

Odette Parry: What sorts of skills do you think it imparts, the actual process of doing a PhD?

Dr. Throstle: It's a very big question. Again I think in anthropology you learn a whole lot of things that you don't normally learn in a PhD, which is partly to do with fieldwork. That trains you to carry on on your own both academically and personally, it's social skills training of a very exacting kind.

. . .

I think one of the peculiarities of anthropology is that unlike most other disciplines, certainly in the social sciences, you're dealing—unlike history for example—you don't start from one body of documentation and convert it into another kind of body of documentation, you start with people's lives and conversations with them and you have to turn that into an academic text.

Which is why it takes such a long time and why it's so difficult, because these two things are miles and miles apart. And it's very common, I think, for graduate students when they come back from the field to react against what they're doing, to feel that what they're writing is somehow a betrayal or it falls far short of the relationships they had when they were in the field. Writing a rather dull piece of academic work somehow feels like a betrayal.

Nevertheless most students learn to do that, and in the process learn an immense amount not only about the people they study, but also writing skills and how to produce a high-level academic text.

I think one of the problems of fieldwork, if you're away for a long time—and most anthropologists are—you lose touch to some extent with your academic and your home culture, and then you have to get back into it, and it's often a slow process when you come back.

It would be easy to treat this extract in much the same way as we did the first extract, and to deal with it initially in terms of Odette Parry's elicitation. We could thus relate it primarily to the kinds of skills that the question asked about. Below, therefore, we have categorized the data extract accordingly. It will be seen that we allowed ourselves to stick closely to the overarching theme implied in the question about skills.

Odette Parry: What sorts of skills do you think it imparts, the actual process of doing a PhD?

skills from PhD

Dr. Throstle: It's a very big question. Again I think in anthropology you learn a whole lot of things that you don't normally learn in a PhD, which is partly to do with fieldwork. That trains you to carry on on your own both academically and personally, it's social skills training of a very exacting kind. . . .

academic

personal

social

I think one of the peculiarities of anthropology is   writing
   that unlike most other disciplines, certainly in the
   social sciences, you're dealing—unlike history
   for example—you don't start from one body of
   documentation and convert it into another kind
   of body of documentation, you start with people's lives and conversations with them and you
   have to turn that into an academic text.

Which is why it takes such a long time and why it's   writing
   so difficult, because these two things are miles
   and miles apart. And it's very common, I think,
   for graduate students when they come back from
   the field to react against what they're doing, to
   feel that what they're writing is somehow a betrayal or it falls far short of the relationships they
   had when they were in the field. Writing a rather
   dull piece of academic work somehow feels like a
   betrayal.

Nevertheless most students learn to do that, and in   writing
   the process learn an immense amount not only
   about the people they study, but also writing skills
   and how to produce a high-level academic text.

I think one of the problems of fieldwork, if you're
   away for a long time—and most anthropologists
   are—you lose touch to some extent with your
   academic and your home culture, and then you
   have to get back into it and it's often a slow
   process when you come back.

We can see here that so far we have produced a very thin and flat set
of categories. They reproduce only the bare bones of skills and do not
appear to do justice to the dense descriptive language of this particular
academic. Another way of approaching the task, therefore, is to pay
much closer attention to the categories of expression that the informant
actually uses. Rather than using the interview extract as an extended reply
to our one question, therefore, we pay much closer attention to the
content of the talk. Here, therefore, we approach the data once more,
and now try to identify themes that reflect the informant's views more
closely. It is not necessary for us to use precisely the same words to index,

or code, those themes; we are interested in exploring them and linking them with other data segments, not only in labeling them.

Odette Parry: What sorts of skills do you think it imparts, the actual process of doing a PhD?	skills from PhD
Dr. Throstle: It's a very big question. Again I think in anthropology you learn a whole lot of things that you don't normally learn in a PhD, which is partly to do with fieldwork. That trains you to carry on on your own both academically and personally, it's social skills training of a very exacting kind. . . .	fieldwork normal PhD academic independence personal independence social skills exacting
I think one of the peculiarities of anthropology is that unlike most other disciplines, certainly in the social sciences, you're dealing—unlike history for example—you don't start from one body of documentation and convert it into another kind of body of documentation, you start with people's lives and conversations with them and you have to turn that into an academic text.	peculiarity disciplines social science history people lives conversation academic text
Which is why it takes such a long time and why it's so difficult, because these two things are miles and miles apart. And it's very common, I think, for graduate students when they come back from the field to react against what they're doing, to feel that what they're writing is somehow a betrayal or it falls far short of the relationships they had when they were in the field. Writing a rather dull piece of academic work somehow feels like a betrayal.	time difficult difference return from field writing relationships in the field dull academic work betrayal
Nevertheless most students learn to do that, and in the process learn an immense amount not only about the people they study, but also writing skills and how to produce a high-level academic text.	people writing high-level academic text

I think one of the problems of fieldwork, if you're away for a long time—and most anthropologists are—you lose touch to some extent with your academic and your home culture, and then you have to get back into it, and it's often a slow process when you come back.	fieldwork time absence academic culture home culture return

In indexing the data in this kind of way, we can start to develop a much denser set of themes and categories. We can start to glimpse some of the recurrent preoccupations of this particular anthropologist, and we can use such categorizations to build systematic comparisons and contrasts with the views expressed by other faculty members. In looking at the data in this way, moreover, we can start to identify some further themes and issues.

Having begun by staying close to the informant's own categories, we can start to see how they might be categorized further, possibly in relation to linking categories of our own devising. Take, for example, the first paragraph of the informant's reply. It will be seen that here she is prefacing a response about "skills" by saying that there is something distinctive about anthropology as a discipline that makes it different from others, certainly among the social sciences. This helps us to identify a superordinate category, which we might identify as *the distinctiveness of anthropology*. If we identify that as a category and code the data accordingly, then we can use that to search for other data extracts in which the anthropologists express what is special and distinctive about their subject.

There is also a potentially intriguing theme to be constructed from this anthropologist's words. Writing is identified as a major academic skill to be acquired, but that thought is expressed in a particular, and striking, way. Dr. Throstle talks of the difference between the academic text that the student must prepare and the people who were studied. People's lives and conversations have to be turned into text, and students find the essential difference between the social and the textual to be a problem. Not only is this a very interesting comment about anthropology, but it also connects with our previous category in two ways. First, it is offered as an example of how anthropology differs from other disciplines (the requirement of constructing a body of text out of lives and conversations). Second, it picks up on the significance of difference in a new way.

Let us look ahead in the data once more before commenting further. The informant talks about the importance of fieldwork. Fieldwork is introduced as one of the distinctive aspects of the anthropology PhD at the beginning of the extract. The topic reappears later. Toward the end, for example, fieldwork is contrasted with coming back, and there is a contrast between fieldwork, on one hand, and academic culture and home culture on the other. Again we see Dr. Throstle describing things in terms of difference, in this case differences between cultures. We can see now that there is a potential superordinate category relating to difference that relates to all these aspects of the interview extract. The differences that are described are different in content, but they all seem to relate to a coherent set of underlying issues: the distinctiveness of anthropology, the significance of fieldwork, and the separation of field-work from other aspects of the anthropologist's life. We should note that this theme, which relates closely to the content of the data, is clearly one that we have constructed. It is also one that takes us toward concepts of a more analytic, even theoretical, relevance. We have thus moved our coding process from identifying categories that remain close to the original data to those that imply much broader analytic issues. We may therefore return to the data once more and apply a further set of codes.

Odette Parry: What sorts of skills do you think it imparts, the actual process of doing a PhD?

Dr. Throstle: It's a very big question. Again I think in anthropology you learn a whole lot of things that you don't normally learn in a PhD, which is partly to do with fieldwork. That trains you to carry on on your own both academically and personally, it's social skills training of a very exacting kind. . . .

> distinctiveness   contrastive
> of anthropology   rhetoric
>
> significance of
> fieldwork

I think one of the peculiarities of anthropology is that unlike most other disciplines, certainly in the social sciences, you're dealing—unlike history for example—you don't start from one body of documentation and convert it into another kind of body of documentation,

> contrast anthropology
> with other disciplines
>
> difference between the
> field and academic texts

you start with people's lives and conversations with them and you have to turn
that into an academic text.

Which is why it takes such a long time and
why it's so difficult, because these two
things are miles and miles apart. And it's   difference between field
very common, I think, for graduate stu-   and academic texts
dents when they come back from the
field to react against what they're doing,   metaphor:
to feel that what they're writing is some-   betrayal
how a betrayal or it falls far short of the
relationships they had when they were in
the field. Writing a rather dull piece of
academic work somehow feels like a betrayal.

Nevertheless most students learn to do that,
and in the process learn an immense
amount not only about the people they
study, but also writing skills and how to
produce a high-level academic text.

I think one of the problems of fieldwork, if   difference between the
you're away for a long time—and most   field and academic
anthropologists are—you lose touch to   culture
some extent with your academic and your
home culture, and then you have to get   difference between the
back into it, and it's often a slow process   field and home culture
when you come back.

In attaching codes in this way we have indicated some key generic
issues. That work has been done as more than a mechanistic exercise in
segmenting the data. It reflects a series of readings and re-readings of the
data, in which the details of the interview and our own emergent concerns interact. We may also note while dealing with the interview text at
this level that the repeated references to differences and distances suggest
two further issues. In identifying these categories, we have also started
to move from a consideration of the content of the anthropologist's talk
in order to pay some attention to its form. We can note that his or her
descriptions draw on a recurrent pattern, a series of contrasts: anthro-
pology/other disciplines, fieldwork/home, and people's lives/academic

texts. In Chapter 4, we will consider in more detail how we can examine such formal properties, and we will discuss this particular property again when we consider *contrastive rhetoric* (Hargreaves, 1984) as one device that actors use in producing their accounts of the social world.

In considering form and content here, we have noted one further aspect of this academic's talk. We have identified the graphic way in which the distance between field and text is expressed. We are told that student anthropologists may feel that their work is a *betrayal*. Again, we will return to discuss the exploration of such figures of speech in Chapter 4, but we note that it may prove useful to identify figures of speech such as metaphors during the process of coding. We have therefore added two codes to the extract above, one identifying the use of contrastive rhetoric, the other identifying the location of this particular metaphor.

We have been through this one extract from our data and applied to it different, complementary sets of codes. For the sake of clarity, we have displayed the data and the codes separately. In the course of repeated examinations of the data for the purposes of a comprehensive analysis, we would not necessarily have recourse to such separation. We can think of the successive passes at the data as resulting in overlays of different codes, reflecting different levels of specificity or generality as well as reflecting different sets of analytic themes. These different approaches to the data could result in different physical disaggregations of the data: physically cutting up different copies or cutting and pasting segments into different files with the word processor. If we were using computer software to perform these tasks, we would be able to retrieve the coded segments by using different codes or combinations of codes to identify them.

Our illustrative example is not an exhaustive treatment of the data. Any other analyst could conceptualize them in different ways. The point is not to search for the "right" set of codes but to recognize them for what they are: links between particular segments of data and the categories we want to use in order to conceptualize those segments.

Beyond Coding and Toward Interpretation

Coding qualitative data enables the researcher to recognize and re-contextualize data, allowing a fresh view of what is there. Because coding inevitably involves the reading and re-reading of data and making selections from the data, it involves interpreting the data set. However, a key issue is what to do with data once they have been selected, cut up, fragmented, coded, and categorized. The move from coding to interpretation is a crucial one, as Wolcott (1994) suggests. Interpretation involves the transcendence of "factual" data and cautious analysis of what is to be made of them.

Once coding is achieved, the data have to be interrogated (Delamont, 1992) and systematically explored to generate meaning. There is a case that coding, while reorganizing data, also involves a certain amount of information loss. To some extent, that depends on how thorough and detailed the coding has been. The data loss is much greater if one does not move from the process of coding to an exploration of how codes and categories relate to the original data, to other data, to theoretical ideas, and so forth. Ian Dey (1993) argues that categorizing enables one to think about the data in a new way. This is only the case if we move beyond the codes, categories, and data bits back to what the "whole" picture is or may be.

The move from coding to interpretation has a number of discrete levels. First, the coded data need to be retrieved. This essentially means that recontextualized data need to be displayed in such a way that they can be read easily. The data bits that relate to a particular code or category need to be presented together in order for the researcher to explore the composition of each coded set. Huberman and Miles (1994) argue that data display is a key element of the analytical process. This can be achieved by organizing all the data under a particular code physically in the same place; by producing diagrams, matrices, and maps of the code; or by using a retrieval function on a microcomputing program. Whichever way it is done, the idea is that the codes or categories and the data need to be in such a form that they are accessible both for reading and for exploring.

Second, the move from coding to interpretation involves playing with and exploring the codes and categories that were created. Dey (1993) provides many ideas about how you can go about doing this. He suggests that once data are displayed in a coded form, the categories can be retrieved, split into subcategories, spliced, and linked together. Essentially, the codes and categories you have selected should be used to make pathways through the data. It is worth remembering here that such codes are *not* cast in stone. As you chose and selected them, so you can abandon, change, re-sort, rename, and so on. Similarly, once you are in a position to look at all the data across the codes, you should not be tempted to ignore incidents, events, individuals, or chunks of data that do not "fit" into the codes. The exceptions, misfits, and "negative" findings should be seen as having as much importance to the process of coding as do the easily coded data.

This leads to a further level of the process of moving from coding to interpretation, that is, the transformation of the coded data into meaningful data. Here, the emphasis is on what to look for in the codes and categories. Delamont (1992) suggests that one should be looking for patterns, themes, and regularities as well as contrasts, paradoxes, and irregularities. One then can move toward generalizing and theorizing from the data. The emphasis on the "negative" exceptions as well as the "positive" patterns remains crucial. Huberman and Miles (1994) work from a similar continuum. They suggest no less than 13 "tactics" for generating meaning or data transformation. These move from descriptive through explanatory tactics. At the one end of the continuum are things such as noting patterns of themes, the "counting" of phenomena occurring from the data, and comparing and contrasting the data sets. At the opposite end are the moves toward generalizing, noting and questioning the relations between variables, and finding conceptual and theoretical coherence in the data.

We already have illustrated how codes can represent categories of different sorts. Some of those already imply interpretive frameworks and link data segments to emergent concepts. Hence, we do not need always to think of coding first and theorizing afterward. Our decision making implies analytic ideas at every stage of the coding process. Furthermore, we already have seen that our codings can imply systematic relationships among categories and concepts. These relationships can form one basis for the development of interpretations. For example, if we return to the second of our data extracts, we can see that our codings start to suggest possible relationships. The different levels of coding suggest that some categories may subsume a number of others. This is so for several different codings. For example, Dr. Fitton's responses in the first extract suggest the following kinds of relationships:

Student motivation   Academic career
                              Intrinsic interest
                              Altruistic commitment

Good PhDs   Originality
                                   Theoretical knowledge
                                   Logical coherence
                                   Quality of fieldwork

In a different way, we have seen how Dr. Throstle's coded comments can be linked through a common use of difference and distance, which could linked in the coding scheme through a code of *contrast*. In other words, our codes not only establish linkages between data and concepts; they also can start to map out dimensions within conceptual categories and to establish superordinate links among concepts. We can summarize this set of more abstract ideas as follows:

Difference   Home culture/Field
                                   Field/Academic culture
                                   People's lives/Academic texts
                                   Anthropology/Other disciplines

We will suggest in Chapter 6 that although there is more to it than linking codes, the establishment of ordered relationships between codes and concepts is a significant starting point for reflection and for theory building from qualitative data.

Strauss (1987) develops the use of coding as part of the process of interpretation and analysis. That is, Strauss links the initial process of coding (which he refers to as *open coding* and which is essentially what we did with the interview extract with which we exemplified our earlier discussion) to a more refined process of using categories to generate broader conceptual frameworks. Strauss identifies a set of procedures that allows initial categories to be elaborated and developed.

We are not going to follow Strauss's own model closely. We do not recapitulate all the steps and analytic strategies that he identifies or has codified in his work with Corbin (Strauss & Corbin, 1990). Indeed, it is worth noting in this context that Glaser (1992) accuses Strauss of taking the general inspiration and strategic approach of "grounded theory" and transforming them into unduly prescriptive recipes for analysis. Nevertheless, the general approach to coding that is to be found in Strauss's methodological writing is valuable in encouraging the researcher to move beyond local codings to generate ideas and broader conceptual frameworks.

In essence, Strauss's approach encourages us to go beyond the essentially "summary" approach to coding in which the data are simply reduced to a limited set of categories. Strauss does not encourage us simply to index the data, as it were, or to use the code words merely to mark and retrieve segments of data. On the contrary, his general approach exhorts us to expand on rather than to reduce the data, to take categories and exhaust their full analytic potential. One point is to use our codings and categories to think with and not to remain anchored in the data (notes, transcripts, etc.) alone.

From this general perspective, the process of coding is about asking oneself questions about the data. Those questions help to develop lines of speculation and hypothesis formation. In accordance with more general principles of grounded theory, they may also direct further data collection strategies. In the course of open and axial coding, then, one takes as a topic a "phenomenon" (in Strauss's terms) and attempts to identify its dimensions, its consequences, and its relationships with other phenomena.

For example, if we return to our previous data extract, we start to think more creatively about some of the themes that we have begun to identify in our coding. Consider once more the same interview extract (see pp. 38-39). When we first coded that, we were able to identify stretches of the transcript that seemed to refer to theoretical sophistication, analytic value, originality, fieldwork, indeterminate knowledge, contribution to the discipline, and empathy with the people studied. These were all in an informant's response to the question of what makes a good PhD, and all those separate code words, and the fragments they refer to, all seem to bear on one major phenomenon, that is, the essence of what it takes to produce a successful PhD in social anthropology. We can, therefore, start to think about the various possible "dimensions" of such abilities or competencies.

In this one account, we find the established anthropologist constructing his own characterization of how the competencies are (or should be) combined in one ideal-typical doctoral candidate. In thinking more about this phenomenon, we need to ask ourselves, and to ask of the data, what sorts of abilities or competencies are recognized and described. Our first informant has given us the abilities to theorize, to organize and structure coherent arguments, to empathize with the people studied, to make an original contribution to the discipline, to do fieldwork, and to integrate fieldwork and theory. Further, we note that these abilities are generally characterized as indeterminate qualities rather than being rendered explicit. In looking at other interviews, we note that other categories and codings bear on the same general phenomenon. They are expressed in different ways, for example, the abilities to turn other people's lives and conversations into academic text, to do scholarship, to be original, to be critical, to add to human understanding, to put a new slant on what's been written before, and to contribute to the ongoing debates. Successful anthropologists should also have a distinctive approach and exhibit openness, humility, and the ability to reflect upon themselves. The open coding of a series of interviews would therefore give us a wide range of dimensions of "ability" or "competence" or "quality" (the general phenomenon is very general indeed).

We can also go on to think about some further features. For example, under "axial" coding, Strauss recommends thinking about such features as *consequences*. Following that line of reasoning, we can go beyond the data immediately at hand and ask ourselves such further questions as "What happens if . . .?" For example, we can ask "What happens if there isn't any fieldwork?" That question can inform further inspection of the data, further data collection as the research develops, or both. Inspection of our anthropology data suggests that there may be different answers to that question, depending on the antecedents or causes of fieldwork being absent (another of Strauss's features of axial coding). For example, fieldwork may not take place because the graduate student has decided to pursue "library research" (a term used by our informants). Further exploration of consequences and antecedents shows that library research is often discouraged, and the absence of fieldwork, though deliberate, may be stigmatizing. On the other hand, fieldwork may be incomplete because of conditions beyond the student's control (such as civil disorder). This is not stigmatizing, though it may prove to be a major handicap and is unfortunate. Such observations again help us to open up questions about the significance of fieldwork in the construction of a professional career and an academic identity.

In the same vein, we can ask ourselves what the consequences are for the writing and organizing of the thesis. What are the consequences of not having the ability to integrate theory and fieldwork, or of not making a "contribution" to the area of specialization? Such a reflection perhaps would take us to other aspects of the data. We might look for academic supervisors' accounts of how PhD theses get examined and what aspects of organization and style are rewarded or penalized. We also need to explore the students' accounts of their writing, looking for such things as their strategies for writing, their experiences of writer's block, and their strategies for writing. We need to examine our data (or, ideally, collect further data) on how our anthropologists recognize and reward "a contribution" to the discipline or to a particular debate within it. In procedural terms, this means cross-reference to the "open" codings identified elsewhere in the data. In intellectual terms, it means using the various elements in the data to pursue lines of interrogation and speculation—moving between data and codings to explore and expand on key analytic themes.

We might also follow others of Strauss's analytic strategies in coding—thinking about conditions and antecedents, perhaps. We can ask ourselves, for example, about the antecedents of fieldwork. This approach would probably lead us to think about and to search out data concerning the necessary preconditions (organizational, personal, academic) to embarking on fieldwork. We would then find ourselves asking—and interrogating the data—about when fieldwork is possible and who gets to decide about it (where, under what circumstances, with what intellectual preparation). We would also start to explore some of the more mundane antecedents and conditions, the practical tasks and relationships that go into the practical work of fieldwork. We might thus start to generate ideas and themes that lead us to think seriously and systematically about academic and practical dimensions of anthropological fieldwork. One would hope to be generating themes that facilitated comparative thinking and exploration, for example, contrasting with other travelers to exotic parts, such as war correspondents, travel writers, workers in international transport, or others who live on a long-term basis away from their home base and creature comforts.

Conclusion

In this chapter, we have explored some of the rationales for coding qualitative data and introduced some of the different approaches to be found in the methodological literature and in practice. This discussion has not been intended as a comprehensive cookbook as to how to

perform coding. We have preferred to discuss contrasting and complementary strategies rather than prescriptively recommending a single
orthodoxy. We also have tried to suggest from time to time that "coding,"
however it may be conceptualized and carried out, is not the final word
on qualitative data analysis.

The segmentation of field data and retrieval of marked data segments
is a valuable resource in the management of qualitative data. It is an
established approach that in recent years has been reinforced by the
development of microcomputing strategies (Weaver & Atkinson, 1994),
many of which essentially recapitulate the same logic of data handling.
They substitute rapid and comprehensive searching supported by software for the uncertain and slow process of manual searching and filing.
In and of themselves, however, such procedures by no means exhaust
either the possibilities of the data or, therefore, the possibilities of data
exploration. In particular, it should be apparent that the fragmentation
of data, dependent on code-and-retrieve approaches, or what Tesch
(1990) called the decontextualization of data, does little to preserve
formal features of those data.

Our interview informants may tell us long and complicated accounts
and reminiscences. When we chop them up into separate coded segments, we are in danger of losing the sense that they are accounts. We
lose sight, if we are not careful, of the fact that they are often couched in
terms of stories—as narratives—or that they have other formal properties in terms of their discourse structure. Segmenting and coding may be
an important, even an indispensable, part of the research process, but it
is not the whole story. Consequently, we turn to a consideration of
narrative analysis in the chapter that follows. We will see how one can
look at the same sort of data from a fresh perspective, paying due
attention to its more formal properties and being sensitive to the *storied*
quality of many qualitative data.

Suggestions for Further Reading

Dey, I. (1993) *Qualitative data analysis: A user friendly guide for social scientists.* London:
    Routledge and Kegan Paul.
    *An unusually detailed description of the processes of categorizing and coding qualitative
    data. Illustrated with data extracts from Woody Allen and Victoria Wood scripts.*

Addressed to the management of coded data on computer. Dey is the developer of the software application called Hyperresearch.

Miles, M. B., & Huberman, A. M. (1994). *Qualitative data analysis: An expanded sourcebook* (2nd ed.). Thousand Oaks, CA: Sage.

An exceptionally systematic and formal approach to the classification and representation of qualitative data. A uniquely rich source for analytic ideas, with a strong visual emphasis.

Strauss, A. L. (1987). *Qualitative analysis for social scientists.* Cambridge, UK: Cambridge University Press.

An unusually detailed account of Strauss's own approach to data analysis. Illustrated throughout with extracts from Strauss's postgraduate seminars, giving a particularly privileged insight into his preferred approach.

Strauss, A. L., & Corbin, J. (1990). *Basics of qualitative research: Grounded theory, procedures, and techniques.* Newbury Park, CA: Sage.

An accessible introduction to coding procedures, following Strauss's approach to grounded theorizing. Goes beyond coding itself to discuss the development of ideas and theoretical frameworks.

Tesch, R. (1990). *Qualitative research: Analysis types and software tools.* London: Falmer.

Combines a general discussion of analytic strategies with a survey of computer software packages for qualitative data management and analysis.

3

Narratives and Stories

Collecting and Analyzing Stories

This chapter focuses on the storied qualities of qualitative textual data, that is, the ways in which social actors produce, represent, and contextualize experience and personal knowledge through narratives and other genres. We do not make elaborate distinctions between stories and narratives. There are many definitions and discriminations in the research literature, and for some purposes, such definitions may have value. As Riessman (1993) points out, however, the variety of narrative styles, on one hand, and the variety of analytic distinctions, on the other, defy summary definition. We concentrate therefore on outlining a simple approach to "doing research with first-person accounts of experience" (Riessman, 1993, p. 17).

For some purposes, it makes sense to use narrative and narrative analysis as inclusive categories, restricting the use of "story" to those genres that recount protagonists, events, complications, and consequences. We cannot present a comprehensive review of the field, and we do not therefore attempt to describe all the varieties of narrative performance that can be identified (see Riessman, 1993). We use this chapter to explore how, as qualitative researchers, we can collect and analyze the stories and narratives of our informants. In the recent past, storytelling and the creation of literary and narrative accounts have been utilized by qualitative researchers (from differing perspectives) as mechanisms for collecting and interpreting data. In this chapter, we concentrate on the identification and analysis of narratives in interview and similar data. In Chapter 5, we pay particular attention to how we can utilize the literary ideas of stories to produce texts of our research endeavors.

We argue that thinking about stories in our data can enable us to think creatively about the sorts of data we collect and how we interpret them. Using examples drawn from our anthropology data, we try to emphasize that stories our informants tell can be seen, on one hand, as highly structured (and formal) ways of transmitting information. On the other hand, they can be seen as distinctive, creative, artful genres. In presenting and exploring some of the ways in which we can interpret and analyze stories or narratives, we are not overly inclusive. Our ideas about the ways in which narratives can be analyzed should not be seen as the only ways of approaching the task, nor should they be seen as prescriptive. The ideas we discuss here should be seen as points of departure toward more detailed analytic tasks.

The collection of stories and narratives in qualitative research extends what Riessman (1993) calls the "interpretative turn" in social science. Denzin's (1989) description of interpretive biography provides a framework with which we can contextualize a narrative account. Denzin describes a narrative as a story of a sequence of events that has significance for the narrator and her audience. The story (as do all good stories) has a beginning, a middle, and an end, as well as a logic that (at least) makes sense to the narrator. Denzin (1989, p. 37) also suggests that narratives are temporal and logical:

> A story . . . tells a sequence of events that are significant for the narrator [the respondent/social actor] and his or her audience. A narrative as a story has a plot, a beginning, a middle and an end. It has internal logic that makes sense to the narrator. A narrative relates events in a temporal, causal sequence. Every narrative describes a sequence of events that have happened. Hence narratives are temporal productions.

We should make it clear here that, while concentrating on the genre of storytelling, we are not suggesting that there is only one form of story or narrative.

Narratives and stories can be collected "naturally"; for example, by recording stories as they occur during participant observation in a research setting. Alternatively, they can be solicited during research interviews. Mishler's (1986) work in particular considers interview responses in terms of the stories they embody. As Riessman (1993) notes, during research interviews respondents often hold the floor for lengthy runs and organize their responses into stories.

Precisely because it is a form of discourse that is known and used in everyday interaction, the story is an obvious way for social actors, in talking to strangers (e.g., the researcher) to retell key experiences and events. Stories serve a variety of functions. Social actors often remember and order their careers or memories as a series of narrative chronicles, that is, as series of stories marked by key happenings. Similarly, stories and legends are often told and retold by members of particular social groups or organizations as a way of passing on a cultural heritage or an organizational culture. Tales of success or tales of key leaders/personalities are familiar genres with which to maintain a collective sense of the culture of an organization. The use of atrocity stories and morality fables is also well documented within organizational and occupational settings. Stories of medical settings are especially well documented (Atkinson, 1992a; Dingwall, 1977). Here tales of professional incompetence are used to give warnings of "what not to do" and what will happen if you commit mistakes.

Similar tales have legendary status in the oral culture of schoolchildren (Delamont, 1989, 1990, 1992; Measor & Woods, 1984). Urban legends about the transfer from primary to secondary school, folklore about the evil (or gay) teacher, the rat dissection, the big bullies, and the head down the toilet on a birthday provide particularly memorable examples. The story genre also has been used to understand the culture of teachers within school settings. In particular, the use of the life history method has enabled the collection of rich teacher narratives (Casey, 1993; Goodson, 1992; Sparkes, 1994). Narratives are also a common genre from which to retell or come to terms with particularly sensitive or traumatic times and events. Riessman (1993) provides several key studies of how narratives and storying can be used as an approach to the study of trauma and traumatic life course events, such as divorce or violence.

To summarize, the storied qualities of qualitative textual data, both "naturally" given or research driven, enable the analyst to consider both how social actors order and tell their experiences and why they remember and retell what they do. The structuring of experience can hence be analyzed alongside meanings and motives. What follows in this chapter is a discussion of how, as analysts, we can approach the exploration of these stories that we may collect as part of our qualitative research endeavors.

Formal Narrative Analysis

Narratives have rather specific, distinct structures with formal and identifiable properties. Propp's (1968) quasi-algebraic (Manning & Cullum-Swan, 1994) analysis of the Russian fairy tale provides an important early example of this form of analysis. Propp proposed that fairy tales could be understood using four structural principles: The roles of characters are stable in a tale, the functions/events in a fairy tale are limited, the sequence of functions is always identical, and fairy tales are of one type with regard to structure. Propp's argument is that tales unfold linearly in terms of a number of functions. The characters and patterns of events are relatively stable within a structured format. Propp's main emphasis is that stories convey meanings in standard structural forms.

Labov (1972, 1982) developed a sociolinguistic approach to narratives and stories that, to some extent, built on this idea. Labov has argued that narratives have formal, structural properties in relation to their social functions. These formal structural properties have recurrent patterns that can be identified and used to interpret each segment of narrative. A number of analysts have applied this type of approach to narrative analysis. For example, Cortazzi (1991, 1993) systematically applied Labov's analytical framework to the study of occupational (teacher) narratives. Riessman (1990, 1993) also considers narrative analysis as a formal methodological approach and has applied such approaches to a study of personal relationships.

Riessman's work goes beyond searching for formal structural properties, but she does suggest that the unpacking of structure is a significant early stage in narrative analysis. By beginning with the structure of the narrative, Riessman argues that researchers should avoid reading simply for content. Attention to the structure of the narrative might include looking at how the story is organized, how the tale is developed, and where and how the narrative begins and ends. Riessman suggests that this can be done as the transcriptions of the narratives are read and worked, and she provides one way of beginning to find a focus for analysis.

There are various specific approaches to the organization of narrative, and it is not our intent in this section to review them all. Here we outline and exemplify one of the most basic of those approaches, one that captures some of the more general characteristics of this style of analysis. As is apparent, the interest here is not solely in the formal analysis per se but also in using the structures to identify how people tell stories the way that they do: how they give the events they recount shape; how they make a point; how they "package" the narrated events and their reactions to them, and how they articulate their narratives with the audience or audiences that hear them. We will base our discussion on the model outlined by Labov, which has been called an "evaluation model" (see Cortazzi, 1993). Labov identifies a number of elementary units of narrative structure. The elements can be viewed as answers to the audience's implicit questions. They are summarized below (adapted from Cortazzi, 1993, p. 45):

Structure	Question
Abstract	What was this about?
Orientation	Who? What? When? Where?
Complication	Then what happened?
Evaluation	So what?
Result	What finally happened?
Coda	[Finish narrative]

Labov himself suggests that such narrative elements occur in an invariant order, although there may be multiple occurrences embedded and recurring within a single narrative. For our purposes, it is not necessary to maintain Labov's strong claims for the pervasiveness of the elements and their sequencing; rather, the point is to see how the identification of such structural units can help us think about our data, in order to facilitate more general and more sociological kinds of analysis.

We will try to illustrate this principle with an extract taken from the anthropology interviews. Narrative analysis can lend itself to certain kinds of interview data anyway, as the conversation exchange of the research interview often implicitly or explicitly invites the informant to recount stories. Our interviews with graduate students and supervisors contained various storylike features, but we should not exaggerate their presence in this particular corpus of data. The research interests of the research team were not focused specifically on the anthropologists' "tales from the field" (fascinating though that topic is), but in the course of their personal accounts, it was inevitable that some of them produced narrative responses to particular questions. Given below is an extract from an interview with a graduate student, in which she retells her experience of anthropological fieldwork.

Well the first year was trying to sort out the questions, really, that I needed to ask, and so I started my fieldwork in eighty-five, and had envisaged doing a year of fieldwork and then writing up for a year afterwards and that being that. But then I got pregnant in eighty-five, which in many ways was a good thing, particularly with my main informant, because she was just pregnant and I was just pregnant and that really meant our relationship changed a lot and became much deeper as we were going through the same thing, we could talk about things that perhaps I wouldn't have thought about before. But I also had problems with the pregnancy and had time off, so apart from having maternity leave anyway I also had time off because I couldn't work after the fifth month. And then other things happened as well. I had a miscarriage and my father was ill, then I was pregnant again and had more maternity leave, so I had various reprieves from the ESRC [Economic and Social Research Council—a government-funded council providing funding for postgraduate research].

So in real terms I'm now coming up to the end of my fourth year as defined by ESRC. So the fieldwork got really punctuated and I could add it up if I went back to the books, but it was off and on, off and on, and once I'd had Ben I went back and did more fieldwork and then had another break and went back, and so obviously that caused problems. Because I was known in the clinic it wasn't a problem of establishing myself. I could turn up whenever I knew there was a room free and that side of it was fine. But in terms of what was happening in the news changed. I mean IVF [in-vitro fertilization] was very much in the news then and that did actually change the course of what I studied in the end, or how I approached it—trying to get at people's ideas of procreation through their understanding of new reproductive technologies and so on. And I mean, I suppose if I'd done my fieldwork in a block then a lot of those issues wouldn't have been around, and people wouldn't have read so much about them, and so it was something they were more familiar with. But it meant that the background to the research was shifting quite a lot, so it was elongated, really.

Turning to Labov's structural units, we can see how they might be applied to this data extract. Labov suggests that the abstract is optional, and there is not a separate one in this instance. Typically, when the abstract occurs "it initiates the narrative by summarizing the point or by giving a statement of a general proposition which the narrative will exemplify" (Cortazzi, 1993, p. 44). (In interview data, the interviewer's question normally elicits the narrative, and the informant may feel no obligation to provide such a prefatory statement, which normally has the function of establishing the opening of the story and claiming a narrative-like turn in the conversation.) It is clear, however, that the anthropology student's narrative begins by giving an orientation. She establishes the situation (the fieldwork), the time (the first year of her doctorate, 1985, the year she started her fieldwork), and the person (herself). This occupies the first sentence.

Orientation is followed by complication, which normally carries the major account of the events that are central to the story. It comprises the bones of "what happened." In other words, complication consists of the narrated events. In this particular example, the events are the student's pregnancies, periods of maternity leave, and father's illness, as well as how they were related to the progress of her fieldwork. In accordance with Labov's analysis, they are recounted in the simple past tense. They narrate turning points, crises, or problems, and how these were made sense of by the teller.

Evaluation in this particular case is closely linked with the result. The evaluation typically highlights the point of the narrative, while the result, which follows either the complication or the evaluation, describes the outcome of the events or the resolution of the problems. Starting from "And I mean, I suppose if I'd done my fieldwork in a block," the student provides an evaluation of her fieldwork experiences and gives the audience a sense of the outcome. The result is emphasized in the final clause: "it meant that the background to the research was shifting quite a lot." Her evaluation was that if she had done her fieldwork in an uninterrupted block of time, her ideas would not have developed in the way that they did. She implies that her fieldwork benefited from her pregnancies and related experiences.

In the same way that an abstract is optional, narratives may finish with a coda. The coda marks the close or end of the narrative, returning the discourse to the present and marking a possible transition point, at which the talk may revert to the other parties to the encounter. (In interview talk, it may indicate closure of a response to a question, indicating that the interviewer may follow it up with another prompt or a fresh topic.) The anthropologist's story does end with an abbreviated coda: "so it was elongated, really." This final clause takes the story full circle, back to the issues of how long the fieldwork took and why. It is of interest that at the outset of the story, there is an implied or projected story of what did *not* happen, that is, the simple version of events that the student had predicted and that was overturned by the complications and resolution of what actually transpired. That too has its implied coda: "that being that." This finishes the implied or projected narrative and moves the narrator on to the actual story being told.

We do not wish to suggest that Labov's categories map onto this narrative, or to all narratives, with perfect regularity. We also wish to avoid creating the impression that all analysts of such data need to search obsessively for the equivalent narrative units and their defining characteristics. There are other ways of looking at the data, and other analysts identify different structural features. It is worth noting, however, that even with our simplified treatment of Labov's analytic framework, and with our fairly restricted data, we can identify some issues of potential significance. The framework provides us with an analytic perspective on two things: It allows us to see how that narrative is structured, and it offers a perspective from which to reflect on the functions of the story. Drawing on these closely related aspects, we now have a sense of what the key themes and issues are and how the student constructs the story in order to convey her point. We can see how the informant's personal narrative of lived experience is organized into a narrative form. Although the reported biographical events may be unique to the individual, they are structured according to socially shared conventions of reportage.

It clearly would be unproductive merely to examine large numbers of narratives—whether or not derived from interviews—in order to demonstrate that they have the same underlying structure. We are not suggesting here that the qualitative researcher should mechanistically submit all narratives to analyses based on Labov's formal schema. It is useful to be able to identify recurrent structures, but that is not the whole story. We can also look for characteristic uses or functions of narratives, as well as for distinctive types or genres.

Narrative Forms and Functions

As we indicated earlier, as well as thinking of narratives as formal structures with identifiable properties, we can also think of them in terms of functions. The analysis of narratives can also focus on the social action implied in the text. This can involve taking a slightly less systematic and structured approach to narrative analysis, deriving more context-dependent infrastructure and focus to explain the effect (intended or unintended, implicit or explicit) of the story or tale. This emphasizes the idea that individual narratives are situated within particular interactions and within specific social, cultural, and institutional discourses. For example, in the narrative extract used in the previous section, rather than concentrating on the structural properties, we could think about the possible functional qualities of the story. The story serves to illustrate the relationship between planning and luck in the research endeavor and the negative and positive effects of forced breaks on fieldwork, for example. The emphasis shift here is not a strict or rigid one. In analyzing structure, we alluded to the functional qualities. What we are suggesting here is that the idea of function can be brought to the fore and used as a principal analytical unit.

Anthropological perspectives on narratives in different cultures have revealed a range of variation in the functions of narratives. For example, Preston (1978) suggests that a main function of Cree narratives in Canada is to define and express basic cultural categories in the sharing of individual experiences. Toelken (1969, 1975) provides an example among the Nvago narratives of moral functions. Similarly, folkloristic approaches to occupational narratives (Cortazzi, 1991, 1993; Dingwall, 1977) also reveal that stories can have functional qualities within the occupational culture. Cortazzi (1993) gives examples of functional types of occupational narratives such as cautionary tales of accidents and disasters (whose function is to teach learners to avoid them) and organizational sagas, which function to give a collective understanding of the rationale of an organization and a rationale for workers' commitment. Cortazzi's evaluation of teachers' narratives revealed that teachers' stories

have functions of self and cultural identity, entertainment, moral evaluation, and news. They provide media for reflecting teachers' cultural
context in the work they do.

To illustrate the functional properties of narrative, we have chosen
two particular forms. These by no means exhaust the possibilities, but
they provide some indication of the general analytic strategy. Using data
from the interviews with anthropology graduate students and supervisors, we explore how narratives can be analyzed in terms of content and
function. The two forms we use to illustrate this are stories that present
a moral fable (of either success or of failure) and stories that are told as
a way of chronicling an individual's life experiences.

SUCCESS STORIES AND MORAL TALES

The story with a moral or a point has a long tradition within the
realms of children's stories and fairy tales. Endings of "and they all lived
happily ever after" pull together a tale and present the end result as one
of success. Similarly, the moralistic tale, which often presents a sad or
unfortunate story, serves as a collective reminder of what not to do or
how not to be. These stories also provide the reader with an ending, this
time along the lines of how to avoid the fate described in the story. Stories
of our own and others' experiences are often told with a point in mind.
Such narrative accounts of atrocity and of success can be analyzed both
in terms of what they tell us about the individuals or the research setting
and in terms of how the stories are developed and built up.

To illustrate these ideas, we can turn again to our anthropology data.
Dr. Teague of Southersham University describes doctoral students he
has supervised.

Extract 1

Anyway, this person had done an MA by coursework, then went on to a PhD,
did fieldwork in Newfoundland in a fishing community—the PhD was on
Newfoundland fisherman. That was good, because although I don't have any
experience of Icelandic fishermen, we were interested in the same areas of
anthropology. The difference between the first person I mentioned and the
second, was that the first one—I got to supervise her in the first place because
one of my interests at the time was supposed to be on ethnic minorities,

because I'd done fieldwork on Canadian Inuit, but I had no particular knowledge about ethnic minorities in Britain, so—in that case it didn't really matter because the student had strong enough opinions of her own; in the second case it was different because I felt it was someone who was interested in the same sort of issues as I was, and that worked out very well, he was a good student, and he's now the leading anthropologist in an Icelandic university. He's trained up a whole series of anthropologists who are now in various places in the United States, Canada and here, so now we're getting students in this department that he's trained. He's written a couple of books, so he's doing fine.

Extract 2

Number four was an ESRC funded student. She did an MA here first of all for which she got a grant from a fund for the daughters of vicars! That got her through her MA year, then she got the ESRC grant. She went to study Francophone separatists in a town in Quebec and again, in my area, which was nice, she coped with the fieldwork, which everybody had told her would be impossible, she coped very well and wrote her thesis on time, in fact she got the thesis written before the grant finished, which was a record, and it was a very competent thesis, which was supposed to be a book, and should be coming out at any moment, and after that she married a Thai research student who was here, and went out to Thailand for a while, but then things went wrong with the marriage and she came back here and had a research job. So those were the four.

These "vignettes" can be thought of as serving a purpose. A recurrent theme in the two extracts from Dr. Teague is the overcoming of difficulties and the achievement of success. This is similar to the story retold by the PhD student in the previous section. Like that student with her pregnancies and her father's illness, the students described by Dr. Teague had also expressed difficulties in the course of their fieldwork. Dr. Teague quantifies success—locating the student in the first extract as a leading anthropologist in the University of Iceland, as a successful "supervisor" in his own right, having trained and placed a whole series of anthropologists, and as a productive author. The story is one of a magnitude of success that goes beyond the supervision and the PhD topic.

The second extract is about the scale of success in the face of some difficulties and adversities. The story begins with success—the funding of the student's MA and PhD. The student was told by "everybody" that her fieldwork would be impossible; however, she "coped very well." Again Dr. Teague presents tangible measures of success in the form of a thesis written ahead of time, perhaps to become a book. The student's marriage and its subsequent failure also is presented as an adversity that the student surmounted to come back (to research and a job).

Both stories focus on key turning points, both difficulties and successes. The supervisor highlights fieldwork as a key part of the doctoral program, emphasizing the centrality of this aspect of anthropology. Dr. Teague also indicates what is viewed as important and significant in the junior anthropological career—publications, jobs, and students of one's own. The extracts give us some insight into the cultural organization of anthropological work and the signifiers of success.

Anthropology supervisors also tell less hopeful stories of graduate students. There are stories that tell of things going wrong or being too difficult, and of failure. These also serve particular purposes, giving indications of what does not work and what students (and supervisors) should not do.

Extract 3 (from interview with Dr. Dorroway, University of Kingford)

Another thesis I examined, it makes an anecdote, and there's a point to it, I think, a long time ago, in Masonbridge, a Sudanese student, whose supervisor had wanted it to be an MPhil thesis because he felt it wasn't up to scratch, but the guy insisted on presenting it as a PhD, and it wasn't PhD standard and it wasn't passed. About a month later the guy died of a liver disease, but the story went round in Khartoum that it was because of disappointment at not getting his PhD. There's a moral in that that supervisors shouldn't have their arms twisted.

Extract 4 (from interview with Dr. Feste, University of Kingford)

Yes, this is the woman I'm seeing through to the end, who's actually been supervised as far as I can tell, by everyone else in the department. . . . Well, she started with not a very coherent idea with Jeremy Styles, I think—she's doing ideas of procreation and birth—and it wasn't coherent when she started out, and she was moved on to both Ian Felgate and Ralph Dorroway, both of whom she did not get on very well with, and she seems to have been through several other people, and ended up with Carolyn Brackenberry after seven or eight years—it's been a long, drawn out saga, and Carolyn's managed to get her through to the point where she's almost ready to submit.

Everything's just about ready in draft, and she had to go on leave, so rather than saying "take another nine months" she arranged to bring her to me, so that she would finish by June 30th. Which is the ESRC deadline, although she's missed it by several years, as far as I can tell. The department had more or less written her off, and it's quite clear from her fieldwork material, as Carolyn Brackenberry pointed out, that she was not adequately supervised at various points, so that questions the supervisor would have said "Have you asked your women this?" particularly as she was right here in London, are missing from the material, because there was no one there to suggest things, so there were gaps, which even if you're in the field, you write to your supervisor and get a letter back saying "Try this" etc. And she's had great blanks of supervision where she was on her own so it has been a problem.

Extract 3 contains both anecdote and rumor but appears to be told to some (explicit) purpose by the supervisor. The story links the failure of the doctoral thesis to a student's failure to take the advice of a supervisor. There is, of course, a parallel moral for supervisors that they should "not have their arms twisted" and should stick to their convictions. The story is told, however, as the student's fault. The failure is clearly seen as the student's, in that he did not take the supervisory advice he was offered. We could use this insight to elaborate on the nature and importance of the supervisory relationship in the (successful) pursuit of a doctorate, at least in anthropology. The (poor) supervisory relationship is identified as the problem. How this is manifested—failure to listen, lack of respect—could form a wider analysis of what makes a good or bad supervisor and supervisory relationship.

Extract 4 expands on this central part of the PhD experience, presenting a protracted tale of a student's relationships with several different supervisors. The moral tale begins with the student's lack of clarity over her research topic and then continues with a number of supervisors with whom she did not get along. The supervision by Carolyn Brackenberry is presented as somewhat successful: The student finally got to the point of being almost ready to submit. The story continues with a missed deadline, which the department seems to be ignoring, and the belief of Dr. Feste that she will finish eventually. This story contains further data that we can feed into our analysis of the nature and significance of the supervisory relationship. The "moral" of the tale seems to be a warning about multiple supervisors and blanks in supervision. This is prefaced by a description of a difficult, incoherent student. The structure of the narrative itself thus helps to deflect potential blame from the supervisor and the department by locating it implicitly with the student.

Here we begin to explore how anthropology supervisors make sense of and justify supervisory relationships, as well as looking at PhD successes and failures. It seems to be that supervision is important and, if done well, produces good students. The exact effects of supervision, however, are presented as rather less determinate than that. Students sometimes achieve success in spite of, rather than as a result of, supervision. Similarly, even with supervision some students fail.

These success stories and moral tales are useful starting points for a more thorough analysis. They provide a mechanism for exploring how social actors frame and make sense of particular sets of experiences. In considering the supervisors' extracts, we can begin, as we have indicated, to develop ideas and questions about the work of anthropologists and the nature of the supervisory relationship. For example, we have mentioned measures of anthropologic success, the overcoming of adversity, good and bad supervisory practice, and explanations for success and failure. These are all analytic points of departure from which we could re-read and explore our data set in more detail.

It is worth mentioning here that we can continue to think of these stories as having certain structural properties. In particular, with "moral tales" social actors tell their story with a purpose. With that in mind, we can also think about the ways in which the stories are organized to give their delivery impact. Biographical details are used to contextualize stories, and comparisons with other events and theses set up a story. Some tell the listener that "there is a point," and so on.

The extract about the Sudanese student offers an example of a story structured to give impact. It is relatively short and to the point. The opening gives the impression that there might be a long story to tell. The impact therefore comes with the "and then he died" scenario. The forms that stories take can provide insight into how experiences are structured and how information is transmitted to give the desired impact. Some stories "rev up" and provide a detailed and drawn out account; others hit you early with the punch line. Some tell you the purpose at the beginning. Others add mystery and suspense by delaying the point to the story. In terms of analysis, our point is that stories that have meaning and purpose relay their context in morally contextual and socially acceptable ways. Stories are discursive structures that reflect cultural norms. We can consider how stories are told to full purpose as well as why they are told.

The next section follows this theme, moving our discussion to the autobiographical qualities of narrative. Structural concerns with the formal properties and social functions of narrative are only some of the ways of thinking about stories in an analytical way.

NARRATIVE AS CHRONICLE

As social actors, we are all involved in retelling our experiences and lives. In doing so, we chronicle our lives in terms of a series of events, happenings, influences, and decisions. Narrative, as autobiography, describes the way in which people articulate how the past is related to the present (Richardson, 1990). Time is placed into a personal history, where the past is given meaning in the present. Social actors organize their lives and experiences through stories and in doing so make sense of them. This chronicling of a life, or part of a life, often starts from a point of "how it all happened" or "how I came to be where I am today."

Analytically, a recognition that social actors organize their biographies narratively provides a potentially rich source of data. How social actors retell their life experiences as stories can provide insight into the characters, events, and happenings central to those experiences. How the chronicle is told and how it is structured can also provide information about the perspectives of the individual in relation to the wider social grouping or cultural setting to which that individual belongs. The data extracts that are drawn upon in this section are the narratives of anthropological faculty recounting how they came to be anthropologists working in particular institutional settings. An initial analysis of these narratives suggests that they can reveal a number of different characteristics and events central to the anthropological career. The concept of career has long been of interest to social scientists, in particular, to sociologists.

As a concept, "career" is both retrospective and often narrated. All of us have stories about our careers, as students, or teachers, or parents, or academics. Career is most often associated with a notion of a working life, an occupational career. In sociology, the concept also has been applied to other social roles, allowing insight into the careers, for example, of parents, children, and patients. Our understandings and explorations into the concept of career have allowed distinctions to be made between objective and subjective careers (Evetts, 1994) and between notions of personally and structurally oriented or enforced career paths. Careers are both individually constructed and structurally determined. Social actors have their own stories to tell and their own perspectives on what has gone before and what is to come. These stories are mediated by structural dimensions and social arrangements that at least seem outside the control of the social actors (Acker, 1994). The following chronicle illustrates how these individual, collective, and structural factors are all present in the retelling of a career.

Interview With Dr. Talisman (Southersham University)

My first degree was at Cambridge, 1975-1978, in archaeology and anthropology, specializing in anthropology. After that I had a year off because I didn't know what I wanted to do next, and then decided after a year that nothing interested me as much as carrying on in university and doing some research of my own. And in my year off, before going up to Cambridge, I'd spent time on a kibbutz in Israel. I very much liked the farming and the outdoor life, and the community of the kibbutz as well. I felt rather alone in Cambridge, and I liked the togetherness of the kibbutz. So I thought I'd do some research on a kibbutz, combining something academic with a style of life that I liked.

So I decided to go to Manchester to do a PhD, because with Max Gluckman, the previous professor, there'd been a strong link with Israel, and lots of research projects started from Manchester. His field of interest was Manchester, but he was a South African Jew, and when his family left South Africa, he was the only one who came to England, the others went to Israel, and I suppose he knew how to get money to do research in Israel. There was a man called Bernstein who funded a lot of projects, and Gluckman's links with Bernstein were such that he was able to fund a lot of research projects in Israel.

So I went there rather than stay in Cambridge or go somewhere else, and was really pleased to go there. It was a small department, very together, intimate, and I thrived, I really liked it. I really liked the anthropology there, it was more individualistic, less emphasis on social structure, more on the flux of social life, the creativeness of social life, really relating to my interests in the self and the individual. So I did my PhD there and I finished in February 1983, which was just over three years. Then I went to Australia, on a postdoctoral fellowship in Western Australia, and ended up spending two and a half years there altogether. It turned out that my first research wasn't in Israel, the professor who was in charge there at the time, Emrys Peters, was quite keen to alter the focus of the department. He was an Arabist himself, worked in Libya and the Lebanon and convinced me that the kibbutz was old-fashioned to study, and I was also very interested in Europe, so I ended up doing my PhD on a small French farming village in the Normandy, looking at communication, worldview, perception, interaction, how the farmer saw the world.

In Western Australia, where I did my second piece of research, I looked at how people talk about violence or why people talk about violence so much, it sort of took the place of the weather in English conversational exchange, and wrote a book on the nature of urban interaction—I was doing fieldwork in the only real city in that part of Australia—and doing covert participant observation in the university itself, and in bars, and hospitals and courts of law. Anyway after three and a half years there I'd had enough. I wanted to move back to England, but jobs are very scarce here still—that was 1987—so after a year as a fellow here at Southersham, doing some work as a tutor, I got a lectureship in Israel in 1988, and went out to Israel. . . . I was teaching there and also doing some research on a new town in the middle of the desert, looking at why the American immigrants who were there had come and whether what they'd come for they'd found. After a year there I managed to get a lectureship here in Southersham, and I started in October 1989. So I've been here an academic year.

This extract recounts a section of an anthropologist's academic career. The biographical experiences told in the process of the story can be analyzed on a number of different levels. The story maps the anthropologist's past (and his biography) along a particular time frame. The listener is taken chronologically through the anthropological career, beginning with the first degree and ending with the present academic post. Key events are related to this career: a year in an Israeli kibbutz, the decision to change institutions between first degree and higher degree, a fellowship in Australia, the publication of a book, a move back to England, and a lectureship in Israel. Key social actors also are related to this career: Professor Max Gluckman, Bernstein, and Emrys Peters.

These key events and actors are signposts on the career path of the anthropologist in the informant's own terms. The narrative reveals the actor's own "story" of why he is where he is today. The narration also embeds a more general story about the development of the anthropological discipline. As well as mapping the individual career, the events and actors described provide insight into the development of anthropology as an academic discipline. We get a sense that different sorts of anthropology are done at different institutions, that anthropology is institutionally structured. The move toward studying the familiar and the local also is charted as a significant moment with the discipline. Furthermore, we are given the names and stories of key characters in anthropology—for example, Gluckman and Bernstein—and the individual anthropologist's relationship to these figures. The narration also reveals the focus and orientation (and how they have shifted) of different, key anthropological departments.

The story also can be analyzed in terms of the accounts and explanations that the social actor uses to make sense of his career. The biography is peppered with turning points and conversions. The year off in an Israeli kibbutz altered the perception of the style of life he wished to have, and Israel provided a source of possible PhD fieldwork. The decision to go to a different institution to study for a master's degree marked a key turning point in the sort of lifestyle and the kind of anthropology that was desired. Emrys Peters provided influence that converted the subject studied; this in turn influenced future work in Australia.

Alongside the turning points is the tension between career and life planning, on one hand, and circumstances and luck, on the other. The chronicle is told as a planned and ordered set of experiences but is one that also turns on luck. The kibbutz experience came about because of indecision about the future and became a critical point in shaping future career decisions. Similarly, the lectureship in Israel almost seemed to come about because there were few jobs in England, yet it was a key point in the anthropologist's career.

To summarize, then, this particular autobiographical narrative can be analyzed in terms of what it reveals about the individual's career, the anthropological discipline, key characters and events, key turning points, and influences. It also can be considered in terms of how the social actor tells the story, the sorts of vocabularies and rhetorical devices used, how present and past experiences are contrasted, and the different institutions and people discussed. We also can use the story to explore how the tensions between luck and judgment or intent are told and explained.

If we were to develop this analysis, we might look for other narratives of career among the anthropologists, picking out the key characters and events and the ways in which the story is constructed, told, and framed. The data extract below demonstrates how we might build on our initial analyses.

Extract From Interview With Dr. Telpher (Southersham University)

I started in Engineering at Ohio State University. At the end of the first year when I'd enjoyed myself very much, I was asked to leave, because I hadn't done very well in my engineering exams. But we had to do courses outside, and I'd done English, and I'd done extremely well at English, and they thought that perhaps I was ill-suited to the course that I had chosen. Anyway I'd run through my money as well, so I transferred to another university, which was closer to home, so I could work and support myself, and I still continued with science subjects, I was doing physics and maths, and in the course of that I was in a programme where we were streamed and the upper 5 percent of the university was put into what was called an honours college and we had special classes where we were taught by special members of staff, and the standard of teaching was much higher.

And in doing that I was still doing science subjects and the head of the programme called me in one day and said "Why are you doing all this stuff?" And I said "Well that's what I want to do professionally." And he said "This is probably the only chance in your life you'll have to try something else, so why don't you do something different?" I thought why not, and said "What do you suggest?" and he said "You could do some philosophy, or English, or anthropology." So I thought "Alright." So I took a course in symbolic logic, thinking I wasn't risking very much, and I did a course in anthropology, and I thought they were fantastic. I loved them both.

So I finished in that line, and by the time I graduated I was doing almost nothing in the physical sciences. I almost completely changed over to the arts and social sciences. By that time I'd decided I wanted to go on and do something in sociology and social anthropology so I applied to graduate schools in the States and I was given a fellowship in Northeastern University in the African Studies programme. And I was in the Department of Sociology and Anthropology, so I went there. When I first went to Northeastern Paul and Laura Bohannon were both there on the African Studies Programme, and the first year I worked with Paul Bohannon, and was completely bowled over by British social anthropology which I was encountering for the first time. The clarity of the vision and the way in which problems were phrased seemed quite strikingly different from American anthropology which I'd got acquainted with up to then. And I thought "Yes, that's what I want to do."

Unfortunately the Bohannons left, at the end of my first year, and there was virtually no one around to do anthropology. But because of an arrangement at University I was able to go over to Harvard and I had two seminars, one with Tambiah on religion, and another with Darryl Ford who was visiting that year on African religion, and that confirmed my previous experience with Bohannon, that it was the kind of social anthropology that I wanted to do. How this all relates to what I'm doing now—there is a connection, and that is that the head of my department at Northeastern was Gary Joplin, a sociologist who'd done fieldwork in Turkey, and he had a project in which he'd invited two Turkish scholars to come to Northeastern to do community study techniques, and they needed a dogsbody to work with the Turks and help them with their interviews and all their statistical apparatus, and as it happened I had the most experience in maths and statistics by far, most of the other students being innumerate, and I was given by Joplin to work with the Turks on the project, to teach them a little bit of statistics and do the results.

And as a result of that I was invited to go to Turkey at the end of this project and do some research when I got back home, and again they wanted someone to come and help them train interviewers and do the practical aspects of the data process. So I was invited to Turkey and spent the summer there, five months, working with the Turks. Having had no interest or training in that part of the world previously, that was the summer of the Anatolian earthquake, and it was in Anatolia that I was working, and the earthquake put an end to that project, and I had to leave because of the earthquake. I was moving to the University of Lockport which had just started a little PhD programme in social anthropology. It was a complete unknown, I was going in as one of the first of their postgraduate students, but having looked around at other universities I decided that I preferred to do something that was unknown in social anthropology, rather than some- thing that was more mainline American university anthropology. That wasn't what I wanted then, though it meant taking quite a gamble.

It turned out to be excellent, one of the few good choices I've made in my life. The programme was very well taught, an awful lot of energy went into the training of my students. I thought on the basis of my African Studies experience in Northeastern that I wanted to do fieldwork in Africa. But that seemed to be increasingly unlikely because of political problems then be- tween the U.S. and Uganda where I was thinking of doing my fieldwork. A friend of mine from Northeastern days, working in Uganda, was sending back frantic letters about the difficulties he was having getting permission to do fieldwork. So the head of my department at Northeastern said I should look around for some other place to do work. And I thought about going to Central Brazil to work with Lewis, but that seemed like hero stuff, and I didn't think I was quite up to that. Then there was the possibility of going back to Turkey, and it was really on the spur of the moment after dithering for months that the head of the department called me in and asked where I wanted to do my work and I said "It's very complex, because on the one hand . . . on the other hand . . ." and I outlined all the complexities, and he said "I know all the complexities I just want to know where you want to do your work." I said "It's extremely difficult to answer that" and he said "I know, but where do you want to work?" and I said "I can't answer that" and he said "That's alright, you've got a half hour to make up your mind, I just want to know before you go out of that door." And I blurted out "Turkey."

That was the summer of '63. It was a five-month project, a sociology project—that was the first time. My own fieldwork was done from '67 to '68, I think. The dates are a bit hazy without having a c.v. to refer to. Then I was back again in 1970. So that's a long answer to how I got into my training. . . .

While I was a student at Lockport, Freddie Bailey was a member of staff for a year. Vic Turner, who was at Cornell, came to Lockport, for a term, and he gave the Morgan lectures. Max Gluckman was in the country and he came to Lockport for a time. I went to Cornell to attend a couple of his seminars. So the Manchester School as it's known, was very much at the forefront of my consciousness, and I knew that it was a very interesting department. And then when I first started teaching, I was teaching in a small college in upstate New York, and one of my first undergraduate students went to Manchester as a postgrad. So I was aware of what was going on in the department through him. And I always fancied my chances of going there. And several years later I was at Carnegie Mellon University, working on a project that was coming to an end, so I was looking around for something else, and there was a job going there at Manchester, so I thought, "If I don't put in for it I'll always wonder what might have happened" so I decided to put in for it, and lo and behold I was offered the post. It only lasted two years, though, while one of the permanent staff was away on fieldwork, so I came on here to Southersham.

This autobiographical chronicle displays many of the analytical points we drew from the previous autobiographical abstract. The narrative here also talks in terms of key anthropological figures, key turning points, and the influence of particular academic departments. The relationship and balance between decisions and luck is also highlighted. Key anthropological influences are featured, including social actors such as the Bohannons (a married couple of anglicized American anthropologists), Joplin, Bailey, Turner, and Max Gluckman again. The story is replete with turning points: doing poorly in engineering examinations, the interview with the head of the department, the relationship at Northeastern, and the invitation to Turkey. The tensions between planning and luck show perhaps even more strongly in this material: running out of money, being a "dogsbody" to visiting Turkish scholars, the earthquake, and getting to know Manchester through coincidental contacts. These are all told as luck but all had an influential impact on the life course and career of the social actor. This extract also is replete with contrastive rhetoric, particularly in how the respondent compares anthropology in the American and British traditions. We get a sense of the different approaches to anthropology and different people and places associated with those approaches.

In pursuing such a line of inquiry, we find ourselves explicating how actors construct their biographies and careers. We see how the past is shaped by narrative form. Simultaneously, we see how key events and other social actors are represented through the narratives of experience. We thus start to explore what Denzin has described in terms of "interpretive interactionism" (Denzin, 1989): the relationship between social processes and personal lives. Sociologists and anthropologists have become increasingly interested in the production and analysis of lives. This has included the investigation of whole lives, for example, through the collection of oral and life histories, as well as the investigation of key life events.

Well-established sociological concepts can be viewed in terms of their relevance to a concern with the biography or life story. For example, we have well-developed sociological interests in concepts of the self, the life course, and the career. Indeed, there has been a recent resurgence of interest in (auto)biography in sociological inquiry. The turn to textuality and a concern with intertextuality has led many to question the distinction between biography and autobiography, between representations of reality and reality itself. Central to this theoretical and empirical interest is the place of the narrative—as biographical producer, account, and framework within which to locate the telling of lives. In other words, an attention to narrative forms and functions allows us to develop aspects of our data in particularly useful ways. We can explore not only the elementary structures of narrative but also how they are used to perform particular kinds of account.

Ethnopoetics, Oral Performance, and Voice

We have so far treated narratives as unproblematic, in that we have said very little about the contexts in which they are produced or how they may be encountered in the course of fieldwork. By illustrating our argument from our interview data, we do not mean to imply that social science interviews are the only occasions in which personal narratives are produced or from which such data may be culled. Stories are told, experiences are shared, and similar kinds of performances are enacted as part and parcel of everyday life. Work, leisure, bureaucracies, and indeed the entire range of social institutions and occasions are full of stories. The narratives of everyday life are used to construct and to share cultural values, meanings, and personal experiences. They also express—and indeed enact—the social conditions of power and influence in everyday life. Talk—and stories form part of everyday talk—is selected and performed to an audience. As such, talk can be contextualized in terms of it being an oral performance.

The data on which we draw in this book do not lend themselves especially well to analysis in terms of oral performance. The stories that are told are located within an interview format and are prompted, to some extent at least. As such, the performance quality is to some extent bounded by the answers to prompted questions. Even here, however, the anthropologists "told" their stories in certain ways and gave a performance of sorts to the interviewer. More lengthy (and in-depth) history interviews and the observation of naturally occurring speech lend themselves rather better to an analysis of the oral performance of the narrator and its poetic qualities. Our point here is that we can think about how actors orally "perform" and what that reveals about the social and cultural setting.

We can think of this concern with oral performance as a concern with the *ethnopoetics* of everyday life. Attention to the performance element in oral traditions and events is summed up by Bauman (1986, p. 3) who describes performance as

> a mode of communication, a way of speaking, the essence of which resides in the assumption of responsibility to an audience for a display of communicative skill, highlighting the way in which communication is carried out, above and beyond its referential content.

Thinking about how stories are performed enables us to think about analysis in terms of how social actors self-present to a public or an audience, and how that presentation is achieved. How are relatively standardized verbal forms manipulated and performed to capture audiences, whether familiar or strange? Related to this is how successful or competent the social actor is in the performance. Why are some social actors better than others at getting their story across? Oral performance also can be a way of thinking about the competencies of performing (and therefore of individual social actors). Crocker (1977) suggests the significance of this by arguing that the "many details of visual life" are the result of social audiences witnessing skilled oral performances. Similarly, a noncompetent oral performance is not greeted readily by the audience: "[T]he joke may fall flat, the poet's writing remain so obscure as to exasperate his [sic] readers, the actor is booed off the stage, the content is ignored" (Crocker, 1977, p. 45).

In terms of analyzing social interaction and "oral data," then, one can look at how oral performances are acted and performed by social actors. As well as looking at the skills of performance and the tools of performance (voice tone, actions, nonverbal communication skills), there is also interest in the success or competence of the performer and the relationship between performer and audience. Oral performances capture "ethnopoetics of everyday life." That is, attention to the performance enables the qualitative analyst to consider both the social and cultural world of the individual social actor as well as the situated and institutional context of those performances. On one level, each oral performance can be viewed as unique and emergent, a display of individual and cultural personality. On another level, one can look toward identifying conventionalized, patterned organizations of performances, the ways in which such performances are consistent (or not) with local understanding, situationally and institutionally contextualized. Performances then are fundamentally social and situational, or as Bauman (1986) suggests, situated social accomplishments of people engaged in the practice of social life.

Analyzing oral performances requires consideration of the structure of the performance event and how the situational factors feed into the event. These include the performer and the performed to (or audience), the expressive skills employed by the social actor in creating a performance, the norms and strategies used in performing, how performances are interpreted and evaluated by the audience, and how performance is sequenced to create a complete performance. By considering all of these, in the context of looking at the telling of the narrative we are able to recognize that oral data have form as well as content, art as well as science, creative structure as well as means. We are also reminded that qualitative analysis is as much about "how things are said" as about what is said. What we are concerned with here is a recognition that storytelling is culturally situated and relies for its success on culturally shared conventions about language and the hearing of stories.

In analyzing qualitative data from interviews alone, we are not in a position to report directly on the full range of oral performances in which anthropologists and their graduate students may engage. There are many occasions when they perform. A full ethnography of our academic departments and their doctoral training programs would provide plenty of opportunities to observe and record such events, among them seminar presentations, debates and disputes, and oral examinations. On the other hand, there is little doubt that our interview data have close affinities with more "natural" performances. There is, for example, every likelihood that the kinds of stories that were produced in our research interviews (genealogies, reminiscences of field research) had been and would again be recounted in other settings. Although one must always be mindful of the fact that research interviews are particular social contexts and that extrapolation from them is always problematic, one should also recognize that the narratives and reminiscences that are produced in the interview are not necessarily unique to that context. Many will have been rehearsed, either as part of a private repertoire of recollections or as part of a collectively shared stock of narratives. Many stories are worked up and are recounted on repeated occasions. Often the research interview provides an additional situation for their telling rather than a uniquely novel encounter. Moreover, there are normally cultural expectations that actors will have appropriate recollections and stories to share. Members of an occupational subculture have shared expectations about such stories; oral performances about anthropology and anthropologists are certainly not confined to research interviews. We should be alert, therefore, to those occasions—including interviews—when oral performances are enacted and shared. We can examine not only the content and form of such performances but their functions as well. Among other things, we should pay close attention to the ways in which social actors construct their self-presentations and negotiate their identities vis-à-vis their fellow actors. The researcher may sometimes provide just such an audience.

It is perhaps important at this point to say something about the nature of the narratives that we collect as social researchers. Goodson (1995) makes the distinction between stories of domination and oppositional stories. That is, stories can be used to relay dominant voices or can be appropriated to "give voice" to otherwise silenced groups and individuals. Goodson suggests that stories prolific in the cultural heritage of a particular society or the occupational culture of a particular group are often carriers of dominant messages. That is, stories relay messages of dominant sectors. There are oppositional stories that also may be part of a cultural storying, but Goodson argues that these are often in a minority form and are less powerful as agendas. Goodson makes this distinction to argue that as social researchers we should be reflexive about the stories and accounts we collect. We would not want to argue strongly that the anthropologists' stories are dominant, yet they do carry messages about which are the accepted leading figures and moments in anthropology as a discipline. The extracts we used in this chapter are matched by much of the rest of the data in providing a united picture of who was and is influential in forming the discipline, what types of anthropology and academic departments are more acceptable, and so forth. Goodson suggests that in analyzing such stories we should give some attention to whether social actors are transmitting a dominant message and how these messages manifest themselves in the storytelling. The anthropologists do not question the messages they are giving in the stories, yet they could perhaps be said to reveal a *dominant* picture of what anthropology is and to say who does it and where it is done best. The caveat here is that we should be sensitive to the kinds of stories we collect and the influences on the recollection and telling of the story. That is, in any cultural or social setting, storytelling voices are differentiated and stratified (Becker, 1967).

Such attention to the voices of storytellers and other social actors is of profound significance to various contemporary perspectives on social research. By giving due analytic weight to the nature of personal narratives, we can help ourselves to avoid subordinating otherwise muted voices. Various feminist and postcolonialist critics have argued for the presence of voices of women, people of color, and other oppressed people in the studies that so often make them the object of scrutiny. Commitment to a dialogic methodology, for example, implies the representation of actors' own narrated lives (cf. Guba & Lincoln, 1994).

The stories that are collected during social research are subject to and are part of literary and cultural norms about the form of the story. Although storytelling is ubiquitous, it is not therefore naturally occurring but is part of the representation of social reality as text. Storytelling is subject to conversational norms and structures (Atkinson, 1990, 1992b). Stories are not naturally occurring in this sense but are part of a set of culturally specific mechanisms for the constructing of textual representations. In other words, narratives cannot and should not be divorced from their location as social constructions within power structures and social milieux (Emihovich, 1995; Goodson, 1995). That is, narratives are not "naturally" occurring in that they are shaped, formed, and told according to connections and cultural understanding. As Passerini (1987, p. 28) argues, "When someone is asked for his life story his memory draws on pre-existing story lines and ways of telling stories, even if these are in part modified by the circumstances." This should not distract or discourage us from collecting and analyzing stories. Rather, it urges us to be reflexive in our collection and critical in our analysis.

Conclusion

In this chapter, we have shown how narrative analysis is an especially valuable approach to the analysis of qualitative data. It complements and counteracts the "culture of fragmentation" (Atkinson, 1992b) that is so characteristic of data analyses based on coding and categorizing. We already have outlined the importance of that approach, especially as it facilitates the exploration of content in interviews, fieldnotes, and the like. We also have noted, on the other hand, that such fragmentation does little to preserve the *form* of qualitative data. Naturally occurring interaction and explicit exercises in data collection are often grounded in storied sharing of personal experience. It is, therefore, essential to remain sensitive to those narrative forms and genres. We do not wish to imply, however, that there is anything uniquely privileged about personal narratives. It is not the case that ethnographic interviewing, or the collection of life histories, grants us privileged access to private experiences or to the essential identities of individual actors. On the contrary, and as we have noted, narrative forms are as conventional as any other form of individual or collective expression. In being so constructed, they are equally susceptible to cultural conventions of language and to dominant forms of expression. There are no formulae or recipes for the "best" way to analyze the stories we elicit and collect. Indeed, one of the strengths of thinking about our data as narrative is that this opens up the possibilities for a variety of analytic strategies. Such approaches also enable us to think beyond our data to the ways in which accounts and stories are socially and culturally managed and constructed. That is, the analysis of narratives can provide a critical way of examining not only key actors and events but also cultural conventions and social norms.

Suggestions for Further Reading

Bauman, R. (1986). *Story, performance and event: Contextual studies of oral narrative.* Cambridge, UK: Cambridge University Press.

A valuable introduction to the study of narrative and other performances in their cultural contexts.

Cortazzi, M. (1991). *Primary teaching, how it is—A narrative account.* London: David Fulton.
Cortazzi, M. (1993). *Narrative analysis.* London: Falmer.

A useful, complementary pair of books. The first presents and analyzes teachers' accounts of everyday life and work in schools. The second is an especially useful summary of a range of analytic strategies for narratives and accounts.

Heyl, B. (1979). *The madam as entrepreneur: Career management in house prostitution.* New Brunswick, NJ: Transaction Books.

A particularly telling use of the life history method. Based on personal narratives gained from multiple interviews with a key informant.

Kleinman, A. (1988). *The illness narrative: Suffering, healing and the human condition.* New York: Basic Books.

Examines how illness (especially chronic illness) is understood and expressed through personal narratives and suggests that narrative renders suffering meaningful.

Mishler, E. G. (1986). *Research interviewing: Context and narrative.* Cambridge, MA: Harvard University Press.

Stresses the importance of narrative in a critique of standardized survey interviewing, which Mishler argues does violence to the narratives of personal experience.

Myerhoff, B. (1978). *Number our days.* New York: Simon and Schuster.

An especially engaging and sympathetic exploration of talk and narrative among elderly Jewish Americans.

Plummer, K. (1995). *Telling sexual stories: Power, change and social worlds.* London: Routledge and Kegan Paul.

Explores a number of genres of personal, sexual narrative. Examines in detail the coming-out narratives of lesbians and gays, rape stories, and accounts of recovery. Places narrative in a wider framework of contemporary culture and in the tradition of symbolic interactionism.

Polkinghorne, D. E. (1988). *Narrative knowing and the human sciences.* Albany: State University of New York Press.

An important general statement of a narrative approach in contemporary cultural disciplines.

Riessman, C. K. (1990). *Divorce talk: Women and men make sense of personal relationships.*
    New Brunswick, NJ: Rutgers University Press.
Riessman, C. K. (1993). *Narrative analysis.* Newbury Park, CA: Sage.

   *An especially useful pair of monographs. In the first, Riessman demonstrates an
   approach to narrative analysis that is based on detailed empirical research and owes
   something to Mishler's general approach. In the second, she outlines a rationale and a
   variety of approaches to narrative analysis.*

4

Meanings and Metaphors

Meaningful Data

In turning from coding to narrative, we began to explore not only what was said in our data but also how it was said. We not only looked at the content of the data but also started to look at their form. We suggested that in a narrative analysis, form and content can be studied together. We also suggested that a narrative approach can help to alert the analyst to research problems and themes that coding and content analysis may not uncover. A concern with narrative can illuminate how informants use language to convey particular meanings and experiences.

Narrative analysis by no means exhausts analyses of this general sort. We can examine qualitative data from a number of related perspectives, some of which are related to varieties of semiotic analysis (Denzin, 1987; Feldman, 1994; Manning, 1987). The latter term implies a much broader set of theoretical and methodological commitments than we attempt to cover here: "a mode of analysis that seeks to understand how signs perform or convey meaning in context" (Manning, 1987, p. 25). How people convey their meanings through language can be looked at from a variety of complementary perspectives. It is possible, for example, to examine how language is used figuratively. In this context, we use metaphor to include all figurative tropes; analogies, similes, and other kinds of imagery can be considered under this general term. As Lakoff and Johnson (1980, p. 5) state, "the essence of metaphor is understanding and experiencing one kind of thing in terms of another." For example, "the field" is a metaphor readily used by anthropologists. They *go out* into the field; *return from* the field, and *construct and deconstruct* the field. They do fieldwork and collect fieldnotes and other field data. Fields have *boundaries,* and they can be *managed, produced, created,* and so on. As a metaphor, the field and its meanings are implicit in the everyday language of anthropologists, drawing on the analogy of the field as a physical entity. We suggest that a sensitive examination of such aspects of language use can illuminate how individuals and groups organize and express their experiences.

A broadly semiotic approach also can lead us to look at the use of specialized vocabularies in our data. It is always important to pay close attention to how members of particular groups or communities use ordinary language in special ways or use local specific variants. Such issues are not simply questions of folklore or the search for exotic local color. The organization of cultural categories through linguistic resources is a fundamental topic for virtually any kind of qualitative inquiry. Likewise, it is important to examine interview and other kinds of data in terms of their status as accounts. In other words, it is important to recognize that when informants provide responses by recounting past events or by describing general states of affairs, they may be performing particular kinds of speech acts. They may be giving accounts that justify, legitimate, excuse, and so on. They may be locating their own and others' actions or evaluations within particular frames of reference. They may use particular *vocabularies of motive* to account for social actions (Mills, 1940). They may be using kinds of accounting devices to produce coherent and plausible constructions of their world of experience.

In the course of this chapter, we will outline and exemplify a number of these analytic strategies. Again, they will be illustrated from our anthropology data. We do not intend to imply, however, that such perspectives can be brought to bear only on data derived from interviews. Interviews are common sources for such data but by no means the only ones. The analytic approaches outlined here can and should be applied to data of all sorts. They are especially relevant when one is analyzing data derived from naturally occurring spoken interaction, that is, data such as transcribed recordings of face-to-face encounters, telephone conversations, meetings, judicial proceedings, medical consultations, classroom instruction, mass media transmissions, and so on. The particular data set we draw on here should not imply unnecessary limits on the general use or relevance of such analytic strategies.

Metaphors

As we indicated above, spoken interaction is constructed through a variety of rhetorical and semantic devices, one of which is the characteristic use of metaphorical imagery. Metaphorical imagery can provide a useful way of thinking about and interpreting textual data. Metaphors are a figurative use of language, a ubiquitous feature of a culture's or an individual's thinking and discourse. This is accomplished through comparison or analogy. At its simplest, a metaphor is a device of representation through which new meaning may be learned. At their simplest, metaphors illustrate the likeness (or unlikeness) of two terms (or linguistic frameworks).

A metaphorical statement reduces two terms to their shared characteristics, enabling the linguistic transference of one to the other. There are variations on the general type of metaphor that serve to broaden their usage and their analytic mileage (see Lakoff & Johnson, 1980; Lodge, 1977; Sapir, 1977).

For the purposes of qualitative analysis, we also need to consider metaphor in a broader context. In the analysis of interactional or textual data, we might be concerned not only with how metaphors are structured but also with the ways in which they are used and the ways in which they are understood. In terms of data analysis, metaphors can be considered in a number of different ways. For example, we can explore the intent (or function) of the metaphor, the cultural context of the metaphor, and the semantic mode of the metaphor. Metaphors can be thought of as rhetorical devices serving a particular purpose for the speaker. Analytic questions might then focus on what the speaker is trying to express, what information he or she is trying to impart, or how his or her interests are being served by the use of the metaphor. From the analytic viewpoint, we should be interested here in the outcome of metaphor in terms of function and in the meaning imparted by the metaphor.

The use of metaphor by social actors in their interactions with one another, and in the course of research interviews, is revealing. This is particularly the case if we think of metaphors in terms of their cultural or social contexts. Metaphors are grounded in socially shared knowledge and conventional usage. Particular metaphors may help to identify cultural domains that are familiar to the members of a given culture or subculture; they express specific values, collective identities, shared knowledge, and common vocabularies.

Metaphorical statements have a number of features that deserve analytical attention. They can reveal shared understandings and situated realities of the social actor or social group. What terms are used in a metaphorical statement and what shared characteristics are implied can reveal common knowledge and what is taken for granted as shared understandings. In the same way, a "failed" metaphor can reveal levels of ignorance. How metaphors are structured and performed by social actors can reveal the taken-for-granted usage of metaphor and may prompt an analysis of the contexts in which metaphorical statements are utilized.

Turning to the data on anthropology and anthropologists, on the surface they do not seem especially rich in metaphorical usage. In other words, the informants do not spend much time likening their experiences to other things or producing vivid imagery. This may be a result of the relative formality of interviews themselves or the academic subject matter that occupied much of the spoken interaction. The naive investigator might be disappointed and conclude that the data were not fruitful from this perspective. On closer inspection, however, many of the descriptions of the work of the anthropology student and the nature of the social relationship between supervisor and graduate student do draw on a number of metaphors.

Among anthropologists (and indeed among academics from a wide range of disciplines), the supervisory relationship is regarded as a delicate one that potentially can give rise to particular kinds of problems. For the anthropologists, the delicacy of the relationship, and the problems around anthropological research more generally, were focused on the experience of distant fieldwork and the processes of transforming that work into a thesis. Talking of these issues, one anthropologist said,

One can advise but not dictate. And I think the student has got to be balanced from the point of view of personality to begin with, to put up with this isolation. I don't know if you've heard of Mary Douglas . . .? [interviewer— Yes] I remember her saying she regarded this isolation in the field as an important part of the training of an anthropologist, because one is on one's own. She had this idea that it was a sort of *rite de passage.* One is going through a period when one is marginal, on the borders of one's career, but also being involved in another society. But from the point of view of the fieldworker's personality, they have to be able to live with it and take it, and a number of people who have been attracted to research have been attracted because they don't feel positive about other opportunities, and I think that's not good enough. They have to be positive about research . . . and the problems arise that they were slightly depressed, easily diverted by all sorts of nonacademic alternatives and none of these has delivered the goods. . . .

Here the metaphors (of a *rite de passage,* of marginality) are so firmly based in anthropology and other social sciences themselves that their status as tropes is less obviously discerned than it might be in other contexts. Nevertheless, in developing our analysis of this set of data, we would want to do two closely related things. First, we would want to examine the full range of metaphors applied to the crucial phases of graduate work and the supervisory relationship. Second, also as illustrated here, we would want to look at how concepts derived from anthropological discourse itself are applied reflexively to the processes of becoming an anthropologist. We would see that the metaphor of a *rite de passage* is applied frequently, if apparently rather self-consciously. We also would want to go beyond the overtly metaphorical in order to examine how particular terms are used in the context of a given subculture—in this case, that of academic anthropologists.

The same data fragment reveals a further set of metaphors, not so much to do with the supervisory relationship but rather relating to the work and intellectual endeavors of anthropology. If one takes a slightly broader view of metaphor, then it becomes clear that there are a number of terms used by the supervisor that have metaphorical properties. For example, *balanced, isolation, the field, marginal, borders,* and *delivered the goods* are all metaphors. That is, they all use physical terms and concepts to refer to and describe what are actually *intellectual constructs* about the nature of anthropological work. Inspecting the data, then, we would want to ask ourselves which linguistic terms seem to have special significance for the anthropologists. We would then want to retrieve and examine these usages in more detail. We would want to do more than merely noting their occurrence. We would want to explore the range of denotations and connotations that such terms seem to have, in particular contexts. In other words, we do not assume that such local terms (which we might think of as elements in an occupational register, or as terms in a situated vocabulary) each have a fixed meaning. Rather, we should inspect their use in the data at hand.

Consider, for example, some further extracts from the data that convey metaphorical images of anthropological fieldwork. In the following extract, a faculty member articulates some familiar, but highly evocative, images of the field:

> [M]y general feeling is that the more immersed you get, the longer it takes to produce a PhD. And I have a second theory about that which is that I suspect, for reasons to do with the cultures we study, that most women doing fieldwork get more immersed, because women tend to be less able in the societies we study to keep a marginal resistance, to keep mobile between communities. They're plonked dead in the centre. They tend to get more immersed as fieldworkers, and I suspect, for that reason, to take longer to write up. . . .

Metaphors of the field—such as that of *immersion*—are so familiar to social scientists, not only anthropologists, that it would be easy to overlook them in these data. Taken together with other images, however—such as the spatial metaphors of *centrality, marginality,* and *mobility* in this example—these metaphors help to convey a pervasive set of cultural assumptions about the discipline of anthropology and its most characteristic work.

In a similar vein, there are recurrent metaphors about the process of academic supervision and research training. Consider, for example, the following extract from a faculty member:

> [A]ll this business of training I think is largely spurious, it's something that's learnt by the experience of doing it, it's rather like teaching music. You can't teach people to play without a piano, it's only by playing that they learn. And I think fieldwork is like that.

The metaphor of teaching music here is used to capture a particular image of the practical experience of learning and doing. It also conveys the image of a direct, personal pedagogical relationship between the teacher and the learner. A full analysis of all the data would benefit from an exploration of the imagery used in this and similar contexts. Attention to these and other metaphors in the data help us to gain analytic purchase on how faculty members and students conceive of their work and their working relationships. Their imagery helps to convey key features of their shared culture.

It is also of more than passing interest that anthropologists use anthropological concepts to refer to themselves and their peers. In addition to the imagery of *rites de passage* to describe the process of socialization, the anthropologists not infrequently refer to themselves as a *tribe*, liken their intellectual disputes to *community feuding*, and refer to the senior professorate as the *elders*. This is usually done with arch self-consciousness, but it is characteristic of the discipline's local culture.

Metaphorical statements enable the analyst to explore the linguistic devices used by social actors and how such devices reveal shared meanings and understandings. Metaphors also can be seen in a wider context of specialized vocabularies. Language is used in specific and particular ways. Cultural categories are organized through linguistic resources. Metaphors are therefore part of a wider use of linguistic symbols to convey (or create) shared cultural meanings. Analysis of this general sort can be referred to as domain analysis, and we now turn to that as a way of continuing our discussion of how we can analyze informants' language in order to reveal shared cultural understandings. We have already noted the centrality of "fieldwork" in the interviews with anthropologists. We use this to illustrate the fundamentals of domain analysis. First we outline the approach in general terms.

Domain Analysis

Analysis of this general sort draws on the cultural significance of linguistic symbols to create and maintain shared meaning. The emphasis is on an understanding that social actors order their experiences through a series of symbolic references. This is not limited to linguistic usage and can include action, movement, and facial expression. As Spradley (1979, p. 9) notes, "because language is the primary means for transmitting culture from one generation to the next, much of any culture is encoded in linguistic form."

The aim of this type of analytic strategy is to explore the linguistic symbols or "folk terms" used by social actors, both individually and collectively. In doing so, we are concerned with identifying patterns and systems of folk terms as a mechanism for understanding the cultural knowledge of a particular social group. The task of the analyst, in this context, is to work toward an exploration of the structure of a culture's cognitive universe, drawing on the data (Tesch, 1990). In terms of analytic strategy, we need to break down the sequential and linear order of texts into "non-linear, network like semantic structures that underline their texts" (Werner & Schoepfle, 1987, p. 30). We also note here, and explore in more detail in a later chapter, that many computer software programs can be of great help in creating and exploring semantic structures.

Domain analysis is often described as though it were a single analytical event. In practice, it involves a number of separate, though related, tasks. Central to this type of analysis is the identification of the linguistic (and cultural) symbols themselves. Spradley (1979) suggests that a symbol has a triad of elements. These are (a) the actual symbol—for example, the folk term used by an informant or social actor; the sounds, words, and analytical terms taken from the culture itself; (b) the referent or referents—these are the things to which a symbol refers or what a symbol represents; and (c) the relationship between the symbol and the referent(s)—that is, the relationship in which the referent becomes encoded in the symbol, where attention is focused on what the symbol refers to, the symbol itself being taken for granted. Simple examples of linguistic symbols are "car" and "tree." Both of these are in common everyday linguistic usage in the United Kingdom and the United States. We know from those words what people are referring to. By *car*, we are actually referring to a vehicle for transporting four to six people, with four rubber wheels (tires), a petrol (or gasoline) engine, and so on. Similarly, by *tree* we refer to a large living structure, rooted in the ground, with a wooden trunk, leaves, branches, and so on. We might associate it with being climbed or with its distinctly "wooden" properties.

Such symbols and symbolic codes are taken for granted within our cultural context and carry implied, shared meaning. Clearly, meanings that are attached to such symbols can simply denote or can have wider connotations. One symbol may have more than one meaning, and most do. Trees come in many shapes and varieties, and cars have different manufacturers, features, and performance levels. Take Spradley's (1979) example of the term *flop*. Spradley studied individuals living on the street as down-and-outs or tramps. In the culture of tramps, *flop* is a word that refers to a place to sleep. On closer inspection, Spradley showed that a *flop* denotes many different kinds of places, including doorways, stairwells, graveyards, and park benches. As a folk term or symbol, *flop* means various physical spaces that on the surface might appear to have little in common, yet they are all related as a type of *flop*, a place to sleep.

Analysis of these linguistic symbols implies the identification of these symbols (folk terms) for a given social group and an exploration of the patterns and relationships among such symbols. The symbols may be thought of as categories or as *organizing schemes* (Tesch, 1990, p. 139), and the task of the analyst is to identify the rules and relationships among the symbols. In this context, a *domain* refers to a set of symbols that share meaning in some way. Spradley (1979, 1980) describes a domain structure as having four characteristics: (a) a core term or overall category title (e.g., *car, tree, flop*); (b) two or more included folk terms that belong to the category (for *tree,* these might be elm, ash, oak, willow; for *flop,* doorways, park benches); (c) a semantic relationship that links the core term to the included terms (e.g., inclusion, cause-effect, attribution); and (d) a boundary or parameter, the terms of which should be defined by the native informant/social actor.

The emphasis in this type of analysis is the semantic relationship among folk terms. This enables speakers to refer to folk terms while imparting or drawing on shared meanings and understandings. Certain types of semantic relationships appear to have almost universal usage; for example, a relationship of inclusion (*x* is a kind of *y;* a park bench is a kind of flop; an oak is a kind of tree) or a relationship of cause-effect (*x* is a cause of *y*) have particularly wide cultural usage. Other semantic relationships between folk terms may be particular to the social setting.

Spradley (1979) offers a step-by-step approach to the technicalities of domain analysis, so we do not provide a detailed exegesis or the whole approach here. The overall schema is to start by selecting single semantic relationships and then identifying "core" folk terms and "included" folk terms. The overall goal is to be able to identify categories of expression and gain an overview of the social or cultural scene being studied through the linguistic domains and classifications being used. Spradley also demonstrates how one moves from domain analysis in general terms to the in-depth analysis of a single domain. Referred to as taxonomic analysis, this enables the exploration of the meanings and relationships of one domain. The development of a folk taxonomy identifies the relationships among the folk terms; such relationships can be expressed diagrammatically and enable the analyst to build up visual representations of how sets of cultural knowledge are interrelated. We exemplify such a taxonomy in Chapter 5 when we discuss the value of visual displays in the representation and reconstruction of cultural phenomena (see also Miles & Huberman, 1994).

This analytic approach is concerned with exploring the folk terms and linguistic symbols used by social actors in particular cultural settings. We argue that developing an understanding of the folk term usage has analytic mileage in terms of exploring the tacit cultural knowledge of the social setting. There are at least two caveats to this kind of approach. First, domain and taxonomic analyses are meaningful only if we use the symbols, categories, and relationships that are used and identified by the "native" speakers, that is, the social actors from the particular social or cultural setting. In the process of trying to create order and patterns out of the folk terms, we must resist the temptation to impose our own categories from our own folk taxonomies and domains. Second, the domain analysis or completed taxonomic structure will never fully match the cultural knowledge patterns of the native culture. Such analysis can only approximate the way the social actors actually organize and gain meaning from their cultural knowledge. It should not be described and seen as a direct replica of cultural knowledge.

What follows is an example of how these sorts of ideas can be used to gain insight into a particular social setting. Drawing on the anthropology data, it is possible to begin to analyze the folk term *fieldwork* and its meaning to anthropology students and faculty. Fieldwork has a number of relationships attached to it and a number of different semantic meanings stemming from it. As a folk category, it is rich in linguistic symbolism, as our discussion below indicates.

"Fieldwork": A Domain Analysis

It seemed to us from reading the data from anthropologists that most of them associated the discipline with a sustained period of "fieldwork."

That is, all the anthropologists talked about researching a field or doing fieldwork, and indeed they ordered their student and disciplinary experiences around this period. From this observation, we began to look back over the data, attempting to ascertain how the anthropologists talked about fieldwork, how they conceptualized it and consolidated the experience they gained from it. We began to ask the data a series of questions based on this emerging idea about fieldwork as a symbol: When was "fieldwork"; when did it happen? Where was fieldwork; where was it located? What was fieldwork like; how was it experienced? What was it for? What were the products of fieldwork? To foreshadow these ideas in a slightly different way, we began to think about the relationships among the folk term *fieldwork* and other folk terms: What were the places for fieldwork? What were the times of fieldwork? Were there different activities that could be counted as fieldwork? What were the effects of fieldwork? This series of questions enabled the anthropologists' stories and accounts to be looked at in a particular way. Taking a theme that is talked about by all the anthropologists, we are able to begin to construct a domain analysis in which *fieldwork* is the core term and the domain is constructed from the answers to the questions we ask of the data. Fieldwork in this context is symbolic and functional.

To illustrate this, we take an interview with a PhD student and an interview with a faculty member. Both provide accounts and information on how fieldwork is constructed and experienced. We retrieved these particular examples by taking the student and supervisor interview transcripts from the same institution and sorting for one of each that specifically talked about fieldwork in some detail. By then applying the questions of who, where, what, and so on, a preliminary analysis could be undertaken.

WHERE IS FIELDWORK?

Anthropologists talk about fieldwork as being "away" in the "field." The sense we get is that fieldwork is traveled to—you arrive and you come back. It is distant and somewhere you "get to." Extracts from the data illustrate this. A PhD student talked about fieldwork in the following ways:

> I was upgraded to a PhD student before I went out into the field. Then I went to do my fieldwork in October '88 . . . the year before I went away.

I think that's something strange about anthropology, that really you have no idea what you're going to study until you get to the field.

The student also uses phrases such as "since I've been back" and "those who've returned from fieldwork." As well as traveling to field-work, you also return from it. A PhD supervisor gives similar insight as to where the "field" is, adding the emphasis that as well as fieldwork being "away," it may also be distant: "you would keep in touch—correspond."

[S]o long as I know that everything there's alright, that the student's alive and well and collecting material, then I would want to keep as much distance as possible. It's part of my responsibility to make sure they are alive and well, but as long as I have that assurance, which comes basically from the fieldnotes coming in, and the odd letter, I don't require more.

"Away" and "distant" are also captured by phrases of coming back and settling down, of being "sent off" to "sit on your own, organize your own research." *Fieldwork* seems to be bounded by this sense of distance and sense of a *place* you travel to and return from. In that sense, fieldwork is described as a physical entity in itself. Students and supervisors do, of course, talk about particular geographical locations, for example Papua New Guinea, but they characterize fieldwork as an entity or place that is generalizable. That is, it can be talked about outside the particular: Fieldwork occurs in a place that is definable, away, and distant but self-evidently there.

WHEN IS FIELDWORK?

Supervisors and students locate fieldwork along a time line. This is bounded by both formal university arrangements on one hand and more tacit understandings of beginning fieldwork, doing fieldwork, and end-ing fieldwork on the other. For example, the supervisor and the PhD student both describe formal processes of when it is appropriate or acceptable for students to go to do their fieldwork.

Student

Well as I understand it, the university has regulations that you can either start a PhD with an MA, or you have to spend a year doing work aimed towards an MA. So you have to spend a year here before you can do fieldwork. I wasn't clear at the beginning whether I would submit an MA, but towards the end I decided I didn't want to have to write a whole thesis, so what the university requires is a putative first two chapters of a PhD thesis which have to be judged to be of a standard that shows you're working towards a PhD. That's before they allow you to go into the field. So up to that point I was registered as an MA student for a year. Then at the end of that I submitted the two chapters with a synopsis of the whole thesis. It was approved by my supervisor, who then went to the faculty and they approved it as well. Then I was upgraded to a PhD student before I went out to the field. Then I went to do my fieldwork in October '88.

Supervisor

Yes, they can't go to the field until they've been upgraded. Nobody does fieldwork—except for very exceptional circumstances—for an MA. So they register for the MA in the initial period. At the end of one year they're supposed to submit something substantial in writing which need not be a whole thesis, but work towards it, and if this is deemed to be OK they get upgraded to PhD. What we've done now is to institute a more formal arrangement, whereby right at the start of the course the student and supervisor have to agree on a date at which a thing called a research proposal or transfer report is to be submitted. And that consists of a ten-thousand-word piece, which includes a substantial review of the literature, a discussion of the objectives of the proposed research and so on, and a chunk on methodology, practical methodological problems surrounding the research. So there's three parts to it, a literature review, research objectives, and methodology, which is put into ten thousand words, formally submitted and read by a panel in the department which consists of the supervisor and two other members of staff. Then there's a sit-down session, rather like a PhD viva, from which the student can get feedback and so on, and if it's all OK, then we recommend the student for upgrading. This is the first year we've operated this more formal system, and it means that when students come we can tell them this is what they're going to do—"By such and such a date you have got to have produced this." And I think that's much better.

So, fieldwork happens once a student has "upgraded," that is, once they have "graduated" or moved from an MA registration to a PhD registration. Fieldwork is something students are "allowed" to do once they have completed a year of "preparation." It is a *rite de passage* from master's degree level to doctorate, something that is worked toward and for which there is a formal procedure of admission. As we mentioned above, "when fieldwork happens" is also located within more indeterminate but still agreed boundaries. Fieldwork "begins and ends." You "go" and you "come back." Supervisor and student talk of the "time" spent in the field in terms of calendar time—away in 1988, back in April of this year, a year or more, and so on. They also talk in terms of phases of the fieldwork: early in my fieldwork, a long period of time, later on in the fieldwork. Fieldwork is also bounded by the "before" and the "after." If people (anthropology students) are not doing fieldwork and therefore away, they are either "pre-" or "post-fieldwork." Early work is geared toward preparation ahead of fieldwork. Coming back includes "a debriefing session with my supervisor" and a period "when they're settling down." Leaving the field and returning from fieldwork are also described by the anthropologists as potentially difficult.

> There's a real feeling, especially among those who've returned from fieldwork and are writing up, and the younger members of the teaching staff that coming back from fieldwork is a strange experience, you feel lost, and to get on with academic work again, and the arduous job of writing up—there's a lot of support for people. The young members of staff that we're getting in at the moment are especially useful for this—it's really nice to have them around.

> [T]he psychological problems of being back from your fieldsite, and change of perspective, and I think these are very hard to deal with in any kind of course, or through groups. You really depend very much on the goodwill and understanding of your supervisor, and his or her ability to deal with personal problems.

Fieldwork, then, occurs within different time frames—calendar, chronological, early/late, before/after, pre/post. These not only provide a physical time location for the fieldwork but also enable the career of the student anthropologist to be mapped and kept track of.

WHAT IS FIELDWORK LIKE?

The anthropology data are filled with rich descriptions of what the experience of fieldwork is actually like. Generalizations and contrasts can be made. The supervisor describes fieldwork as "very much an independent business"; of her own fieldwork, she reflects on the "chance to do fieldwork," a PhD being "a wonderful opportunity to do fieldwork and spend a couple of years thinking and writing about something I was interested in." Fieldwork is highlighted as the special aspect of anthropology and its essential difference from other subjects. Fieldwork is what makes a "proper" anthropologist:

> [I]t's a unique subject in that you do get sort of, sometimes to central Glasgow, sometimes to Papua New Guinea, sometimes to places in between, where for a year or more you sit on your own, organize your own research very much. . . .
> It is very much like that in the sense that before you go away you are just one of the kids and are treated as such, maybe not consciously, by members of staff, but when you come back you can be talked to like an adult. You have passed your initiation—well, you've undergone it, whether you've passed it or not you'll find out later, but that's the most important thing about talking to anthropologists, it's such a strange subject in the sense that you have to do this fieldwork.

So fieldwork is a chance, an opportunity, special, where you think and write, where you are independent. Fieldwork also is necessary to become a proper anthropologist—it is in essence an initiation into the discipline.

Student accounts of fieldwork bring out some similar aspects. The independent, private nature of fieldwork experience comes across, the notion that you have to find your own way of doing it, that "you really have to be flexible about your work." Fieldwork in that sense is still described as independent and individualistic, but students also give other views of what fieldwork is like. Above all, this particular student talks about how you cannot prepare for it.

> [I]t's common to find that until you get to the field you don't know what you'll be doing. . . . I think if you're too primed to do fieldwork that can backfire, you can plod along on your own course and be less receptive to the way things are going. It is a problem with the requirement to go and immerse yourself into a society for such a long period of time, you really have to be flexible about your work, and if you're too prepared and you have too many methods you want to employ, if you've structured your time too much before you arrive, you can mess it up by not being receptive enough.

This student also talked about fieldwork as immersion: the way "you just get in there and participate in the social life of the place as much as possible and observe." This is not without its problems. The student talked about a concern with personal security and the sense of "going into the wild." The student perspective then is smattered with the uncertainty of fieldwork, how you cannot be prepared for it, and how it may be dangerous and difficult. What comes across is a sense of privacy, isolation, and ambivalent response. There is less emphasis on the opportunities and joys of fieldwork. Having said this, like the supervisor's account there is a sense of a *rite de passage*. As we discussed earlier, leaving the fieldwork and "returning" are both signifiers of a particular stage in the anthropological career, and both have psychological consequences attached. From our data, we might suggest that these are similar and different for the student and the established scholar.

WHAT ARE THE "PRODUCTS" OF FIELDWORK?

Both supervisors and students talk about fieldwork as generating a number of "products." Fieldwork, in this context, is a productive activity. There are, of course, the physical products: the "fieldnotes," the "genealogies," and the "writing up." There are other tangible products talked about—the paper, the draft of the first chapter, the PhD thesis, and the intended book manuscript. Other products are less tangible— the "product" of the *rite de passage* and becoming a proper anthropologist. Students also talk about the product of fieldwork being about changing ideas about what you are going to study. The product in this sense is in developing the focus and perspective of your anthropological niche. The product of fieldwork is then described as both tangible "things" and more elusive roles and developments. This aspect of analysis could be followed through further by viewing fieldwork as an end in itself—the work in order to complete the dissertation or a means to an end, the experience of developing and becoming an anthropologist. In this sense, then, fieldwork is both real and symbolic.

Even this very preliminary domain analysis of "fieldwork" reveals many aspects that could be followed up with a more thorough analysis. Figure 4.1 summarizes the analytical framework we have described. How fieldwork is talked about and conceptualized highlights the centrality of it for the anthropological career. Figure 4.2 (p. 100) summarizes how the same analysis can be viewed in terms of a series of semantic relationships of inclusion, product, emotions, and time. This analysis could be taken

Where is fieldwork?	away distant "the field" "there"
When is fieldwork?	after upgrading after preparation early/late
What is fieldwork like?	independent a chance an opportunity thinking and writing special on your own an initiation private individualistic immersion uncertain insecure "a void" dangerous
What are the products of fieldwork?	thesis fieldnotes papers a *rite de passage* becoming a proper anthropologist a focus real and symbolic

Figure 4.1. Preliminary Analysis of Anthropological Fieldwork

further than we take it here, relating fieldwork to wider semiotic and organizing schemes. In this way, a picture could be built up about the linguistic symbols and shared cultural knowledge of anthropologists and anthropology.

Accounts

So far in this chapter, we have concentrated on the use of vocabulary and linguistic symbols as means by which shared meaning is derived and

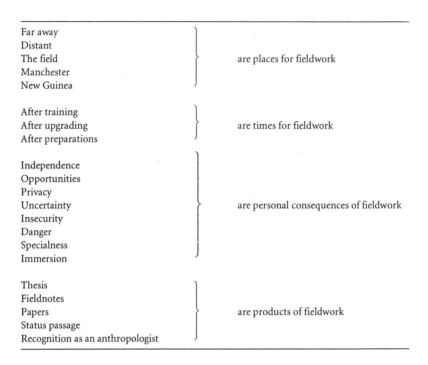

Figure 4.2. The Relationships of the Folk Term *Fieldwork*

hence may be explored. As we have discussed so far, informants use language to convey particular experiences and meanings. Social actors also draw on particular sorts of vocabularies in order to account for their social actions. Mills (1940) refers to these particular sorts of rhetorical devices as "vocabularies of motive." Certain types of vocabulary and speech devices can be used to produce coherent and plausible accounts of social events and social action. These can be examined as part of the analytic strategy.

Interview data and other data that encompass talk can be examined in terms of their status as accounts. Examining textual and oral data in terms of accounts enables us to think of talk itself as socially meaningful text. That is, as individual social actors recall and retell events or describe past experiences, they may be performing particular types of speech acts. Social actors may be describing events in certain sorts of ways that account for, justify, excuse, or legitimate action or behavior. Accounting devices are used by social actors to produce plausible and coherent constructions of the social world. Lyman and Scott (1970, p. 112) suggest that the giving and receiving of accounts are part and parcel of everyday talk, employed by social actors to explain unanticipated, untoward, or unusual behavior. They are situated accounts that may be dependent on the status of the interactants and the physical or social location. The important thing about accounts, as conceptualized in this way, is that they tend to be standardized within cultures and subculture groups; hence, we can identify the content of accounts and their literary and idiomatic style as a way of exploring the situated culture within which they are embedded. Different types of accounts are employed by social actors in differing situations, and different forms of delivering accounts can demonstrate the situated and cultural nature of the production of accounts.

Some accounts can be conceptualized in terms of two types—excuses and justifications (Lyman & Scott, 1970; Potter & Wetherell, 1987). Excuses can be thought of as socially approved vocabularies designed to mitigate or relieve questionable action or conduct. By contrast, justifications neutralize or attach positive value to informed or questionable acts rather than denying responsibility. Lyman and Scott (1970) put forward a number of ideal types of excuse vocabulary, including the appeal to accidents, biological drives, fatalistic forces, lack of information, and scapegoating. Excuses are used by social actors to account for the available evidence (Wetherell & Potter, 1989). Justifications also can take several forms, relying to a large extent on what Sykes and Matza (1957) termed *techniques of neutralization*. Justifications therefore are socially approved vocabularies that may situate the act in a justificatory context, trivialize the consequences or the victim of the act, and in other ways justify the act as acceptable (if not desirable). Like metaphors, successful accounts should be coherent and plausible, and they must draw upon shared knowledge and understanding. In order to excuse or justify actions, accounts must also be persuasive.

Accounts have idiomatic form employed to suit the social circle in which they are introduced, and this will tend to conform to the norms of a culture or situation. Examples of idiomatic form might include rather formal styles, in which the account giver and receiver are social strangers or in which the audience is too large to allow coparticipation of giver and receiver. At the other end of the continuum, accounts may have more informal or casual linguistic form that includes jargon, slang, omissions, and so forth. Such styles are appropriately employed in dyads or small groups in which parties are well known to one another. The linguistic style and form of account is hence dependent upon the situated context of the interaction and the identities and relationships of the givers and receivers of accounts.

In addition to excuses and justifications, there are many more specific "accounting devices" that actors use in order to produce plausible explanations of their own and others' actions. An important analysis of interview data that examines actors' accounting devices is the study of scientists' descriptions of scientific discoveries reported by Gilbert and Mulkay (1980). They report how scientists' talk draws on a repertoire of accounting devices in the construction of plausible (if internally contradictory) explanations of scientific success. In particular, they use two repertoires of account. On one hand, scientists use explanations that are couched in terms of contingent factors, such as luck and the personal characteristics of scientists themselves. On the other hand, they refer to the inexorable revelation of scientific truth in response to evidence and experimentation. This latter repertoire Gilbert and Mulkay call TWOD (Truth Will Out Device). The scientists they interviewed used the devices together in producing their accounts of scientific work and discovery.

In a similar vein, the students and faculty members in anthropology produced characteristic accounting devices to describe and account for their distinctive disciplinary knowledge. Understandably, their repertoires were different from those of the laboratory scientists interviewed by Gilbert and Mulkay. Anthropologists' accounts include the "indeterminacy" repertoire, imputing academic success and research performance largely to personal qualities that escape formal training. Such accounts often emphasize the apprenticeship mode of intergenerational transmission and stress the element of *rite de passage* in fieldwork. For example,

> participant observation is not, I would say, a research method which can be taught in the classroom and applied in the field, whereas statistical methods can be taught in the classroom and applied in the field. But of course participant observation is hardly a method. I think it's the *sine qua non*. It's something you can only learn by doing. . . . The way knowledge is constructed out of observation, interaction between the informants and the investigator,

the general reflexivity of the process is very much the stuff of the training before going into the field . . . there remains a certain mystique about it. Yes, in order to do the *rite de passage* properly you've got to do it by yourself.

It is perceptible from these and similar uses of the repertoire that some features of these accounts take on almost proverbial status. They have the air of craft-based wisdom, readily expressed in terms of maxims and tags. Phrases such as "taught in the classroom and applied in the field" and "it's something you can learn only by doing" sound like maxims that are part of an almost formulaic craft knowledge and are indeed echoed in other anthropologists' accounts.

When we think about the anthropology data in terms of accounts and accounting devices, we open up a vast array of potential analyses. We should acknowledge that data drawn from interviews and other kinds of spoken interaction cannot always be taken at face value. By that, we do not mean that informants lie or otherwise systematically misrepresent themselves and others, and we are not exactly concerned with methodological problems of "bias" in the data. Both of those concerns imply that we could—in principle and in practice—establish a gold standard of reality from which accounts observably depart and through which speakers willfully seek to deceive. We do not believe that the relationship between accounts and the realities they describe could ever be that simple and transparent. On the contrary, we have to recognize that accounts necessarily shape those realities. This is the principle known as the reflexivity of accounts.

We thus can inspect our data with a view to establishing *how* accounts are constructed—and so how realities are constructed and reconstructed through them. Among other things, we can look for the use of specific devices or structures that are used to generate characteristic accounts, and so to construct plausible and reasonable descriptions. In principle, we could identify a number of genres of accounts in the anthropology interviews. To some extent, we already have seen characteristic accounts when we introduced some of them as narratives. Here, from the current analytic perspective, we look not so much at their storylike qualities but instead as devices used to construct accounts. In considering accounts as speech acts, we recognize, as we have indicated, that they are used to perform acts in their own right. In other words, they embody particular kinds of claims, legitimations, or justifications. They may reconcile otherwise contrasting versions and perspectives. They may be part of the teller's self-presentation as an actor (rational, sensitive, courageous, stoical, or whatever). In other words, accounts have moral functions in placing the speaker in a rational or moral order.

To exemplify our argument, we can turn to one accounting device that is used repeatedly by the academics who were interviewed as part of the anthropology study. Academics drew on a particular device to describe their own practices, their own departments, and their discipline. The general form of the device is that of "contrastive rhetoric" (Hargreaves, 1981, 1984), that is, accounts in which the speaker and his or her practices or values are legitimated or justified by means of comparisons with what goes on elsewhere, what has been done in the past, or what others do. The contrasts are constructed so as to provide the hearer with the opportunity to recognize which state of affairs is to be preferred. Consider how the following, very experienced, anthropologist talks about his discipline:

> I think the PhD has changed. I can parody how it's changed. The old anthropologists—not old, the generation of the forties and fifties—went out to some unknown part of the Empire, acquired the language, wrote up their PhDs which then became monographs, on the basis entirely of their field data. There was very rarely even a bibliography, and certainly very little reference to major theoretical debates. Theory was embedded in the ethnography. These were highly original thinkers, producing highly original work, but of an unprescriptive kind. I think the subject's grown enormously, it's become more complex and more specialized, and become more theoretically oriented, so the focus has been to examine some sort of theoretical issue in a particular ethnographic context. And it's become much more scholarly, and there's a much more substantial theoretical overview, much earlier on in the thesis and the theoretical aspects are made much more explicit and much more in terms of debates than they used to be. And what is expected of a PhD has increased, and I consider that a problem which the profession must sink its teeth into, because the level of expertise both in terms of fieldwork and other types of research, and in terms of ethnographic reading and theoretical debate has increased enormously. . . . We're squeezed between different models of what a PhD is. The North American market is quite important to us now, the American PhD is very long, seven years in anthropology, working towards a higher level of scholarship. The ESRC model is three years. We've screamed for two decades that you can't do a PhD in anthropology in three years, but the model the ESRC is promoting is a three-year piece of research training. Even the language of research training

isn't the language in which PhDs were discussed by the Oxford professors in the 1940s and 1950s. A PhD was a contribution to original scholarship. The bulk of original work done in anthropology was done by people doing PhDs.

The key features of this account are quite transparent, not least because the teller acknowledges that he is creating something of a parody. He does so in terms of a series of contrasts—the past with the present, the United Kingdom with North America, the nature of the monograph and the place of theory within it over time. He constructs his current views on the PhD in anthropology in terms of a complex set of contrasts. It is also apparent that through his accounting practices, he is able to convey—and to some extent reconcile—conflicting views. This is not a view that celebrates a golden past, nor does it altogether denigrate it. The present is not celebrated uncritically.

The comparison with elsewhere hints at some degree of ambiguity. Indeed, the anthropologist himself concluded this section of the interview by saying "some of the things that are happening I applaud, and others I'm a bit worried about." Such perspectives are captured well in his various uses of contrastive rhetoric in the construction of his own account. He uses this device to justify how the PhD has changed and his views about that change. It is justificatory in that he demonstrates that there are reasons for the change and his views of it. This does not mean he considers all the changes, but it does mean he has vocabulary and rhetorical devices for justifying them and making sense of them to himself and others. This example could be used to develop a much broader analysis than we have attempted here. We could explore more of the data for other instances of contrastive rhetoric or search out other accounting devices that are explored. We could concentrate more on when particular kinds of accounts are used—to justify specific activities, events, and states, or to excuse particular behavior or circumstances. These could be explored for regularity or peculiarity.

Conclusion

We have not attempted to provide a rigorous discussion of the whole range of approaches that might be called linguistic or semiotic analyses. Our purpose in this chapter has been to demonstrate the potential value of exploring how cultural categories and identities are organized through the use of language. What we have been particularly concerned with is thinking about how social actors use a variety of linguistic resources and devices to convey meanings and motives. The value of such analytic approaches is in the opportunity they afford us to think about the experiences of social actors in their own terms. The "down side" of such approaches is that we should endeavor not to impose our own meanings and imagery. Such analytic strategies are useful only if we think about them in terms of how individuals and groups are using linguistic devices and imagery to organize their own experiences and express those experiences. We are interested in the meanings that the social actors and cultural groups attach to their linguistic expression, not our own interpretations. Without "going native," it is virtually impossible to construct a complete replication of the linguistic resources of a social group, and even then there are no guarantees. The sorts of approaches we have outlined in this chapter, however, provide some ideas of how we can be reflexive in our analyses of how local language is used figuratively, metaphorically, and rhetorically.

Suggestions for Further Reading

Fernandez, J. W. (Ed.). (1991). *Beyond metaphor: The theory of tropes in anthropology.* Stanford, CA: Stanford University Press.

  An interesting collection of essays that explore various aspects of the metaphorical as a topic for anthropological inquiry.

Gilbert, G. N., & Mulkay, M. (1980). *Opening Pandora's box: A sociological analysis of scientists' discourse.* Cambridge, UK: Cambridge University Press.

  A detailed analysis of scientists' accounts of scientific discoveries, in which the authors stress the methodological imperative to regard interview talk as accounts rather than taking them at face value.

Lakoff, G., & Johnson, M. (1980). *Metaphors we live by.* Chicago: University of Chicago Press.

  The classic, standard text on the pervasiveness of metaphorical expression in everyday thought and language.

Manning, P. K. (1987). *Semiotics and fieldwork.* Newbury Park, CA: Sage.

  Introduces the application of formal models derived from linguistics and semiotics to the analysis of qualitative data. Covers issues similar to what we have referred to as domain analysis.

Noblit, G. W., & Hare, R. D. (1988). *Meta-ethnography: Synthesizing qualitative studies.* Newbury Park, CA: Sage.

Includes an examination of root metaphors in ethnographic texts as one way to undertake meta-analysis and synthesis of ethnographic research.

Spradley, J. P. (1970). *You owe yourself a drunk: An ethnography of urban nomads.* Boston: Little, Brown.

An ethnography that exemplifies some of Spradley's characteristic uses of semantic categories and relationships in the explication of culture.

5

Writing and Representation

Analyzing and Writing

Analysis is not simply a matter of classifying, categorizing, coding, or collating data. It is not simply a question of identifying forms of speech or regularities of action. Most fundamentally, analysis is about the representation or reconstruction of social phenomena. We do not simply "collect" data; we fashion them out of our transactions with other men and women. Likewise, we do not merely report what we find; we create accounts of social life, and in doing so we construct versions of the social worlds and the social actors that we observe. It is, therefore, inescapable that analysis implies representation.

We have emphasized that the existence of complementary strategies for data analysis implies choice. We do not follow any one analytic strategy in an uncritical fashion. One should certainly not adopt any one approach without principled reflection. One should be able to make disciplined, principled choices about how to represent and reconstruct social worlds and social actors, social scenes and social action. Among other things, such choices direct how we write our accounts, such as monographs, theses, or journal articles. They also direct us toward new ways of representing our research endeavors.

The writing of qualitative research has never been monolithic: It has reflected differences among disciplines (e.g., sociology and anthropology), rational academic styles, and the influences of subject matter. Conventions of authorship and representation also have not been unchanging. There have been shifts from one generation of scholars to another, even within the same field of specialization. It is, however, only in the recent past that social scientists have begun to reflect critically and self-consciously on how they produce their texts and how various audiences read those texts. Such reflection is part of an intellectual movement that has impinged on many disciplines. It has had particular implications for the writing of ethnography and other qualitative research in anthropology, sociology, and cognate disciplines. It is not our intent to review those intellectual accounts in all their complexity. Rather, we wish to identify a number of themes and issues that should be of practical relevance to all researchers using qualitative data. Our general approach is to suggest that—as with all the strategies we have identified so far—we are able to exercise a degree of choice and control over how we write and represent.

As we will indicate, in recent years social scientists (and others) have tried out various kinds of literary and other forms of representation. We will not be advocating experimentation for its own sake, nor gratuitous innovation. There is no merit in a mindless pursuit of the avant-garde any more than there is in the unthinking adoption of tried-and-tested approaches. The net effect of recent developments is that we cannot approach the task of "writing up" our research as a straightforward (if demanding) task. We have to approach it as an analytical task, in which the form of our reports and representations is as powerful and significant as their content. We also argue that writing and representing is a vital way of thinking about one's data. Writing makes us think about data in new and different ways. Thinking about how to represent our data also forces us to think about the meanings and understandings, voices, and experiences present in the data. As such, writing actually deepens our level of analytic endeavor. Analytical ideas are developed and tried out in the process of writing and representing.

As in the previous chapters, we will illustrate our arguments with reference to data about doctoral students in anthropology and their mentors. We have not, as a matter of fact, completed ethnographic reports on those data in a variety of styles or formats. We cannot, in any case, display the full range of writing possibilities within the confines of one chapter. We will, however, illustrate some of the strategic issues with example write-ups of the data. Our examples should not be taken as models. We hope that readers will use them as points of departure in reflecting on their own possibilities and practices.

Analyzing and Reading

The analytic process of writing is paralleled by that of reading. As writing is a positive act of sense making, so too is reading (or so it should be). An active and analysis-oriented approach to "the literature" is an important part of the recurrent process of reflection and interpretation. Glaser and Strauss (1967) commend the creative use of written sources, including published studies, in the production and elaboration of analytical concepts. In common with them, we draw attention to the need to read and to use "the literature" in order to generate ideas and analyses. One of the most important disciplines for analysts, therefore, is the ability to read the work of others as part of their craft skills. That reading need not be confined to the work of other social scientists. There are many genres in which authors explore social worlds, both fiction and nonfiction. Many of the most successful authors are able to use diverse sources to develop fruitful and productive ideas.

A general value of wide and eclectic reading is the development of "sensitizing concepts" (Blumer, 1954), or general analytic perspectives. We do not have to look to published sources for "the answers" to our analytic questions and problems. We do not use the literature in order to provide ready-made concepts and models. Rather, we use ideas in the literature in order to develop perspectives on our own data, drawing out comparisons, analogies, and metaphors. Likewise, we can look to other sources for ideas of how to construct our own narratives of social life. We write narratives as well as analyze them, and there are many models to draw on in constructing our stories. Fiction and nonfiction sources alike can provide information for writing. Davis (1974) illustrated this when he pointed out a number of thematic parallels between classic works of fiction and sociological classics. Davis recognized that sociologists tell stories. Like any other storytellers, they construct narratives of tragedy, irony, and humor. There are parallels between the work of the novelist and the interpretive schemes of the sociologist:

> For example, the equivalent of the anomie story of Durkheim is, perhaps, *The Great Gatsby*. A good piece of work in family sociology dealing with the kind of interaction which underlies a phenomena [sic] like Bateson's double-bind is Eugene O'Neill's *Long Day's Journey into Night*. Certainly a fine story on the meaning of a vocation, as Max Weber could have analyzed it, is the Thomas Mann short story "Tonio Kroger." (Davis, 1974, p. 311)

There is no shortage of literature from which to draw in developing sensitizing concepts for our data on anthropologists. In the first place, a fair number of anthropologists themselves have written their own autobiographical accounts of anthropological work, especially on the experiences of fieldwork. The confessional tale is often a highly personalized (and self-absorbed) account of fieldwork and has an important role to play in allowing the researcher's subjective fieldwork experiences to be revealed and discussed. Our own narrative of students' and supervisors' accounts could usefully draw on such sources. We would note that in addition to sober autobiographical narratives and methodological reflections, anthropologists have on occasion fictionalized their personal recollections (Bowen, 1954) and have transformed their anthropological fieldwork into colorful accounts that, if not exactly fictionalized, are certainly some way from documented accounts of sober, scholarly work. Barley's accounts clearly have been worked up to appeal to a lay readership, and in the process certain dramatic and humorous aspects of the fieldwork experience have been played up (e.g., Barley, 1986, 1987).

Likewise, there have been even more highly colored personal accounts (e.g., see Davis, 1986; Donner, 1982). It is not necessary to treat all these sources as essentially the same or equally authentic in order to use them either to develop or to try out ideas about the personal experience of fieldwork. In various ways, our reading of such sources should make us think about some of the ambiguities of the situation and the helplessness and incompetence of the anthropologist despite her or his expert knowledge and background. We could examine such accounts for images and metaphors of the encounter of the anthropologist with "the other" (personal, cultural, and material). We could explore how—despite themselves, perhaps—anthropologists describe the exotic aspects of their field settings and of their fieldwork. We could probably be struck by the ways in which anthropologists' accounts included representations of personal and intellectual isolation.

In writing and analyzing accounts of anthropologists, then, we would read and draw on different models of the accounts of fieldwork. Our search for sensitizing concepts and narrative models would not stop there. We would probably look to accounts of similar experiences, such as narratives of explorers and other travelers. We would not have to stick to such obvious precedents and comparisons. Having identified themes such as "conversion" and "isolation," we could develop our analytic frameworks by examining accounts of personal survival in extreme situations; of religious and secular conversions and identity transformations; or of solitary life led by Christian recruits, Hindu holy men, and perhaps athletes in training. We would be able to examine *rites de passage* in order to illuminate the transformative experience of fieldwork. Those, and doubtless many other, possibilities are available not only for gratuitous "literature reviews." There is nothing more tedious to read or to write as a ritualistic summary of "the literature"; even the best summaries can render the most exciting of intellectual fields tedious. As we have suggested, such reading should be used actively and creatively to suggest and to help develop analytic insights. The literature should be used alongside writing as a tool for thinking and analyzing. Reading as well as writing can be viewed as an analytic activity.

Units of Narrative, Levels of Generality

In the literature on standard research methods, we are usually presented with discussions of "units of analysis." That is, in much orthodox social research (such as social surveys), we have to ask ourselves what unit of analysis we are dealing with: the individual social actor, the household, a particular social group, and so on. Likewise, we sometimes need to ask ourselves about the "unit of narrative." In other words, we need to think about what level of social analysis our texts will convey. Shall we, for example, construct our account primarily in terms of individual social actors? If so, we might want to write our ethnography as a life history or series of life histories based on and peopled by fully rounded characters. We would want to write about those social actors by making their own experiences and their lives the prime focus. There have been many highly successful studies (monographs especially) that are carried primarily—though not necessarily exclusively—by the characterization of social actors who are described as individuals and who are memorable as named characters. Among recent urban ethnographies, for example, is Duneier's *Slim's Table*. Duneier (1992) develops some very general points about the social world of respectable working-class black American men through a series of vivid, individualized portrayals of a small number of actors who can be encountered in one social setting. The unit of the narrative is, for the most part, those individual actors and their interactions. The general sociological points emerge out of those particular portraits and characterizations.

If we were to write about the anthropology data from such a vantage point, we would need to concentrate on a few key actors (probably from the same academic department). We would develop our arguments about young anthropologists and their intellectual careers by focusing on them as individual social actors. We might, for example, trace some of their careers through their individual and collective experience of critical incidents and turning points. For example, as we have already glimpsed in data fragments, for many of our novice anthropologists, the first experience of the discipline was, metaphorically, a personal and intellectual conversion. Some of them took master's degrees, having read a different undergraduate subject, and so theirs was, in conventional academic usage, a conversion course. For many it seemed to have gone well beyond that. Their "conversion" was more akin to a personal revelation, even with connotations of a religious conversion. Consequently, we could focus part of our narrative on the re-telling of such deeply personal views of intellectual change, evoking the personal experience that the respondents had recounted. (In practice, we would need more detailed data about a small number of anthropologists than we have at hand in order to do full justice to such an approach.) In this context, our account would try to convey the lived experience of the anthropology students, probably in rich detail. We would use their own words often in order to convey their particular—even unique—perspectives on the reported events and reflections.

Here is a fragment of how we might write up such an account. It tries to convey some of the emphasis on the individual social actor as the unit of analysis:

Fieldwork is a disciplinary prerequisite and a personal commitment. It may be pursued overseas in places that are remote, isolated, and even dangerous. Emily Coughlin, for example, undertook her fieldwork in Sri Lanka even though she knew it was unstable and politically dangerous at the time. Her choice of research setting reflected a personal and a political interest in the Tamil language, which she described as "a very understudied, underrated language." She was also committed to research on language and discourse under the influence of Michel Foucault's work. In order to get into Sri Lanka while she could, capitalizing on some existing links that could be activated, she was allowed by her department to go into "the field" earlier than normal, and so she embarked on the research when still in the first year of postgraduate studies. Her period in the field, away from department and supervisor, was protracted:

I was away for a year and a half. . . . It was a very difficult time because everybody wanted me to leave, the embassy and so on. During the disturbances there were only four people left at the embassy. But I was up country, and I refused to leave, in fact.

Her supervisor was supportive, but for long periods of time there was little communication. Isolation was extreme:

You're supposed to send back a report after six months. But during three months of those six when my time was up, it was when the worst trouble was going on in Sri Lanka and I had no way of getting stuff out, and there was nothing coming in to me. I didn't have any news for four months and they didn't get any from me, except what they could gather from the embassy.

Although the personalized version we have just provided gives a detailed account of how the doctoral students in anthropology expressed their recollections and experiences, it is by no means the only approach open to us. The unit of narration might be changed. Rather than the actor carrying the analytic writing, we could shift the focus to the act or the event. We would not focus attention so much on the fully rounded characters as on recurrent patterns of events, speech acts, and descriptions. For the purpose of illustration, we can stick with the topic of conversion, but rather than presenting stories of personal experiences, we could focus instead on how conversion accounts themselves are structured and narrated. In a similar vein, we could look for the common features of such intellectual conversions, as reported by our anthropologists. Such a account might look something like this:

> The experience of becoming an anthropologist is often described in terms that imply a conversion-like transformation in identity. Indeed, when MA courses are described as conversion courses for graduates from disciplines other than anthropology, that conventional label for them seems to take on extra resonance. Like many conversion experiences, the process includes practices of separation and integration, isolation and group membership. The experience that lies at the heart of this identity-transformation is generated by extended fieldwork. Anthropological fieldwork is overwhelmingly described as an intensely personal experience, normally undertaken alone. The novice is physically and socially separated from his or her home department and from the personal tutelage of the supervisor. Physical danger may be part of the experience, as may ill health and privation. For the great majority of young anthropologists, the period of segregation is undertaken "elsewhere"—often in distant, remote places that are culturally and linguistically strange. So powerful is the expectation that fieldwork implies such isolation that those few students whose fieldwork is done "at home" isolate themselves from their supervisor and from the department, immersing themselves in the field for extended periods. The extended isolation of fieldwork is part of the extended status passage through which the student is transformed into an anthropologist.

The two approaches we have outlined above do not exhaust the possibilities for writing. Extending our own example, we might make something like "the discipline" or "the department" of anthropology the primary unit of narrative. Here we would structure our own account not in terms of individual experiences and life histories, nor in terms of the formal properties or actions, but in terms of institutional frameworks or cultural systems of norms and values. If we were to take that as our unit of narrative, we might still be able to draw on the "conversion" data but would do so in order to develop an account of disciplinary or institutional academic culture. The data would be much the same as in our previous treatments, but the focus of the narrative, the main carrier of the argument, would be at a more general analytic level. Consequently, the writing might go more along the following lines:

The discipline of anthropology and its constituent departments in the United Kingdom are strongly bounded. Anthropology is a highly exclusive domain. Few are admitted to membership who have not passed through the extended apprenticeship of a doctorate that includes extended fieldwork. Although anthropologists may build an entire career on a few field trips to just one site, which furnishes the authority to profess anthropology in general. Such an apprenticeship is held to produce the necessary personal, biographically grounded knowledge for which no amount of theoretical work or reading can substitute. Within its symbolic boundary, the discipline expects and generates a high level of loyalty. Although there are frequent disputes—some of them marked by remarkably vigorous exchanges—they are often likened to "family disputes," and the collective identity of anthropologists in general is often strongly expressed and reinforced. Hence anthropologists are often at pains to distinguish themselves from neighbouring disciplines, such as sociology, often emphasizing the unique character of their overseas field-work.

It is equally important to think strategically about levels of generality, for those decisions have direct consequences for how the analysis is conceptualized. It is not always easy to think about levels of generality, partly because they are often implicit, and partly because many authors (especially, but not exclusively, novice researchers) do not address the issue as part of their strategic, analytic thinking. Sometimes there seems to be a vague, and usually forlorn, hope that the right level of generality and significance will somehow emerge. It rarely does. By contrast, it is a good analytic discipline to follow one of the tasks suggested by Spradley (1979). Admittedly, Spradley's own methodological advice is sometimes over-elaborated and sometimes too rigid, but his advice on writing is useful. He suggests that there are at least six levels of ethnographic writing, moving from the general to the particular, and he argues that effective writing includes statements at all six levels. The six levels are outlined below (adapted from Spradley, 1970, pp. 210-211).

> Level 1—*Universal statements:* all-encompassing writing about social actors, their behavior, culture, or environmental situation.
>
> Level 2—*Cross-cultural descriptive statements:* statements about two or more societies, including assertions that are true for some but not necessarily all societies.
>
> Level 3—*General statements about a society or cultural group:* statements that combine generality with specificity, making some general points about a particular group.

Level 4—General statements about a specific cultural scene: statements, still of a
general nature, that capture some of the themes of a particular social scene.

Level 5—Specific statements about a cultural domain: statements about how social
actors use linguistic devices and folk terms to describe events, objects, and
activities.

Level 6—Specific incident statements: writing that takes the reader immediately to
a particular behavior or particular events, demonstrating cultural knowledge in action.

The point here is that such reflection about levels of generality makes us
think about what kind of generalizations—and hence what kinds of analyses—we are trying to promote in our writing. In Chapter 6, we discuss the
importance of generalization through the development of formal concepts.
It is important to relate those generic theoretical ideas to the levels and styles
of writing. These reflections also lead us to reflect on what kinds of conceptual frameworks we are engaging with and to what intellectual fields we are
trying to contribute. It may seem trite to suggest these things. It may appear
to be self-evident that a piece of work is directed toward a particular
discipline (sociology, education, anthropology), but novice authors in particular often need to think very precisely about their engagement with the
texts and perspectives of others.

We have exaggerated some differences for the sake of our argument.
In an ideal world, it would be possible to vary the level of the narrative,
to move from one level to another and thus to vary the focus. Reflection
on the range of published works will show that analyses are not all the
same and that different authors will couch their works in terms of
different levels. It is impossible, however, to write up everything several
times over, from different analytic angles and at different levels. At any
given point in the analysis—and hence in the construction of written
reports—the author needs to reflect upon and make strategic decisions
about the level and direction of her texts.

These are by no means merely aesthetic or stylistic considerations.
How we write is, effectively, an analytic issue. We can and should make
strategic decisions about these and other kinds of writing. As we have
stressed repeatedly, we cannot relegate the production of our scholarly
works to an apparently mechanical and minor aspect of the research (as
is sometimes misleadingly implied in some accounts of "writing up"). It
is important to think about the kind of written work desired.

Audiences and Readers

The analytic work of writing implies the establishment of a relationship between the author and her readers. We know from literary analysis and reception theory that we cannot determine precisely how a given text will be read (Iser, 1978). Reading is an active process, and no text can have a completely fixed meaning. On the other hand, when we do write—and hence inscribe certain preferred interpretations in our books, dissertations, and papers—we do so with an implied audience of readers. Sometimes such an audience is entirely implicit and the outcome of a lack of reflection on the author's part. On other occasions, the author/analyst can make explicit decisions about the implied readership and hence couch the interpretation accordingly.

To a considerable extent, this is a matter of craft knowledge and professionalism in academic writing, and it takes us beyond the remit of this chapter and this book. On the other hand, it is important to recognize that control over the analysis implies the sort of control over the text that comes from a sense of audience. Richardson (1990) gives a clear, personal sense of such decisions. Her own introduction to the writing of ethnography gives a vivid illustration of how the same ethnographic research can be crafted for different audiences. She describes how her own research on single women in long-term relationships with married men was turned into texts of different kinds, including a trade book (i.e., one designed for a general market) as well as conventional academic texts such as papers for major sociology journals. In such contexts, a sense of audience is crucial in the author's approach to both form and content. In that sense, therefore, we must qualify our previous remark. It is not quite the case that the same ethnographic research can be turned into different kinds of texts. We need to think a bit more subtly. In effect, different texts inscribe different analyses—different viewpoints, different emphases, and different subject matter—and thus construct the research itself in different ways.

Let us try to think creatively about our data on doctoral students in anthropology. How could different audiences help us to identify different analytic standpoints? We would have to acknowledge that however much our research excited us, we would be unlikely to find a mass readership, and the option of a trade book would probably not be open to us. (Doctoral students simply do not have the same appeal as adulterous affairs, we suspect.) Even if our scope is restricted to academic readerships, that does not restrict our analyses to one and only one perspective, or our style to a single mode of writing. Deciding who we are writing *for* still implies decisions about what we are writing *about*, for what *reasons*, and from what *perspectives*. For example, if we want to publish a monograph about our data on academic socialization of doctoral students, we have to establish what kind of book it is to be and what sort of publisher will want it. Most commercial academic publishers, for example, are not very interested in detailed accounts of particular social groups or settings unless there is a clear audience. Some publishers have specialized lists and specialized markets for such works and can identify a potential readership or a market niche. For many studies, however, it is far from straightforward to define a readership, a market, and hence a publisher. The need to address such an issue at some stage in the production of the research can pose interesting and important analytic issues.

If we want to write a monograph using our anthropology data, we have to ask ourselves some tough and potentially illuminating questions. We need to persuade ourselves, and subsequently persuade a publisher, of such issues as why enough people would be interested, the overall significance of the work, how it relates to other published work, and the distinctive features of this monograph that will make it original and stand out from all the other books that are likely to be published by academics in this and related fields. If you start to address these and similar questions (which any publisher will ask, even if you do not), then you inevitably start to address problems of real analytic significance. Those questions force us to think about the main themes and issues of the book. We need to reflect on what disciplinary knowledge will be drawn on and developed, and what concepts and theories (if any) will be developed. We need to think, for example, whether we will develop themes and arguments through a narrow treatment of the data or by using our data to engage with much broader, more general themes. We might, for example, use our data on academic socialization to produce a detailed monograph on anthropologists, their work, and their departments, perhaps like Traweek's (1988) account of high-energy physics, *Beamtimes and Lifetimes*. If so, then our analysis probably would be driven by a set of themes and issues reflecting the rather specific focus of the work, such as the organization of fieldwork, anthropology as a discipline, and relationships between doctoral students and their supervisors.

On the other hand, we might try to use the data to develop much more general perspectives and complement our data with insights related to broader domains. We might write about, say, the general theme of "novices," drawing out chapters on conversions and inspirations, rites of passage, initiation into the mysteries of a craft, and so on. Our ideas, literature, and comparisons would probably draw on a very wide range of sources discussing craft apprentices, religious postulants, sorcerers and schemers, and professionals in training. Our resulting text might therefore look more like Lave and Wenger's (1991).

We do not wish to labor the point that one can design and produce different texts from the same research, but we do want to stress that such decisions are part of the process of analysis. There is a close, dialectical relationship between the kinds of analyses we produce and the kinds of texts we use as models and produce ourselves. The same point holds true if we look beyond the rather simple contrast we have just outlined. Most of us are not so naive as to write academic papers in a vacuum and then cast around for a suitable audience and a suitable outlet. We write with a view to, say, a particular conference, a particular edited collection, or a particular journal. Again, the implied readership has a bearing not only on how we craft the works—in terms of a journal's house style, for example—but also on how we conceptualize it. An audience of readers implies shared knowledge and assumptions about what is relevant to our own paper: past research, research methods, key authors, current debates, controversies, and fashions. The implied audience for our projected written work thus suggests lines of analysis and textual organization.

These considerations reflect the extent to which analyses, and the texts they are enshrined in, have the property of *intertextuality*. That is, texts have relationships with other texts: They do not exist in isolation. There are, for example, genealogies of texts. Within a particular discipline such as sociology or anthropology, one can readily trace continuities over time, not only in terms of ideas or personal influences between mentors and protégés but also among texts. A tradition such as "community studies," for example, is recognizable as a tradition partly because of the family resemblances between its texts and a degree of textual stability over time. As authors such as Boon (1983) have pointed out, the classic anthropological monograph of the structural-functionalist tradition commonly displayed an internal organization shared with others of the same genre. Indeed, as Boon persuasively argues, the structure of such monographs closely reflected the main guiding principles of that style of anthropology.

It is safe to say, therefore, that we write our academic texts in the light of styles and genres that are characteristic of disciplines, specialisms, schools of thought, and so on. They are characterized by particular conventions—of organization and language—that are of direct relevance to major analytic perspectives. Analysis, therefore, and the ways in which we choose to represent our data cannot be separated. It is unthinkable to divorce analysis from representation. We certainly cannot conceive of analyzing one or more social worlds without at the same time reconstructing such domains through textual or other formats.

Alternative Literary Forms

So far we have written as if the only texts available to us were those of a highly conventional and traditional nature: the scholarly monograph or paper in a learned journal, written in accordance with the taken-for-granted conventions for such work. For most of us, the majority of our work will appear in some such form. Most social scientists, like most scholars throughout the academy, are only too pleased to see their work in print in quality outlets. On the other hand, that should not blind us to the fact that there are other formats and sets of conventions available to us and that they have important implications for how we analyze and represent our data.

This is not the place for an extended methodological or epistemological exegesis on textual analysis. There is a voluminous literature on a range of issues in that general area (see, e.g., Atkinson, 1990, 1992b; Clifford & Marcus, 1986; Clough, 1992; Richardson, 1994; Van Maanen, 1988). Here we wish to draw attention to the fact that questions of choice about analyses and representations can be extended beyond the normally expected range of textual types. In recent years, authors in a number of disciplines, including anthropology and sociology, have begun to experiment with alternative literary forms for scholarly work. These modes of representation have their own analytic implications and are designed in order to convey particular analytic approaches. To some extent, it must be acknowledged, those new or alternative literary forms are tried out in a spirit of avant-garde experimentation. Sometimes, they find a more coherent justification in the claims for postmodernist perspectives on research and representation.

From a postmodern stance, the apparent authority of the traditional scholarly text is rendered problematic, as are many of the traditional claims to truth or authenticity that they implicitly or explicitly enter. The authorial perspective of the analyst is also rendered suspect. A postmodernist perspective is often held to question the smooth assurance of the conventional authoritative account. It is the complete antithesis of the self-assured voice of an Evans-Pritchard as author of, say, *The Nuer* (1940). Classic works of ethnography that adopt a single dominant perspective—that of the author/observer—are held to embody an essentially "modern" set of assumptions. In particular, they seem to be predicated on the *discovery* of social realities through selectively unproblematic acts of engagement and inspection (and as participant observation).

Under the auspices of postmodernism, the nature of texts and their status as representations of social reality may be treated as much more problematic and uncertain. Not only is there a recognition of the arbitrary nature of representational conventions, but there is also a willingness to transgress cherished boundaries and to explore alternatives. Postmodernist aesthetics do not celebrate consistency of form: There may be a celebration of different, contrasting styles and a deliberately promiscuous combination of them. The approach may be described as one of *pastiche*, drawing on re-creations and evocations of diverse styles and practices. Postmodernism is not the only inspiration here, but it is a useful (if imprecise) way of drawing together a number of related textual experiments.

The textual experimentation associated with postmodern perspectives is paralleled by a feminist interest in textual variety. As feminist authors such as Wolf (1992) suggest, feminism's preoccupation with knowledge and representation provides an especially appropriate vantage point from which to question taken-for-granted styles of writing. Feminist sociology and anthropology throw into relief the ways in which we reconstruct social actors and their experiences (Mascia-Lees, Sharpe, & Cohen, 1989). Among feminist texts, Krieger's account of a women's community (Krieger, 1983) is but one example of an increasingly important genre of writing (cf. Clough, 1992). As authors such as Lather (1991) suggest, feminist epistemology challenges the traditional forms of narrative and representation, turning attention to the need for alter-native forms of textual reconstruction (cf. Olesen, 1994).

New literary forms have been used by a number of sociologists of science. Largely inspired by the work of Mulkay, they have adapted various overtly literary styles to represent particular kinds of sociological analysis (e.g., Mulkay, 1985). As Atkinson (1990) has rather pedantically pointed out elsewhere, those literary forms have not been new in them-selves. Indeed, they have been entirely familiar—as one-act plays and dialogues. Where they have novelty is in their use for "serious" socio-logical analysis. The literary forms that the sociologists of scientific knowledge use are normally particularly pertinent to their chosen sub-ject matter. When reconstructing particular kinds of scientific or socio-logical disputes and debates, for example, it can prove engaging to construct a dialogue between actual or ideal-typical social actors. Here the sociological analysis resides not so much in explaining (much less explaining away) or resolving the contrasting perspectives, synthesizing them into a single narrative or explanation. Rather, the analytic work resides in the juxtaposition of alternative perspectives and their artful arrangement into dialogues.

In a similar fashion, the construction of playlets or sketches allows the analyst to work out and spotlight particular ironies or paradoxes inher-ent in particular positions and cultural conventions. The same is true of reconstructed dialogues or debates. The author who uses such alterna-tive sets of compositional conventions must do so scrupulously. It is all too easy to put words into actors' mouths and to create caricatures such that there is little or no credible relationship between the representations and any other plausible version of social reality. The analyst needs to use a large degree of artistic restraint in these contexts. It is, for example, common practice to base reconstructed dialogue very closely on actual words uttered in interviews or in naturally occurring interactions. The resulting work is crafted by the analyst insofar as he or she selects, edits, transposes, and juxtaposes in order to convey particular effects (such as ironic contrast, humor, or parody). In other words, these exercises are not based on purely fictional invention; rather, they take real data and apply certain sorts of editorial license in the construction of textual representations.

All forms of textual representation involve some degree of "fictional" work. Even those that conform to more familiar patterns are often based on the selection and juxtaposition of data extracts. There is no absolute distinction between fact and fiction in the construction of texts. The new or alternative literary forms we allude to in this chapter are perhaps more self-consciously and evidently stylized, but they are still crafted from the data. Such literary styles do permit additional features, less easily represented in conventional texts, such as the creation and insertion of entirely fictitious elements. The analyst may adopt one or more personae, for example, and insert additional voices in order to introduce a "devil's advocate" or to raise an alternative interpretation.

We believe that such approaches should be used for good reasons and not overworked or used only to achieve a gratuitous sense of novelty. If we were to use such approaches with our anthropology data, we could probably do so with good—and justifiable—effect. The data deliberately were not collected from matched pairs of supervisor and student: The research team members were anxious not to appear to play one off against another in a research situation that could have been delicate. For the same reason, they did not conduct joint interviews with students and supervisors. On the other hand, a contrived dialogue, in which the voices of students and mentors could be juxtaposed, could be an illuminating way of highlighting some of the differences between their respective experiences and outlooks. We already have explored some of the data about anthropological fieldwork, when we used them to illustrate the analysis of a domain. These data also lend themselves to the new literary forms of reconstruction. If we were to do so, we would proceed in something like the following fashion.

Our editorial work would be part of our analysis and our thinking, and our literary work obviously would be predicated on a sense of what messages, impressions, and analyses we wished to convey. We cannot simply select and combine random lists and pieces of recorded data. The writing must have a point; more precisely, it should help us to *make* a point. In reviewing the data on fieldwork, we were struck by the extent to which fieldwork seemed to have very different connotations; hence, we would pick out extracts of the actual data and incorporate them into a dramatic dialogue or confrontation. The result might look a bit like this:

Fieldwork: A Conversation

Supervisor: Anthropology is a unique subject in that you do get to go sometimes to North Manchester, sometimes to New Guinea, sometimes to places in between, where for a year or more you sit on your own and organize your own research very much. It's a wonderful opportunity to think.

Student: But there's also something strange about anthropology, that really you have no idea what you're going to study until you get to the field. I had no idea what I was supposed to be doing when I arrived, it was like, "Where the hell do you start?"

Supervisor: But that's part of it. It's a chance to pursue some critical problems, and it has to be a very independent business.

Student: Independent or isolated? I wasn't prepared for what I was going to find in Papua New Guinea. You seem to think that we can just get out there and do it, and that everyone has to find their own way of doing it, so why should you tell us? I had no idea of what I was supposed to be doing out there.

Supervisor: I didn't want to poke my nose into your fieldwork. I know it's very much an independent business. It could have been awkward, embarrassing, and annoying for you to worry about keeping me informed. So long as I knew you were alive I wanted to keep as much distance as possible.

Student: I may have been alive, but I was ill and worried. The place I was in hadn't been worked by an anthropologist before. It's renowned for being quite a violent place, so I was a bit concerned about personal security and what was going on there. So in that sense I really felt I was going into the void.

We have constructed this dialogue by manipulating the original words of the informants, taken from individual interviews. Nearly all the words used were in the original data. We have changed the order in some cases and combined separate utterances in order to construct the actors' speeches here. Such a reconstruction has potential value. It obviously can provide a more vivid sense of confrontation and contrast. Such a device here emphasizes the clearly contrasting perspectives of a senior academic figure, on one hand, and a graduate student on the other.

There are different versions of fieldwork to be found in the data, and the views we have encapsulated in this dialogue are by no means atypical.

Many graduate students report experiences of isolation and disorienta-
tion, and academic supervisors stress the indeterminacy of personal
knowledge and fieldwork experience as somehow a defining characteristic of anthropology and anthropologists. We explored some of these
contrasts earlier when we used extracts from the same interviews to
explore fieldwork as a domain. We should also emphasize here that
although a dialogic approach has a great deal of potential value (in this
example, comparing and contrasting alternative voices on fieldwork), it
does need to be used self-consciously and reflexively. There are risks of
moving away from the data and inventing dialogue to fit in with our
overall analyses. It is also important to note in our written representations of such dialogues that they are fictionalized versions, at least
to the extent that the conversation as presented did not happen.

A number of authors have gone further than the construction of brief
dialogues or similar kinds of reconstructions (see, e.g., Bluebond-Langer,
1980; Ellis & Bochner, 1992; Mienczakowski, Morgan, & Rolfe, 1993;
Paget, 1990; Richardson & Lockridge, 1991). They have developed a
genre of ethnographic drama or ethnographic theater (Mienczakowski,
1994, 1995). Again, based on the collection and collation of real data,
this style of representation exploits the conventions of naturalistic theater to produce graphic reconstructions of social interaction. They may
be confined to written scripts (sometimes embedded in longer texts) or
acted out. In the latter case, there is a complete cycle between the
dramatic metaphor as a general mode of analysis and the mode of
representation.

A well-known example forms part of Bluebond-Langer's book-length
monograph on the social worlds of dying children (Bluebond-Langer,
1980). This blending of qualitative research with drama is a means of
combining the realist with the poetic. The idea of ethnodrama is to
transform data (dialogue, transcripts, etc.) into theatrical scripts and
performance pieces. This can have several purposes. Theater provides a
way of perhaps more accurately giving voice to those who may consider
themselves without power. Similarly, reconstructing an event as lived
experience with multiple perspectives can give voice to what may be
unspoken but nevertheless present. For example, the work of Mienczakowski and his colleagues in Australia has concentrated on a variety of
sensitive health care settings, for example, psychiatric encounters and
detoxification units. The plays and theatrical scripts that have developed

out of their ethnographic work have been used to give voice to those who have contributed to the work, including otherwise muted health care officials and health chiefs. Similarly, Paget's (1990) ethnographic drama, which takes living with cancer as the theme, and Ellis and Bochner's (1992) drama, based on a reconstruction of the events around their abortion, capture multiple and vivid experiences. Dramatization presents a way of narrating personal experiences through an experiential format. The reader/viewer is invited to live through experiences, often deeply personal ones. Such dramatic representations of social reality can be said to present more "realist" pictures of events (Sparkes, 1995). Dramatic reconstructions can help to promote contested and multiple versions of reality while presenting them in a readable (and perhaps watchable) format. Richardson (1990) argues that the blurring of the oral and the written text is a key characteristic of such approaches. Theatrical representation of qualitative material takes the text from something where one "talks about" to something that "is" the issue, event, or social actor.

Ethnographic fiction takes the idea of drama along a slightly different track. Here the ethnographer-author explicitly draws on literary conventions to construct a fictionalized but authentic account. Krieger's work (1979, 1983, 1984) both draws on and discusses the merits of such an approach, arguing that fiction offers a potentially powerful way of representing the social realities we study. Pfohl's (1992) *Death at the Parasite Cafe* is an exemplary illustration of the use of social science fiction. Tierney (1993, p. 313) suggests that such ethnographic fiction helps to rearrange events and identities "in order to draw the reader into the story in a way that enables deeper understanding of individuals, organizations, or events themselves." Here once more we can see how the process of composition—and indeed, the textual product itself—is an important mode of analysis in its own right.

The boundaries between fact and fiction are sometimes difficult to draw at the best of times. All written work, however factual and authoritative, is composed and crafted; hence, it is not always easy to discern the particular merits of ethnographic fiction. It is sometimes claimed that such a contrivance can allow the ethnographer to write about sensitive issues that might otherwise prove hard to divulge. The fictionalized account may be authentic in conveying general themes and issues while fictionalizing concrete details of the ethnography. Most ethnographic accounts have some such safeguards. Throughout the real analyses and published accounts of the anthropology data, for example, the research team members have been careful to try to preserve the confidentiality of the data by disguising the collective and individual identities of the respondents. In addition to the normal conventions of ethical reporting—such as the use of pseudonyms for people and institutions—nonessential details have been deliberately falsified. Because people's research topics can be instantly recognizable to fellow audiences, as can their individual career in many cases, it has been necessary to change—judiciously—the details of research, such as its subject matter and geographical location, and details of specific departments. Likewise, in an ethnographic study of a very small and localized research group in medical genetics, Atkinson and his collaborators (Batchelor, Parsons, & Atkinson, in press) reserved the right to fudge precisely who had said what and to split one actor into several or combine several actors into one. These little subterfuges are performed primarily for ethical reasons, however, and have little or no analytic import. The more thoroughgoing approach to ethnographic fiction should be used to construct and convey *analyses* of social settings and social action that are given particular point or are impossible by other means.

One of the recurrent analytic virtues of stylistic variation and innovation is that they can help the textual representation to reflect aspects of the *ethnopoetics* of the everyday life under consideration. In all cultures and subcultures, there are characteristic rhetorical and even poetic forms. We already have examined some analytic approaches to narrative and related features. Alternative literary forms can be—and have been—used to point out and emphasize certain aspects of personal or cultural spoken style. Richardson's (1992) is one such essay in literary construction. She has taken the words of a mountain woman, whom she calls Louisa May, derived from life history interview data, and reworked them into a poem. The words are Louisa May's, but the poem is composed by Richardson. The effect is striking and has—for some readers at any rate—an emotional force, coupled with a sense of how Louisa May constructs her life through the telling of it, that might not come through a more prosaic account. Richardson (1992) draws on poetic devices such as "repetition, pauses, meter, rhymes and off rhymes" (p. 24) to represent Louisa May's own words (and life) as poetics.

Here once more, one must be clear that such exercises have an analytic purpose. They enable the author to see familiar social actors and events in new ways, to step into the shoes of the other, and to use individuals' voices and tones in sensitive and meaningful ways. There is a danger in such exercises of producing emotional or aesthetic effects simply for the sake of producing them. They can appeal to inappropriately self-indulgent displays of cleverness on the part of the author. There may be occasions when the ethnopoetics of a given culture may be served better by a faithful rendition of *their* forms, rather than the imposition of an author's aesthetic judgments. The data from anthropology do not self-evidently lend themselves to the construction of poems. The following example is offered in order to illustrate the possibility of such an approach. We claim no great literary merit for the outcome. We start from the following interview extract:

Extract of Interview With Dr. Nancy Enright (graduate of Kingford University, now a lecturer at Latchendon University)

I had the most horrible viva anybody could ever have, I think. I did the most deplorable thing, I got upset and burst into tears, and that was awful, so I have a very bad memory of my viva. Looking back at the one I assisted with, I realized that with mine it was a question of human rights. It was appallingly badly examined. It was probably partly my fault, because you're not meant to know who your external is going to be, but usually there's an unofficial discussion about it. And I was not entirely happy about my external. . . . I was examined by a historian from Reddingdale. There were things he didn't know like the conventions for the bibliography in anthropology—we have a convention where you don't capitalize every single word in a book title—and I had a twenty-five-page bibliography and he went through and put a circle through every single letter he thought should have been capitalized. There were a lot of typing errors, but I got the cheapest typist I could, who typed a lot of things wrong, so that he said things like "This sentence hasn't got a verb in it." And the examiner missed the train, so I was waiting for two hours with the other examiner and the supervisor, so in terms of nervous stress it was awful. . . . And they didn't say "Well done" or anything, it was just "We want the typing mistakes corrected in three weeks." . . .

We could use fragments of these raw data to construct a poemlike sequence, using the informant's own original words. It could look something like this:

And I had the most horrible viva
anybody could ever have.
I think I did the most deplorable thing.
I got upset.
I got upset and burst into tears
and that was awful.
So I have a very bad memory
of my viva.
Looking back, I realize that with mine
it was a question of human rights.
It was . . . It was badly examined
Appallingly badly.
I was examined by an historian
from Reddingdale.
There were things he didn't know
about anthropology.
I got the cheapest typist I could
who typed things wrong.
There were a lot of typing errors
a lot of things wrong.
"This sentence hasn't a verb in it,"
He said, the historian from Reddingdale.
He went through every page and put a circle
through every single letter.
The examiner missed the train from Reddingdale
So I was waiting two hours.
I was waiting with the other examiner
and the supervisor, two hours.
It was a very bad thing to have happened.
It was awful for me.
And they didn't say "Well done"
or anything, to me.

An exercise such as this clearly does not necessarily produce a good poem, and a more poetic treatment might need greater violence to be done to the data. On the other hand, as one can perhaps glimpse from our example here, one can use such a device to pick up and emphasize some of the rhythms of the original speech. One can also point out some of the personal, emotional content of the speech itself. As a textual representation, it is more illuminating and gripping than a conventional format might be. Our own "poem" here helps to capture some of the pathos of this anthropologist's personal recollections of a painful experience. As Richardson (1994) puts it, in discussing the use of such literary devices, it is an "evocative representation."

Experimental or alternative forms of representation for qualitative data should not be seen necessarily as "the way things are moving," although Richardson (1994) does locate such forms as signs of paradigm change, and more journals are now accepting alternative forms of textual representation. We resist the argument that there is a need for a mass movement toward exotic forms of literary composition, nor should the examples we have offered be viewed as the only alternatives, still less as the right ways of constructing a text. The point here is to add to our general argument that there are many ways to shape our data.

If we think of data as material we can use, then it becomes easier to recognize that it is up to us to shape that material in order to meet our aims and reach our audiences. We emphasize that experimental forms of representation allow us to view writing and representation as part of the analysis and as processes of discovery in their own right. The diversity of representations and variety of genres open to the qualitative researcher should be seen as potential tools for the analysis as well as for the presentation of data.

Visual Representations

A consideration of representations and reconstructions should not be confined to textual devices alone. Writing can incorporate a variety of graphic and other visual representations. We do not go into a comprehensive account of them here, but we try to convey some sense of their value. There are at least two major ways in which visual materials can be incorporated into the qualitative researcher's array of techniques. On one hand, there is a rich variety of ways in which data and analyses can be displayed. On the other hand, one can incorporate visual material themselves (such as photographs or reproductions of artifacts).

We begin with a brief consideration of visual displays in the representation of qualitative analyses. These are discussed at length and with great ingenuity by Miles and Huberman (1994), who remind us that extended textual passages—such as long extracts from interviews or fieldnotes—are only one kind of data display. They remark that "in the course of our work, we have become convinced that better displays are a major avenue to valid qualitative analysis" (p. 11). They list matrices, graphs, charts, and networks among those representational devices, and they go on to say that

> all are designed to assemble organized information into an immediately accessible, compact form so that the analyst can see what is happening and either draw justified conclusions or move on to the next step of analysis the display suggests may be useful. (p. 11)

As Miles and Huberman suggest, such graphic representations may be important heuristic devices for the researcher in the course of the analytic process. When suitable displays are also incorporated into the published accounts, then the reader can see "what is happening." Indeed, the imaginative use of displays, such as diagrams, can become a major part of the overall representation of cultures and social processes.

Miles and Huberman draw on an impressive range of qualitative studies to show how ideas can be generated and relationships demonstrated through visual displays. We already have introduced at least one such form of display ourselves. In Chapter 4, we used some of our data extracts to start to build a domain analysis of "the field" in anthropologists' discourse. There we summarized that analysis in the form of a diagram. It conveys a great deal of information about the connotations of anthropologists' use of that familiar term. In addition to being an important analytic tool, a version of such a diagram could be used to good effect in the published account of our analysis of that aspect of our data. Indeed, semantic and similar cultural analyses lend themselves quite readily to such forms of representation. Miles and Huberman, for example, also refer to the use of diagrammatic representations of folk terminologies. They include the construction of tree diagrams to represent individual or collective orderings of particular semantic domains and the construction of componential analyses. These techniques can represent, in graphic form, complex semantic relationships in economical ways. The reader can grasp detailed information from such summary representations much more readily than would be possible from long, detailed discursive representations.

Here, by way of illustration only, we present two summary representations of how British academics (including our anthropology informants) may classify higher education in the United Kingdom and

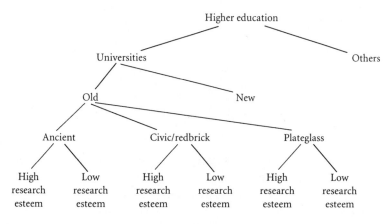

Figure 5.1. A Partial Taxonomy of British Universities

departments of anthropology. (Like many British institutions, an official rhetoric of parity of esteem among universities masks fine gradations of distinction and discrimination.) In Figure 5.1, we use a *taxonomic* approach. It contains no remarkable analysis of our data but helps to capture some of the taken-for-granted cultural knowledge of British academics, and it informs many of the judgments that they form about institutions and departments. In order to understand it, the reader needs to know that British academic life is replete with discriminations among institutions. This taxonomy captures only some of them. There are, indeed, many designations of universities alone. The distinction between "new" and "old" reflects recent changes in the system. Universities referred to as "old" are those that were funded via the former Universities Funding Council; the "new" universities were until recently referred to as polytechnics or institutes of higher education and came under separate funding arrangements. Among the "old" universities, those often referred to as "ancient" include the medieval foundations such as Oxford, Cambridge, Edinburgh, and Glasgow. The "redbrick/civic" were later foundations, often in large cities such as Manchester or Leeds. The "plateglass" were founded in the postwar period, often on campus locations. Relative research esteem is partly a matter of reputation and partly a reflection of nationally published research rankings. In looking at this example, it is important to bear in mind (as with many such

Department	Pure	Recognized	Africa	Asia	Europe
A	+	+	+	+	+
B	+	+	+	−	−
C	−	+	+	−	+
D	−	−	+	+	−
E	+	−	−	+	−

Figure 5.2. Componential Analysis of Anthropology Departments (partial)

representations) that this is only one possible version of how British academics talk and think about their institutions. Other taxonomies could be constructed, using other criteria that are current in the culture. One could certainly introduce other differentiations, such as "Oxbridge" (Oxford and Cambridge thought of as a generic type), "London," "Provincial," and the like.

In the second of our examples, we present a simple (also incomplete) *componential analysis* of departments of anthropology (Figure 5.2). Such an analysis seeks to summarize major components or dimensions that underlie cultural classifications. This is done by identifying a number of features that are used to differentiate cultural items or terms. Here, in diagrammatic form, we can summarize some of the dimensions that were used by our anthropologists to differentiate among departments. In order to avoid any inadvertent disclosure of the actual research sites, we have not undertaken a complete formal analysis of their distinctive characteristics; we have identified only a few dimensions. They include whether the department is a "pure" department of anthropology (as opposed to being in a joint department with other disciplines such as sociology or archaeology), whether it was at the time recognized by the Economic and Social Research Council for the award of national research studentships, and whether it included some research specializations (in terms of regional specializations). It will be seen that in combination, these components help to define uniquely the specific anthropology departments. They are among the criteria talked about by anthropologists themselves in distinguishing among departments and their distinctive academic cultures.

The plus and minus signs summarize the presence or absence of the feature in question. As can be seen, such a representation captures a good deal of cultural knowledge (and analysis on the part of the researcher) in ordering the domain in question. It can readily oversimplify. Such forms of representation should be used with caution and in combination with more sensitive qualitative data on how such cultural domains are constructed, used, talked about, and justified in particular contexts of use. They are, nevertheless, useful representational devices. As we will indicate in more detail in Chapter 7, the construction and use of graphic devices, such as taxonomies, are supported and encouraged by various kinds of computer programs that are currently in use for the analysis of qualitative data.

We turn now to the possible uses of other kinds of visual materials, such as photographs and other images. This is too often ignored by qualitative researchers and relegated to a small enclave of specialist work. As authors such as Ball and Smith (1992) point out, photography long has been associated with ethnographic work, especially in anthropological monographs (see also Collier & Collier, 1986). There is also a small literature of visual sociology, of which Becker's is the most notable contribution (Becker, 1981, 1983). In most cases, visual materials have been used to *illustrate* the text rather than used as the basis for analyzing and representing visual culture itself.

There are many issues that can be analyzed and represented primarily through visual materials, or through an interplay between visual and textual representations. It is easy to think of such visual materials in terms of the more "traditional" aspects of anthropological work, through illustrative styles that represent the colorful and the exotic. This is a style of representation that is familiar through other kinds of reportage, such as the long tradition of travel writing and related genres (see Lutz & Collins, 1993, for a reading of the iconography of *National Geographic*). On the other hand, a detailed analysis of visual culture is a potentially important component of qualitative research and its representation. This analysis of visual culture may include analyses and reproductions of self-presentation and display, artistic and other cultural forms, domestic arrangements, work settings, and the like. Such visual representations need not be confined to "exotic" settings. Published work also includes the use of visual materials in complex organizations (e.g., Sharrock & Anderson, 1979), laboratory scientists' use of graphic representation (Lynch & Edgerton, 1988), and traditions of Western art (Witkin, 1995).

We did not systematically collect visual data about the anthropology departments in which we studied graduate students and academic staff. We could have done so with profit, had we been engaged in more intensive fieldwork with anthropologists alone. Anthropology is a very visual subject, and so are its academic departments and its scholarly practitioners. One cannot visit anthropology departments without being struck by the displays of pictures and material objects that routinely adorn corridors, office doors, teaching rooms, and academic offices themselves. Academic staff often have artifacts from "their" people in the office (usually small objects such as pots or musical instruments). Pictures and posters are often prolifically displayed. Sometimes there are display cases holding examples of material culture. Some departments have museums of material culture attached to them. A visual anthropology of anthropologists would examine how such objects and representations are used to produce individual or collective self-representations. Such an approach might speculate on how the identification of the anthropologist with a region and a "people" is marked through ownership and display.

In a yet more complex manner, the analyst of such visual data might explore some of the contradictions between the explicit messages of contemporary anthropology and the implicit messages of the representations and memorabilia that adorn the academic department. Anthropologists reject the association of their discipline with emphases on the exotic. They denounce "orientalism" in others (within and beyond anthropology itself), yet many of their own manifestations seem to proclaim exoticism and invite identification with the otherness of the (usually) distant other cultures. In the same way that contemporary anthropologists study the indigenous ethnographies and anthropologies of others, so their own processes of self-creation could have been investigated through a visual anthropology. Anthropologists have come close to such reflexive analysis through the investigation of museums and their modes of representation.

A thorough analysis of such artifacts would include visual materials as part of the reconstruction of academic anthropology and its academic subcultures. We clearly could do much more than illustrate our published reports. We could relate text and image in a dense examination of how anthropologists construct concrete representations of their own fieldwork and their intellectual biographies through the accumulation and display of visual materials. (Our own reference to visual anthropology as an analytic resource would have interestingly reflexive effects, just like our own use of accounts of fieldwork to illustrate this book about qualitative research.) We will suggest in Chapter 7 that new forms of information technology—notably hypertext and hypermedia software—are especially well suited to establishing analytic links between textual and visual materials. They also support the construction of research reports that are themselves constructed out of various media and forms of representation.

Conclusion

In this chapter, we have tried to show that modes of writing and other forms of representation are fundamental to the work of qualitative data analysis. There are, as we have indicated, many ways in which ethnographic and similar research can be turned into texts and other forms of output. Some of those are hallowed by tradition among sociologists and anthropologists, while others are more experimental in such a context. The growing awareness among social scientists of the significance of representations, and of their various forms, means that there can be no excuse for failure to be conscious of them. We do not want to preach one or another approach to writing and representation, traditional or experimental. We do, however, wish to commend an awareness of variety, coupled with principled decisions. How we choose to represent our data is no longer (if it has ever been) obvious and unproblematic. We need to be aware of the variety of strategies available. We should not, however, experiment simply for the sake of experimentation.

We also wish to stress that decisions about representation are not optional extras. Any and all of our modes of representation have significant implications for analysis. We inescapably convey messages, explicit and implicit, about social worlds and about our understandings of them. We construct social actors and social actions. We reconstruct cultures though our own acts of representation. It is incumbent on us not only to recognize the fact that we do such things but also to do them carefully, responsibly, and explicitly.

Suggestions for Further Reading

Atkinson, P. (1990). *The ethnographic imagination: Textual constructions of reality.* London: Routledge and Kegan Paul.

Contains detailed analysis of the rhetorical and literary devices used in the construction of sociological ethnographies. Concentrates on how conventional ethnographies are produced, with less emphasis on alternatives and experiments.

Atkinson, P. (1992). *Understanding ethnographic texts.* Newbury Park, CA: Sage.

A brief discussion of the tension between the readability of ethnographic texts and their fidelity to the complexities of social life.

Ball, M. S., & Smith, G. W. H. (1992). *Analyzing visual data.* Newbury Park, CA: Sage.

An extremely accessible and well-documented introduction to this important area of analysis and representation, including anthropological and sociological work.

Clifford, J., & Marcus, G. E. (Eds.). (1986). *Writing culture: The poetics and politics of ethnography.* Berkeley: University of California Press.

A key collection of papers that did more than any other publication to establish a textualist perspective in American cultural anthropology.

Hammersley, M. (1991). *Reading ethnographic research: A critical guide.* London: Longmans.

Takes a different perspective from most of the textualist literature by emphasizing the need to inspect ethnographies for their claims and for the adequacy, validity, and relevance to disciplinary knowledge of those claims.

Richardson, L. (1990). *Writing strategies: Reaching diverse audiences.* Newbury Park, CA: Sage.

Explores how the same ethnographic materials can be crafted into different texts, targeted at different audiences, thus drawing attention to the analytic consequences of written genres.

Van Maanen, J. (1988). *Tales of the field.* Chicago: University of Chicago Press.

Explores some of the different styles or genres in which ethnographers have written. Identifies a realist style in which most traditional work has been expressed, an impressionistic style that is more literary, and the confessional mode of autobiographical accounts in which ethnographers reveal the personal side of fieldwork.

Wolcott, H. F. (1990). *Writing up qualitative research.* Newbury Park, CA: Sage.

An accessible guide to the practicalities of writing up research. Contains excellent advice on getting started, keeping going, editing, and getting published.

6

Beyond the Data

Analyzing and Theorizing

Theorizing is integral to analysis; they are not separate stages in the research process. The strategies for analysis that we have outlined thus far enable us to think about our data, and this is a step along the way to building up ideas and theories. In this chapter, we turn our attention to the extent to which the full implications of analysis take us beyond the manipulation of data.

The conduct of qualitative inquiry is always firmly based on empirical research, and we have emphasized various strategies for the detailed inspection of data themselves. Nevertheless, good research is not generated by rigorous data analysis alone. It does not stop at the coding and retrieval of data fragments, nor is it exhausted by the formal analysis of narrative structures, semantic relationships, accounting devices, or equivalent strategies. The whole point of this book has been to indicate not only techniques of data manipulation but also ways of thinking with the data. That means "going beyond" the data to develop ideas. Having and using ideas can be expressed more formally: We are referring here to the processes of *generalizing* and *theorizing*.

We recognize that talking about theory or theory building can seem slightly daunting to some researchers. The thought that your data and the analysis of them has to use, contribute to, and make sense of or build theory can halt the research process altogether. We can think about theory in terms of having and using ideas, and this seems far less daunting. Everyone can use, develop, and generate ideas. In thinking about the research process, Dey (1993, p. 51) describes theory "simply as an idea about how other ideas can be related."

The interweaving of analysis with the use of ideas can occur at different levels and at different stages of the research. Having ideas is part of every aspect of the research process. For example, you can have ideas about the sort of data you wish to collect, the setting, and the social actors. Those ideas can be about what you aim to explore, find out, discover, confirm, or disprove. These ideas can be wholly your own or can use or transform the ideas of others, such as researchers in the same field, philosophers, professionals, and the respondents themselves. Similarly, the analysis of the data can be informed by your own ideas about what is going on, or it can be informed by your respondents' views of what they think is happening. The kinds of ideas you use, transform, or draw upon also can be influenced by your understanding, sympathy, curiosity, or antagonism in relation to particular "schools" of ideas—for example, critical, Marxist, interactionist, positivist, feminist, or phenomenological.

We do not, incidentally, think that all these theories exhaust the possibilities, nor can they be assimilated into an all-embracing paradigm of qualitative research. On the contrary, we strongly reject the notion that qualitative research substitutes for disciplinary perspectives and theoretical frameworks (Atkinson, 1995). It is, however, important that such broader frameworks of ideas be understood and explored in the context of how they provide different, fruitful ways of thinking about qualitative data (Silverman, 1993).

There is nothing optional about the generation and use of ideas in qualitative research and analysis. As Silverman (1993, p. 46) notes, theorizing cannot easily be divorced from analysis:

> We only come to look at things in certain ways because we have adapted, either tacitly or explicitly, certain ways of seeing. This means that, in observational research, data collection, hypothesis-construction and theory building are not three separate things but are interwoven with one another.

Using ideas is part of any research. We have ideas about our research all the time, throughout the research process, even if we do not consciously think about creation of these ideas as theorizing. We select our data, our research problems, what strikes us as interesting, and what to focus on and follow up with our informants. Our influences on the sort of data we collect and what we do with them, and our hypotheses about what our data are telling us, pervade the conduct of research. That is, in essence, what using theory is. We are making explicit what we all do implicitly. We are integrating our ideas with our data collection and data analysis, generating new ideas and building on existing ideas. Having ideas and theorizing about our data are central to the research endeavor. More important perhaps, in terms of this volume, theorizing and theory building are part of the process of analysis and interpretation of qualitative data.

The kinds of ideas that can be generated as the outcome of qualitative research are various, and therefore what counts as theory in this context is open to a variety of understandings. Glaser and Strauss (1967), for example, draw one important contrast when they distinguish between formal and substantive theory. Substantive theory makes sense of a particular social context, while formal theory is generic in scope. Most of our initial theorizing is derived from the close investigation of one case or a few cases. Consequently, we frequently begin to generate our ideas at the substantive level. It is, however, important to be able to go beyond the local setting of the research and to engage with formal ideas at a more general level. In that sense, one may need to go beyond the data and beyond the original setting of the research. One may need to engage with ideas that are derived from and relate to social settings of many kinds. We will try to illustrate these themes briefly with reference to the anthropology study later in this chapter.

It is not possible within only one chapter to discuss and illustrate how one might engage with the enormous range of ideas and perspectives in the social sciences. It is appropriate, therefore, to point out that we do not believe that there are one-to-one correspondences between particular methods and specific theories. Qualitative research methods have stronger family resemblances and affinities with some kinds of ideas than with others, but we do not believe that they are so closely bound together as to constitute self-contained paradigms. On the contrary, we think that advocates of such a paradigm mentality are fundamentally mistaken (see

Atkinson, 1995; Delamont & Atkinson, 1995). Qualitative methods certainly have relevance for interactionist, ethnomethodological, phenomenological, feminist, critical, and related perspectives, but the researcher needs to be able to distinguish between a general methodological commitment to qualitative work and the theoretical and disciplinary frameworks that subsume particular methods of data collection and analysis.

Some contemporary accounts of theorizing are expressed in terms of "theory building," and—as we will discuss again in Chapter 7— approaches to computer-aided data analysis sometimes stress this image of theoretical work. In particular, they stress the extent to which categories and concepts (such as those reflected in coding schemes) can be brought together and ordered systematically. Whether they are actually supported by computer software, such approaches to theorizing are driven primarily by the procedures of coding and categorizing the data. This is a view promoted by Richards and Richards (e.g., 1994). Although they recognize that theorizing is a creative activity, they also stress the degree to which overarching concepts are derived from the coding of data. In their own work, they emphasize the extent to which codes are representations of emergent concepts, which are theory laden. As we indicate in the following chapter, there is now a widespread view that theory building and theory testing are developed primarily out of the categorization of data through coding procedures, and the construction of systematic, hierarchical relationships among the categories.

There is no doubt that theoretical ideas can and should inform the coding of data, as we emphasized in Chapter 2. Likewise, it is easy to endorse the view that a careful examination of codes can help to generate theoretical ideas. It would be unwise, however, to assume that there is a single activity of theory building that follows a uniform set of procedures. In the same way that we argue throughout this book for an informed awareness of the variety of analytic strategies, we argue against the adoption of a single approach to theorizing. There are different paths to theory, and there are different kinds of theories and ideas that can be produced. It should certainly not be assumed that theory can be "built" by the aggregation and ordering of codes or the retrieval of coded segments. One must always be prepared to engage in creative intellectual work, to speculate about the data in order to have ideas, to try out a number of different ideas, to link one's ideas with those of others, and so to move conceptually from one's own research setting to a more general, even abstract, level of analytic thought.

Theories and ideas may take various forms. For example, one may seek to derive explanatory models, attempting to link themes in terms of causal relationships. This is a common way of thinking about theoretical ideas generally. Qualitative research may have much to say about causal relationships. As Miles and Huberman (1994, p. 147) write,

> We consider qualitative analysis to be a very powerful method for assessing causality. . . . Qualitative analysis, with its close-up look, can identify *mechanisms,* going beyond sheer association. It is unrelentingly *local,* and deals well with the complex network of events and processes in a situation. It can sort out the *temporal* dimension, showing clearly what preceded what, either through direct observation or *retrospection.* It is well equipped to cycle back and forth between *variables* and *processes*—showing that "stories" are not capricious, but include underlying variables, and that variables are not disembodied, but have connections over time.

Here, then, one may stress the value of detailed, qualitative research in uncovering the complex causal relationships at play within given social milieux. As Miles and Huberman also point out, for that reason qualitative research may have advantages over other strategies more often associated with causal explanations, such as experimental research designs, which often tell little or nothing about the actual mechanisms of cause and effect.

It is not necessary, however, to assume that all theories need to consist of causal explanations. Many of the theories generated from qualitative research take different forms. Often they take the form of *ideal types,* that is, patterns or typifications constructed by the analyst out of all the actual cases observed. They are intended to capture the key features of a given phenomenon without necessarily displaying all the particulars of individual cases. Goffman's (1961) characterization of the "total institution" is a well-known example of such a type. It illustrates some general features of such theorizing quite well. Goffman himself undertook detailed field research in a psychiatric institution, and from that research he generated ideas about the setting. He raised his ideas to the level of generic or formal theory by applying them—through comparative analysis—to a much wider range of institutions, such as prisons, military establishments, and monasteries. In doing so, he derived and elaborated the idea of the total institution in order to convey key elements shared by all those institutions. His approach was not primarily in terms of causal models, but of patterns and types.

Such types may capture quite diverse dimensions of phenomena. For example, one might focus on temporal and processual features, producing typical careers of actors, social movements, or institutions. Alternatively, one might characterize patterns of social interaction in social contexts. Cultures or subcultures and their associated values may be identified in terms of ideal-typical patterns. Thought of from this perspective, the guiding principle of theorizing is not causal explanation but the identification of patterns and associations. Such analytic enterprises owe more to the general spirit of interpretation than to explanation.

To these may be added various approaches, the goals of which are to explicate how social actors accomplish social order and shared understandings. These include approaches inspired by ethnomethodological studies of members' practices and other perspectives that address the cultural resources that actors use in their everyday affairs. Gubrium (1988) provides a useful summary of some approaches in this vein. These include what Gubrium (1988, p. 27) refers to as "articulative ethnography": "While articulative ethnography takes an interest in the subjective meaning of behavior, it stresses the native analytic work and categorization practices that inform action." The aim of theorizing in this context is not normally thought of in terms of explanation, nor necessarily in terms of the kind of formal theory associated with grounded theory approaches. It is, rather, the description of the (often implicit) knowledge and skills that actors bring to bear.

These approaches to qualitative research and theorizing have features and goals in common. Not least among them is the desire for analytic accounts to be "conceptually dense" (Strauss & Corbin, 1994, p. 278), in that they incorporate many concepts and multiple linkages among them. They are grounded in the actual social contexts and processes of everyday social life, and they are demonstrably linked to such phenomena. They emphasize the role of local cultures and the situationally specific, and they recognize that social life and social action are essentially meaningful. Both approaches—explanatory and interpretive—enable the analyst to transcend the local settings of his or her primary data collection in order to generalize to a wider range of social domains. We return to this issue of generalization later in the chapter. In addition, the approaches to

which we have just referred share a commitment to types of what might
be called traditional, rationalist approaches to social science. It must not
be forgotten that the variety of approaches goes beyond these.

By no means do all qualitative researchers see the goal of their work
in terms of explanations or formal models such as ideal types. There are
those who stress even further the interpretive or hermeneutic goals of
research. This approach does not imply a lack of commitment to general
ideas; the ideas and their use simply are different. Here the emphasis is
on the investigation and exploration of cultural meanings. Moreover, it
is more characteristic of these approaches that they should emphasize
multiple perspectives and multiple voices, sometimes using experimental
styles of representation (Denzin, 1994). Denzin's own characterization
of his interpretive interactionism is illustrative of one such approach.
Denzin (1994, p. 510) suggests that the overall task of research is to
produce richly detailed narratives of personal experiences:

> The focus of the research is on those life experiences (epiphanies) that
> radically alter and shape the meanings persons give to themselves and their
> life projects. In epiphanies, personal character is manifested and made
> apparent. By recording these experiences in detail and by listening to the
> stories people tell about them, the researcher is able to illuminate the mo-
> ments of crisis that occur in a person's life. . . . (Examples of epiphanies
> include religious conversions, divorces, incidents of family violence, rape,
> incest, murder and the loss of a job.)

Here, then, the emphasis of analysis (and of writing) lies in the
interpretation of lives and narratives. Explanatory models are not at
issue, and the analyst is not necessarily seeking to generate ideal types or
formal models of actors' lives. This does not mean that the work is devoid
of general, theoretical ideas: The notion of epiphanies is clearly such an
organizing idea. The goal of the creative intellectual effort, however, is
primarily interpretive.

This is not an exhaustive mapping of all the different theoretical
perspectives with which qualitative research can engage, but it indicates
some of the variety and helps guard against the implicit idea that there
is but one model of theory building. We do not believe that the researcher
needs to commit himself or herself to the production of only one kind
of idea. On the contrary, detailed qualitative research—as we have seen
in the previous chapters—can give rise to multiple types of analysis and

so lead to ideas of different types. There is no need for the analyst to be confined to only one theoretical perspective.

At this point, we return to our own materials from the study of anthropology. Here we try to indicate some of the lines of thought that might inform our theoretical development and relate them to the issues we have just raised. We try to give some sense of the kinds of ideas that we might wish to explore and some of the theories we might wish to elaborate, as well as to provide some insight into how such ideas might arise in the course of a research project. What follows does not constitute a final analysis of the anthropology data but offers a glimpse of analysis in process. In the fullness of time, some of these ideas might be discarded and modified. Others might be developed and documented more fully. Analysis is never complete. There are always more ideas and more lines of inquiry open to us than we can ever hope to exhaust.

Anthropology Revisited

Many methodology texts, and the methodological appendices or autobiographical accounts that relate to specific projects, are retrospective reconstructions. The logic of research design and the strategies of data collection and analysis may well have been defined only after the project was substantially complete. That was not the case with the illustrative materials used to develop our discussions. Although Paul Atkinson was one of the original research team members, he had not fully analyzed the data; Amanda Coffey came to the data fresh, having been an outsider to the original research project. We knew what general methodological issues we wanted to identify and discuss, but we did not know beforehand precisely how the data would relate to those themes. We did not know in detail what findings would emerge from our various inspections of those data. We described in Chapter 1 how one of our motivations for writing it was the number of both novice and more experienced researchers who seem to collect data and then "get stuck" with what to do with them. We wanted to promote experimentation and a variety of analytic strategies. It seemed appropriate, therefore, to begin with fresh data and no preconceived ideas about them. It is appropriate in this chapter to include a summary account of our ideas that emerged from those data and our reflections on them. We draw on the analytic work and writing of the research team (e.g., Parry, Atkinson, & Delamont, 1994) and demonstrate how analysis and theorizing move us beyond the data. We should remind readers here that the following comments draw on the entire data set and not only on the fragments used to illustrate the book.

Throughout the book, we have used fragments of data to illustrate particular points about analysis, writing, and the generation of ideas. As we have suggested, those examples were chosen with two complementary goals in mind. First, we thought it important to show how data from the same research project, gathered in the same way, could be approached from complementary analytic standpoints. Second, we wanted to use a data set that we hoped would hold some intrinsic interest for our readers: Many of the examples we selected bear directly or indirectly on the organization and experience of fieldwork. Running through this text, therefore, is the subtext of an implicit analysis of accounts of the academic socialization of British social anthropologists.

The original research dealt with a wider range of academic disciplines than anthropology alone. It was not conceived as an anthropology of anthropologists (fascinating though that is in its own right). In approaching those data for the purposes of this volume, we have tried to provide glimpses of analysis in process to provide some insight into how we might think about the data and how we might start to develop our analyses. At this point, therefore, although it would be inappropriate to try to compose a mini-ethnography of the anthropologists, it might prove useful for us to round off our treatment of those data with some general remarks and ideas.

It is important to realize, in contextualizing our ideas about the data, that the original research team did not focus obsessively on anthropological fieldwork as a topic of inquiry. The team members were concerned with a wider range of research problems. For example, in the end-of-award report for the research project on the PhD in the social science disciplines, the team concluded that the anthropologists displayed especially strong disciplinary identities. Only a minority of the 24 social anthropology students (9) interviewed had a first degree in the subject, but through either the first degree or a master's program, they had all experienced a kind of intellectual conversion. The academic loyalty of the anthropologists was matched by geographers who were interviewed, the great majority of whom (19 out of 23) had first degrees in geography. Geographers—on this evidence—come to geography early, and graduate students report a long love affair with the subject; anthropologists come to anthropology late but may experience an intellectual absorption with the discipline and a personal identification with it. We were especially struck by the fact that even a small number of graduate students who had dropped out or failed (they did not submit a doctoral dissertation) still seemed to endorse the core characteristics of the discipline. They attributed their own failure to their own personal inability to shape up to the demands of the subject.

It was noticeable how strongly our informants in anthropology—students and established academics—produced accounts expressing the personal qualities that are required of an anthropologist. There was little emphasis in their accounts on the importance of research methods and techniques. The anthropologists were especially skeptical about the real value of explicit training in methods of research. On the other hand, their accounts emphasized the importance of personal, tacit knowledge and its transmission by means of a personal apprenticeship. It is therefore entirely congruent with such expressions of an academic subculture that our interviews with anthropologists should contain such characteristic lineages and pedigrees: They warrant the general importance of personal transmission from one generation to the next and the particular credentials of the speaker.

We do not believe that such genealogies are unique to anthropology. In one sense, it clearly matters to all academics where they have studied and worked, and with whom. On the other hand, the particular force of such pedigrees in anthropological self-presentations is especially striking. They clearly help to establish the personal manner in which knowledge and experience are warranted and are handed down from mentor to student, generation to generation.

The personal quality of anthropological knowledge and its acquisition was clearly expressed in the accounts of fieldwork. Such accounts had several functions: They often justified fieldwork, in the sense that they placed it at the heart of the anthropological enterprise, and they placed fieldwork in the personal and intellectual biography of the teller. Fieldwork thus marks the most crucial aspect of the apprenticeship. The academic socialization career of graduate anthropologists, as constructed in the interview accounts, fell into three clear stages: pre-fieldwork, fieldwork, and post-fieldwork. Of these—as in most classic *rites de passage*—

the central phase was the most special. As we have seen, it involves reported experiences of isolation and separation. It remains normal for the fieldwork to take the novice "elsewhere." Even when the research site is physically close at hand, the novice graduate student may be symbolically separated from the supervisor and the university department.

As our analysis of the data develop, then, we already find ourselves moving between the specifics of anthropology and concrete detail in the data, on one hand, and some general analytic themes on the other. The minutia of personal career narratives suggest a much broader interest in how anthropologists construct themselves as particular kinds of people and their discipline as founded on particular kinds of knowledge. Moreover, it leads to more general speculation that takes us beyond the particulars of anthropology, even of academic settings altogether. It leads us to think of other settings that have been documented in which socialization is dependent on intensely personal experiences, based on close relationships between teachers and novices, in which the student is required to undergo a prolonged period of apprenticeship. As we shall see, those and other themes might lead us to explore ideas about craft apprentices (now and in the past), about entrants to religious orders and converts, or about the making of artists and musicians. We do not have to think that they are all "the same" in order to derive guiding themes in developing our theoretical ideas.

To return to the substantive level of the anthropology data once more, it is apparent that fieldwork is the central experience in the lives and careers of most of the students and faculty members. It is appropriate, therefore, that we should have explored "fieldwork" as a domain. In undertaking a formal domain analysis, we allowed ourselves to examine in some detail the semiotics of this key cultural theme. This type of analysis forced us, perhaps, to examine those aspects of the data much more systematically than we might have otherwise. It is important to explore the denotations and connotations of a term that covers such an important place—symbolic and practical—in the careers of academics.

Our exploratory analysis of fieldwork as a semantic domain developed and formalized our general impressions of the topic. Such analytic work can help to flesh out cultural categories that assume significance in a more general framework of conceptual development. Fieldwork for anthropologists is more prolonged and more isolating than it is for most disciplines. Although sociology and sociologists did not feature in our sampling of the academic world, we know from other sources (including our own personal experience) that fieldwork does not have the same position in the discipline, nor in the processes of occupational socialization. By no means all sociologists undertake fieldwork in any case, and those who do normally do so for shorter periods, with much less social and physical isolation. The differences are not clear-cut, however, and some exercises in urban anthropology are virtually indistinguishable from urban sociology. It is striking, however, that despite such similarities and the relevance of ethnographic fieldwork to several disciplines, anthropologists speak as if such a research approach were unique to their own discipline. The personal and intellectual connotations of fieldwork are among the symbolic markers that help to demarcate anthropology as a disciplinary field.

In pursuing this aspect of our analysis, then, we can again move from the substantive to the generic. Having identified the elements of fieldwork as a domain, we can look at how they relate to the broader picture of socialization and conversion. Thinking again of, say, religious converts or craft apprentices, we can start to make our comparisons more precise: the role of personal isolation in the socialization process, the cultural significance of separation and danger, the symbolic marking of departure to and return from a period of separation, and the forms of relationship between superordinates and novices.

The various components of disciplinary subculture reflect and reproduce how anthropological knowledge is constructed by academics and their students. As our fragmentary analyses hinted and this brief summary has emphasized, knowledge production and cultural transmission are conceived and talked of as highly personal achievements. They are dependent on competencies—social and intellectual—that remain largely implicit. Within the tightly bounded domain of the academic discipline itself, high levels of commitment and subject loyalty are cultivated and expressed. There are thus close analogies with the experience of initiation or conversion to a "sacred" province of experience. Here, some of our treatment of metaphor and imagery comes to the fore. We identified some of the imagery used to convey the highly personal nature of academic supervision, while the metaphor of the *rite de passage* clearly provided the anthropologists with a self-referential way of describing the personal experiences of students and faculty members in the process of becoming full-fledged anthropologists.

In formulating our ideas along these lines, then, we can see different possibilities for theorizing further. It is open to us to develop formal, substantive theory. We can, for example, begin to construct ideal-typical careers of anthropologists. Student careers are based on pre-fieldwork, fieldwork, and post-fieldwork phases; there are different *trajectories* through those stages; some students may have incomplete careers; and so on. The model could be elaborated by reference to key turning points within each of the main phases (choice of research setting within the pre-fieldwork, or crises in the fieldwork, for example). Clearly, those issues can be addressed from another, complementary angle. Taking a more interpretive stance, following Denzin (1989) we can think of the anthropologists' career narratives in terms of their *epiphanies,* in order to examine how they construct their lives and their lived experiences. Here again, therefore, the analytic purchase gained from close attention to accounts and narratives provides a valuable resource for theorizing.

We can, therefore, assemble these and other concepts in order to develop complex accounts of anthropology as a distinctive kind of social world. It will be seen that these ideas all imply interpretive rather than causal accounts. This is not because we think that causal explanations are entirely inappropriate, but the original research was not conceived with that end in view. Hypothetically, however, it would have been possible to try to combine analyses of departmental subcultures and types of supervisory strategy in order to develop explanatory models for doctoral completion rates and patterns of noncompletion in different departments. We are more interested, however, in linking our substantive accounts of anthropology and anthropologists with more generic formal models.

Building on our ideas to date, for example, we could develop our theorizing with reference to the general issue of *conversion.* Going beyond the data about anthropology, we would use relevant literature—sociological, anthropological, historical, theological, and (auto)biographical—to generate formal theories of intellectual and personal transformation, about the rigors and rewards of apprenticeship, and exploring the components of academic self-identity. This would imply interaction among our data, our substantive ideas, and formal ideas derived from the research literature.

In writing about writing, we offered some examples and ideas as to how such sociological analyses could get written up. We conclude this section with more summary remarks on that issue. In writing, rather than merely inspecting and manipulating the data, we are concerned even more than in any other aspect of the research with making explicit and systematic use of concept and ideas, or "theory." The data we have been using still have not yet been fully written up. Here we can only project what will happen to them. It was agreed among the team throughout the project, however, that future writing would—at least in part—be driven by the ideas outlined by Pierre Bourdieu (1988) and Basil Bernstein (1977, 1990; Atkinson, 1985). Both of those sociologists have proposed general theoretical perspectives on intellectual life, schooling and socialization, and culture and its reproduction. In developing the work of those two sociologists, and others who share similar perspectives, we therefore build on a number of general themes. From both we draw the inspiration of their work on academic disciplines, their symbolic boundaries, and their sacred spaces. We would explore the processes whereby academic disciplines and their associated subcultures are defined and legitimated. We would be building on the ideas of Bourdieu that include the notion of *cultural capital* and *habitus,* in order to capture the sense that academic socialization involves the development of personal qualities that reflect the cultural requirements of academic disciplines as "thought collectives," as Ludwik Fleck (1935/1979) put it. That is, we would seek to document all the ways in which distinctive patterns of thought and action are shared and expressed: how they are enshrined in the hidden curricula of educational and other institutions. In doing so, we would build further on ideas of intellectual apprenticeship and the acquisition of tacit knowledge—building in the notion of the "reflective practitioner" (Schön, 1983) or Lave and Wenger (1991) on forms of apprenticeship and the tacit acquisition of practical knowledge.

As we write, those analyses have not been completed, let alone published. It is unlikely that the anthropology data will actually be written up separately. The publications that have been written and will be written develop those and other, complementary themes in relation to other social sciences and selected natural sciences. As we wrote *this* book, the themes we discuss were genuinely emergent out of the data fragments reported here, as well as other processes of analysis that were going on elsewhere, on other parallel data. What we have tried to do is offer the reader some glimpses of the processes and procedures of data analysis that have allowed us to identify and develop some of those lines of thought.

Precisely because the work is incomplete, we are able to share some of our thought processes and analytic strategies. It is not always possible to say precisely where those ideas "come from." They are derived from multiple sources. Some come from previous research: We and our colleagues have done a good deal of research on professional socialization and have a stock of knowledge derived from that empirical work and its associated literature. Some ideas are derived from wider reading in the sociological, anthropological, and educational literature. Still other ideas come from the least tangible sources of general knowledge and a reading of fiction and biography. It is significant, however, that no amount of reading can provide the qualitative researcher with off-the-peg ideas. Similarly, the data alone will not generate analytic ideas of their own accord. Understanding proceeds through a constant movement between data and ideas.

Theorizing and Generalizing

As we have just suggested, it is vital to recognize that the generation of ideas can never be dependent on the data alone. Data are there to think with and to think about. As we have indicated, ideas about our data go beyond that data. We should bring to them the full range of intellectual resources, derived from theoretical perspectives, substantive traditions, research literature, and other sources. Research methods do not in themselves substitute for disciplinary knowledge. We do not, in our opinion, undertake research—qualitative or otherwise—simply as "researchers." We should not approach the investigation of social worlds only as ethnographers, or field researchers, or case-study researchers. Methods of data collection and analysis do not make sense when treated in an intellectual vacuum and divorced from more general and fundamental disciplinary frameworks. We should avoid treating methods and methodology as proxy academic subjects. A discipline such as cultural anthropology or a theoretical tradition such as symbolic interactionism carries far more than an affinity with particular research approaches. There is more to research than a mere adherence to particular methods. Academic disciplines and the boundaries between them are arbitrary. There is nothing inherent in the world that dictates the separate existence of, say, anthropology, sociology, social psychology, or sociolinguistics.

On the other hand, those disciplines do provide the genealogies of ideas, the key perspectives, and the fundamental presuppositions that inform research practice.

In the course of this book, we have presented and exemplified a restricted, coherent set of research procedures and principles. To some extent, one can trace a consistent direction in our exposition. We have moved from the most mechanistic of issues in categorizing and data retrieval through to the most highly literary and experimental modes of representation. There is nothing especially problematic or paradoxical in the collection and exploration of such apparently contrasting methods of data analysis. Such variety and difference is only a real problem if one remains unnecessarily wedded to the search for one correct method.

Research methods, and modes of analysis in particular, should, we believe, be subordinated to broader goals of social research. Methods are not ends in themselves, and we should always remember that we are using analytic perspectives and techniques in order to make discoveries and generate interpretations of the social worlds we investigate.

In the previous section, we gave some indication of how we might think about the anthropology data, moving from those data to some more general statements and theories. What we discuss in this section is the "getting" and generation of ideas, that is, how one moves from managing and organizing data to interpreting and theorizing about them. We might refer to this process as theory building or generalizing. In practice, we find that this terminology can be unduly daunting. We may not think of ourselves as theorists. Some of us may actually feel inclined to the view that "we do not do theory," but in practice all of us can and do generate and use ideas. It is appropriate, therefore, that we should include in this chapter some reference to the getting of ideas. We need to give some indication of how data are not merely managed, organized, or whatever, but also how they are interpreted. We have tried to show such processes at work when we have presented exemplary treatments of data fragments; we did so again when we explored writing and representation. It is important, however, to emphasize that whatever methods are chosen, their interpretation goes well beyond the technical categorization and description of the data themselves. In significant ways, the real work of analysis and interpretation lies precisely in those intellectual operations that go beyond the data. Our important ideas are not "in" the data, and however hard we work, we will not find those ideas simply by scrutinizing our data ever more obsessively. We need to work at analysis and theorizing, and we need to do the intellectual, imaginative work of ideas in parallel to the other tasks of data management. There is, or should be, a constant interplay between the ideas we work with (play with very often) and the detail of form and content in the data themselves.

One useful way to think about the process of generating ideas is in terms of Peirce's notion of *abductive* reasoning (Peirce, 1979). (See Kelle, 1995b, for a succinct review.) It is not necessary to go into the philosophical issues in detail. It is not even necessary to agree with the pragmatist philosophy in order to use the idea productively and heuristically. It seems to capture how many of us think about ideas, perhaps more usefully than many of the reconstructed logics of social scientific research to be found in methodological textbooks and the like. Abductive reasoning lies at the heart of "grounded theorizing," although again it is not necessary to endorse grounded theory, as formulated by Glaser and Strauss (1967), Glaser (1978), Strauss and Corbin (1990), Charmaz (1983), and other interpreters, in order to appreciate its relevance.

Abductive reasoning and logic were used by Peirce to contrast with the polar opposites of inductive and deductive logic. Inductivism is based on the presumption that laws or generalizations can be developed from the accumulation of observations and cases, that the close inspection of ever more data can be made to reveal regularities. There are good grounds, philosophical and practical, for recognizing that such a view of inquiry is untenable and unproductive. It is likely to lead to the collection of more and more observations and recordings. At best, it will encourage unremarkable and undistinguished descriptions of social worlds and events, with little or no innovation and development.

The polar opposite—a strict adherence to deductive principles—can prove equally sterile. This logical position is founded on the assertion that empirical research can be used only to test theories. A hypothetico-deductive approach to inquiry thus confines the role of research to the context of testing existing ideas. A strict adherence to such a position means that there is little or no basis on which empirical research can inform the generation of new theories. Neither of the polar types (which are normally used to delimit the possibilities of inquiry) is satisfactory in informing the actual generation of ideas. Whatever the niceties of the philosophy of the social sciences, practical researchers need guidance on the actual generation and organization of ideas. The context of discovery must be a major preoccupation for all researchers. The emphasis on *exploration* that is characteristic of much qualitative research really calls for ways of generating new ideas. One needs to break free of the strait-jackets imposed by conventional logic.

One way of thinking about the processes of having ideas is to concep-tualize them in terms of abductive reasoning. This approach, as we have suggested, seems to capture more productively how researchers in all disciplines actually think and work. It allows for a more central role for empirical research in the generation of ideas as well as a more dynamic interaction between data and theory. Abductive reasoning or inference implies that we start from the particular. We identify a particular phe-nomenon—a surprising or anomalous finding, perhaps. We then try to account for that phenomenon by relating it to broader concepts. We do so by inspecting our own experience, our stock of knowledge of similar, comparable phenomena, and the equivalent stock of ideas that can be included from within our disciplines (including theories and frame-works) and neighboring fields. In other words, abductive inferences seek to go beyond the data themselves, to locate them in explanatory or interpretive frameworks. The researcher is not content to try to slot them into existing ideas, for the search includes new, surprising, or anomalous observations. On the other hand, such strange phenomena are not used only to disconfirm existing theories: They are used to come up with new configurations of ideas. There is thus a repeated interaction among existing ideas, former findings and observations, new observations, and new ideas. Abductive inference is thus especially appropriate for quali-tative work, in which an open-minded intellectual approach is normally advocated (Kelle, 1995b).

It is more important in the long run to think in terms of having ideas and using ideas than to become unduly preoccupied with the logic of inquiry, or with the more daunting connotation of theory and theory construction. A lot of people find theory a rather daunting prospect, not least because the social and cultural disciplines too often celebrate grand theories that seem to have little contact with the empirical data of field research. Equally, there is too great a reverence for difficult, obtuse theorizing that does little or nothing to illuminate the realities of every-day social life. What are needed are the generation and imaginative use of ideas that guide our exploration and interpretation of the social world.

Theory can sound like something that is special, divorced from ordinary research skills, yet everyone can have ideas about the world about them. We do and should all think and speculate about our data and—more generally—our experiences. We can all make interpretations. Whether we always grace such ideas with the grandiose label of theory, the important thing is to have ideas and to use them to explore and interpret the social world around us.

If we follow authors such as Kelle, then we can also recognize that theories usefully can be thought of as heuristic tools. In other words, we *use* concepts, theories, and ideas constructively and creatively. We explore them and deploy them whatever their origins, whether they come from our own discipline or another, whether they come from the published literature or from elsewhere. In other words, the kinds of analytic techniques that we have outlined in this book are idle if they are not combined with more general ideas. They undoubtedly give us excellent ways of manipulating our data and of producing systematic descriptions of the social worlds we wish to explore, but that is not the end of analysis. Regularities in data—whether of form or content—must be associated with ideas that go beyond those data themselves. This is a creative enterprise, but creative work does not have to be thought of as inexplicably private. Creative analysis is not confined to the realm of personal inspiration. Like writing, it has many craft elements; it is part of the *work* of research.

Good ideas might often be serendipitous, but serendipity can be encouraged by careful preparation. The aphorism attributed to the golfer Gary Player, "the harder I work, the luckier I get," may be applied usefully to the work of research, and it applies at all stages of the research process. Having ideas is not simply about waiting for an elusive and fickle muse. We should instead concentrate on making ideas and using ideas, emphasizing that these are part of the intellectual craft of research and scholarship.

Heuristic ideas and theoretical frameworks will often have their origins in the published literature of the disciplines. The open-mindedness of exploratory research should not be mistaken for the empty-mindedness of the researcher who is not adequately steeped in the research traditions of a discipline. It is, after all, not very creative to rediscover the wheel, and the student or researcher who is ignorant of the relevant literature is always in danger of doing the equivalent. This is a powerful reason why one cannot treat qualitative methods as if they constituted a paradigm or a discipline in their own right. Research methods alone do not provide the wealth of ideas and the empirical traditions that are a major source for ideas and interpretations. We can engage with the ideas of others, however, in an active sense. Our task as qualitative researchers is to use ideas in order to develop interpretations that go beyond the limits of our own data and that go beyond how previous scholars have used those ideas. It is in that synthesis that new interpretations and new ideas emerge. The point is not to follow previous scholarship slavishly but to adapt and transform it in the interpretation of one's own data.

The processes of identifying, using, and adapting ideas cannot be reduced to formulae and prescriptions. Still less do they lend themselves to practical tips. On the other hand, there are some general principles that can guide the novice and the experienced researcher alike. As we have suggested, reading should be pursued actively. An active engagement with the published literature means that ideas are available for use in research. The work of others is inspected not only for its empirical findings but also for how its ideas can inform the interpretation of one's own research setting. Theories are not added only as a final gloss or justification; they are not thrown over the work as a final garnish. They are drawn on repeatedly as ideas are formulated, tried out, modified, rejected, or polished.

Ideas can come from multiple sources. One of the habits of mind that is especially restricting is a concentration on a very narrow field of specialism. If one's reading and thought are very tightly focused, then the chances of fresh discoveries and insights will be strictly limited. The most creative of qualitative or interpretive social scientists have drawn ideas eclectically from a wide range of sources. Those sources do not have to be confined to the particular discipline of one's own identity. Indeed, they do not have to be restricted to work in the social sciences at all. We have already referred in Chapter 5 to the intertextuality of academic work: There are echoes of other texts and other genres. In the same way, our ideas may be derived from multiple sources: Fictional, biographical, autobiographical, and journalistic writing can furnish ideas as often as academic writing in our own narrow specialty, for example. The most general value of wide and eclectic reading, then, is the generation or borrowing of what Blumer (1954) called "sensitizing concepts."

Such processes of reading and thought should inform qualitative research at all stages. It is inadvisable to wait until the fieldwork is complete and the data all organized before casting about for fruitful ideas and frameworks. Ideas inform the emerging analyses at every step in the research project. Many of the ideas that emerge or that are adopted will be used allusively and by analogy. They may suggest especially fruitful metaphors that will in turn suggest (perhaps) more formal kinds of comparison.

The very logic of qualitative research, with its emphasis on comparative methods, calls repeatedly for metaphorical or analogical thinking, reading, and writing. We wrote in Chapter 4 about the analysis of metaphorical expression in our data and of the significance of such figures of speech in everyday life. We cannot and should not exempt our own thought from metaphorical expression. Metaphors and similes can help to suggest—even to create—comparisons between one's own study and those of others (often in quite diverse fields). This perspective has been explored by Noblit and Hare (1988), who argue for an explicit analysis of such metaphorical borrowing as part of a disciplined meta-analysis of ethnographic work. In taking ideas that link one's own data with other social domains, one is moving toward the production of generic concepts and formal theory. Such ideas transcend the specific, local circumstances of a given research project and its research site(s). They draw together empirical details from diverse settings.

For example, in commenting on the anthropology data extracts used to illustrate this book, we have drawn on various ideas. They emerged out of our own—and others'—transactions with the data, together with explorations of various ideas and sources. We can illustrate our thinking about ideas by reflecting more overtly on some of those processes in relation to the data on anthropologists and how we might proceed toward more fully worked up interpretations. For example, we observed when we examined narrative analysis that our anthropologists quite often produced particular kinds of chronicles of their academic career. Although we have not engaged in comparative analyses here, it is noticeable that such career accounts—in that form—are especially characteristic of anthropologists. Most academics recount aspects of their intellectual biography, but in the course of the research on academic socialization the project team members were struck by the anthropologists' approach. In thinking about it, we reflected in part on the discipline of anthropology itself. Genealogies and lineages are exceptionally important themes in social anthropology, given the centrality of kinship and descent to the societies that have dominated the discipline. (At least they have dominated the anthropological treatment of those societies.) Anthropologists have identified the phenomenon of the genealogical charter, whereby descent is claimed in justification for rights, membership, and relationships. It is, therefore, ironic that anthropologists themselves seem to use their own subject's distinctive subject matter in order to characterize themselves.

The potential significance goes beyond that observation. We can be more sociological or anthropological about it. We can think more generally about other contexts in which such genealogies might be significant. We might note, for example, other cultural fields in which intergenerational transmission is seen to be important. In developing an analysis, therefore, we might turn to a field such as music. A reading of musical biographies, or even program notes, would reveal similar kinds of genealogies, of who studied with whom and where. Performing artists such as pianists, violinists, singers, or conductors are often located in terms of their teachers or mentors, as well as their mentors before them. Within a few generations, a lineage may be traced back to Liszt, say, or equivalent culture heroes. Likewise, composers may be identified in terms of such intergenerational inheritance, the genius of Beethoven deriving, say, from his direct inheritance from Haydn and Mozart (cf. DeNora, 1995).

We might ask ourselves how such lineages function. They seem to be more important than explanations of how particular skills and techniques are handed down from teacher to student. They seem to convey strong claims to personal qualities. They legitimate claims to indeterminate personal traits, such as style, taste, inspiration, flair, and the like. They function to describe the "laying on of hands" in the transmission of genius.

In developing such an analogy into a more worked-up analysis, we might note that our data on anthropologists suggest very strongly that their professional and academic identity is based on personal qualities rather than skills and specific technical knowledge. As one of our anthropologists put it, being an anthropologist is more about the accumulation of cultural capital than about specific knowledge and skills. Many of the students and academics put great stress on the personal, biographical qualities that go into the making of an anthropologist. These tacit, personal qualities may be thought to be fostered by personal transmission. Genealogies and pedigrees thus place anthropologists in lines of intellectual descent, perhaps. As we flesh out such a line of speculation, we might reflect further on other kinds of pedigrees. We might compare how our anthropologists construct their lineages with the autocratic ideas of "degrees of nobility" and the deconstruction of the purity of one's inheritance.

As we pursue this line of thought, we might also note that anthropologists' genealogies are not only about people but also about places. It is apparently important not only who you worked with, and who their mentors were, but also where you have been. The anthropologists' accounts stress the local traditions of particular university departments and their associated schools of thought. People and places are brought together in these autobiographical accounts. Our interpretations and lines of thought therefore would pursue how local identities and loyalties are expressed. We would thus extend our reading and thinking by incorporating sociological and anthropological work on symbolic communities. We would look at how communities define their boundaries and their membership, and how they differentiate themselves from other categories of social actors.

As these lines of comparison and interpretation grow out of the data, then, we would find ourselves engaged in processes of abductive reasoning. We note something about the data at hand. We speculate about possible interpretive frameworks—drawn from our general knowledge and from our specialized reading in the social sciences—that might help to account for those phenomena. We thus go beyond the data themselves toward broader, generic issues. These in turn help to throw light on other aspects of the data, which in turn help us to extend the framework of general ideas and concepts. In this manner, our interactions with the data and with our own research traditions may grow—in an organic fashion—toward broad, encompassing analyses.

We can illustrate this further with the data that we already have introduced. We have raised the issue of "conversion" previously, noting that some of our data include accounts of personal and intellectual transformation through an apprenticeship in anthropology. Without wishing to be too glib in such an approach, we should pursue this line. It is clear that we should extend this by looking at other kinds of conversion experiences and accounts. Religious and political conversions figure prominently in published work of all sorts, popular and scholarly, in many disciplines. Taken in conjunction with the other areas of interpretation and speculation we have identified, we could start to build up quite a strong account of local and disciplinary loyalties, identities, boundaries, and careers.

Conclusion

Many of the issues alluded to in this chapter will probably be familiar to its readers. We could not claim to have outlined a startlingly novel set of ideas about academic socialization in anthropology, nor do we claim to have said anything new about how to go about theorizing and generalizing from our data. We have chosen the themes we discussed in the same way that we chose the data, because we hoped they would be familiar to our readers, or at least readily recognizable. Our point in this chapter has been to make explicit the dialogic relationship between analysis and theory, or to illustrate some of the ways in which we have and use ideas about our data. The processes of analysis do not end with the organization and categorization of the data; they go through to the elaboration of interpretive perspectives and concepts. It is not necessary to plunge into the complexities of grand theory. It is, however, necessary to have, use, and explore ideas.

The sorts of issues we have raised here relate to the generalization of research. This is a vexing question. Students and commentators are often troubled as to the generalizability of qualitative research, which is often small in scale and focused on particular social settings. We do not intend to go into all the debates and positions concerning this problem. We do believe, however, that qualitative researchers need to be clear about how they can and do "generalize." When we study local manifestations of culture and social order, we do not have to assume that such social worlds are representative of wider populations. We do not normally treat our research sites or our informants as if they were samples in a statistical sense. On the other hand, our ideas are not confined to the detailed description of the local. In developing and refining, or indeed creating, concepts we aim—as we have suggested—to transcend the local and the particular. Abductive inferences lead us from specific cases or findings toward generic levels that allow us to move conceptually across a wide range of social contexts.

The relationship between the particular and the generic is of a different order from that between a sample and a population. The generalizability of our inferences and our ideas should be thought about carefully; however, we argue that it should not overly preoccupy us. Wolcott (1994) problematizes generalizability by suggesting that there is no one single "correct" interpretation of a social setting or event. Qualitative research captures multiple versions of multiple realities. We do need to reconcile the particular and the universal, moving from the uniqueness of an individual case or setting to an understanding of the more general processes at work. Transcending the local and the particular is important but should be seen within the context of ensuring that our analyses are methodologically and rhetorically convincing. Miller and Crabtree (1994, p. 348) put one view as follows: "local context and the human story, of which each individual and community study is a reflection, are the primary goals of qualitative research and not generalizability."

We, on the other hand, would not wish to draw such a sharp distinction between the local and the general. We believe that every delineation of the particular should be informed by an understanding of more general forms and processes. The generalizing we engage in should always remain firmly grounded in the empirical details of the local. It is important, however, to recognize that the sort of generalization we aim at is not necessarily the goal of all researchers who seek to generalize their findings. In studying a particular setting, a single case, an individual actor, or a small group of people, we do not normally expect to extrapolate from that directly to a given population (of cases, settings, or persons). We do not generalize in the way that a survey researcher hopes to extend his or her findings from a sample to a population. We do not normally work with that kind of view of representation, for we do not normally think of our local research settings as being "representative" or "typical" of a known population of social worlds.

This is not an excuse for wild speculation, nor for a cavalier disregard for the empirical justification for particular ideas and propositions. What it means, however, is that qualitative data, analyzed with close attention to detail, understood in terms of their internal patterns and forms, should be used to develop theoretical ideas about social processes and cultural forms that have relevance beyond those data themselves. Such intellectual work calls for a creative as well as a disciplined interaction with qualitative data.

Suggestions for Further Reading

Denzin, N. K. (1992). *Symbolic interactionism and cultural studies.* Oxford, UK: Blackwell.

> *An important example of contemporary interpretation and theory in a tradition that has informed much ethnographic research.*

Geertz, C. (1973). *The interpretation of cultures.* New York: Basic Books.
Geertz, C. (1983). *Local knowledge: Further essays in interpretive anthropology.* New York: Basic Books.

> *Two volumes in which Geertz explores and documents the interpretive work of anthropological reasoning.*

Gubrium, J. (1988). *Analyzing field reality.* Newbury Park, CA: Sage.

> *Gives excellent insights into processes of formal analysis from qualitative fieldwork, based on the author's extensive field research in organizational settings.*

Hammersley, M. (1989). *The dilemma of qualitative method: Herbert Blumer and the Chicago tradition.* London: Routledge and Kegan Paul.

> *Examines some of the recurrent epistemological problems and theoretical roots of ethnography and interpretive sociology.*

Stanley, L., & Wise, S. (1993). *Breaking out again: Feminist ontology and epistemology.* London: Routledge and Kegan Paul.

> *Explicitly links a feminist perspective with interpretive approaches to the sociology of everyday life.*

Strauss, A. L. (1995). Notes on the nature and development of general theories. *Qualitative Inquiry, 1*(1), 7-18.

> *A valuable discussion of the relationship between theories of different sorts and grounded theorizing.*

7

Complementary Strategies of Computer-Aided Analysis

Using Computers

Many of the analytic strategies we have described can be supported through the use of computer software. The fact that we have not commented specifically on such software does not reflect a Luddite rejection of information technology on our part. On the contrary, we believe that computing can be a key feature of contemporary qualitative data analysis. We are convinced, however, that it is important to identify the relevant analytic strategies before turning to the computer for analytic support. It is important to recognize that contemporary software can be used to help implement and develop all the analytic approaches that we have outlined.

The structure of this chapter reflects the development of the book as a whole. We will discuss the use of computers to create and store qualitative data and for the general management of the research process. We will describe the use of software in the various tasks associated with coding data and the use of codes to retrieve and sort data. Although software is now being used most commonly for the coding and retrieval of data segments, that is by no means its only application to qualitative data analysis. Appropriate software also can help us to examine textual and semantic features of our data, aiding in the construction of vocabularies, folk taxonomies, and narrative form and content. We also look at ways in which computers can help us to visualize and display our ideas and analyses. This leads us to consider how computer applications can help in the intellectual tasks of developing theoretical ideas.

In the course of this chapter, then, we comment on the use of computers in the development of strategic approaches to qualitative data analysis. We write of specific software to illustrate the more general issues. It is not our intent to provide a systematic and comprehensive review of the entire field, still less to comment on all the available software. Fortunately, there are other sources to which the reader can be referred (e.g., Tesch, 1990; Weitzman & Miles, 1995). We will refer to other publications that deal in greater depth with specific applications. (See also our suggestions for further reading at the end of the chapter.)

We reiterate that no single software package can be made to perform qualitative data analysis in and of itself. The appropriate use of software depends on appreciation of the kind of data being analyzed and of the analytic purchase the researcher wants to obtain on those data. It is, we believe, vitally important that researchers recognize the diversity of approaches that can be facilitated via computer-aided qualitative data analysis. As Lonkila (1995) suggests, there is a danger in the current use of software—reflecting in part the relative prominence of some programs, rather than an intrinsic bias in the technology—that reflects a convergence toward one dominant analytic mode. Such convergence is not necessary, and it is certainly not necessary to endorse a version of technological determinism in order to exploit the value of contemporary computing strategies. Indeed, blind faith in the technology undoubtedly would restrict data analysis and methodological reflection.

Some indication of the functions and variety of applications of software is indicated by the list provided in Miles and Huberman (1994, p. 44):

1. Making notes in the field
2. Writing up or transcribing fieldnotes
3. Editing: correcting, extending, or revising fieldnotes

4. Coding: attaching key words or tags to segments of text and making them available for inspection

5. Storage: keeping text in an organized database

6. Search and retrieval: locating relevant segments of text and making them available for inspection

7. Data "linking": connecting relevant data segments and forming categories, clusters, or networks of information

8. Memoing: writing reflective commentaries on some aspect of the data as a basis for deeper analysis

9. Content analysis: counting frequencies, sequences, or locations of words and phrases

10. Data display: placing selected or reduced data in a condensed, organized format, such as a matrix or network, for inspection

11. Conclusion drawing and verification: aiding the analyst to interpret displayed data and to test or confirm findings

12. Theory building: developing systematic, conceptually coherent explanations of findings; testing hypotheses

13. Graphic mapping: creating diagrams that depict findings or theories

14. Preparing interim and final reports

In the remainder of this chapter, we will touch on most of these. We will not do so in a totally comprehensive fashion. To do so would demand yet another volume, and there are other sources that provide much more extensive accounts than this one chapter (see the suggestions for further reading at the end of the chapter).

In constructing the remainder of this chapter, we have followed the general logic of the book as a whole. We depart from our previous practice of illustrating particular methodological strategies and tactics with our own data. We make cross-references back to the relevant chapters where we did so when we discuss particular methodological tasks. To provide detailed empirical examples in sufficient detail to demonstrate all the various software applications would demand a much longer treatment than is possible here. It is, for example, worth drawing attention to the length of a work such as Weitzman and Miles (1995), which provides a systematic overview of the software with no attempt to work through analyses in detail and runs to more than 300 double-columned, large-format pages. Moreover, the exercise of analyzing the same data via complementary programs already has been published (Weaver & Atkinson, 1994, 1996).

Creating and Managing Data

Most of the data used in qualitative research are textual, derived from fieldnotes, transcribed interviews, transcriptions of naturally occurring action, documents, and the like. The first task for which the computer is perfectly suited, is the preparation of such textual data. It was not long ago that field researchers relied on handwritten notes or typewritten materials. By contrast, it is now routine in academic life to use word processors to create and store files of textual materials. It therefore makes sense for researchers to exploit the taken-for-granted technology and base much of their work on text files created with word processors. As Weitzman and Miles (1995, p. 11) say of word processors:

> These are basically designed for the production and revision of text and are thus helpful for taking, transcribing, writing up or editing fieldnotes for transcribing interviews, for memoing, for preparing files for coding and analysis, and for writing report text.

They go on to note that the potential of word processors for analytic purposes is restricted, and it is necessary to go from the word processor to more specialized programs in order to explore those files in more productive ways. This is not a view that is universally endorsed. Some researchers have come to an informed decision that the facilities and functions of the most advanced contemporary word processors can carry out most of the analytic tasks that the practical researcher needs. This is a conclusion reached by Stanley and Temple (1996). They tried out a number of specialized programs for the analysis of qualitative data sets, including materials from the Mass Observation archive, and compared them with Word for Windows. (Mass Observation was an extensive project in the United Kingdom in which large numbers of people kept diaries and created other kinds of data.) Stanley and Temple (1996, p. 167) examined The Ethnograph, NUD.IST, askSAM, ETHNO, and InfoSelect as examples of specialized software and concluded that

> having used both Word for Windows and the five dedicated packages, our conclusion is that qualitative researchers should consider using a good wordprocessing package as their basic analytic aid, and that only if they want to do something that this package cannot do should they then consider using a dedicated package. That is, for many researchers, the facilities provided in

a good wordprocessing package will be sufficient to the analysis required, or, if not, the researcher would be best advised to use a dedicated package for specific research tasks. The seduction of the dedicated packages is that because they have capacities, these are then used to the limits possible.

This is an extremely sensible piece of general advice in that any researcher should use to their full extent whatever resources are available before seeking out more specialized, esoteric research tools. Many practitioners would dissent from Stanley and Temple. As we will illustrate in the remainder of this chapter, there is a range of software available that allows one to use textual and other materials in useful ways. It is valuable to keep in mind, however, that such software facilitates complementary analytic strategies. It is vital to identify one's analytic goals and interests and to use computer software accordingly. There is no one software package that will do the analysis in itself.

The analytic software that deals with textual materials mostly imports data that are created using a standard word processor. It therefore makes sense to translate textual materials, such as fieldnotes or interview transcripts, into text files. There are, moreover, practical management tasks that can be accomplished in the normal desktop computing environment. Data files can be stored, copied, shared, and transferred rapidly and efficiently on disk. Normal routines of file management can be used to organize data sets into directories (e.g., for different research sites, fieldwork periods, samples, etc.). Fisher (1995) points out that many standard features of personal computers can be used to advantage in the general organization and management of qualitative research. In this respect, qualitative research is no different from any other kind of scholarly inquiry.

Fisher provides a useful review of how desktop computing can promote research management. Relevant tasks include maintenance of databases relating to research sites, informants, samples, research contacts, or gatekeepers, and so on; electronic communication as a means of collaboration with research team members and others; management of references and bibliographies; preparation of materials for distribution and publication; and preparation of materials for presentation to live audiences. The use of such resources for the management of research, maintenance of files and records, and production of research output is now part of the craft knowledge of most researchers and can be used to great advantage in parallel with software that is more specifically tied to the work of qualitative data analysis. As Miles and Huberman (1994, p. 45) remind us, the management of qualitative data involves more than the preparation of raw text from fieldnotes or transcripts. Attention must be given to formatting those materials, such as numbering lines, paragraphs, and pages; cross-referencing and indexing; including contextual and other headings; and including summaries or abstracts of longer data documents. These are all significant tasks in data organization and management. They are all necessary preliminaries to detailed analysis, and many are part of broader sets of analytic procedures. All can be enhanced or aided by the use of computer software.

Coding and Retrieving Data

Following the overall structure of the previous chapters, we turn to the use of computer software for coding qualitative, textual data. Generically, such software implements what is known as a code-and-retrieve strategy. At its simplest, this approach recapitulates the tasks of manual coding and searching. On the whole, however, the software allows—even encourages—the analyst to do more with that strategy than manual techniques would support.

Code-and-retrieve programs are designed to allow the analyst to mark segments of data by attaching code words to those segments, and then to search the data, retrieving and collecting all segments identified by the same code or by some combination of code words. As Weitzman and Miles (1995, p. 17) summarize this software strategy, the programs "take over the kinds of marking up, cutting, sorting, reorganizing, and collecting tasks qualitative researchers used to do with scissors and paper and note cards."

It is arguable that, in terms of general methodology as opposed to practical data management, the code-and-retrieve strategy offers no great conceptual advance over manual data sorting. Many programs use that strategy as their major mode of data handling. They include The Ethnograph, QUALPRO, Kwalitan, Martin, HyperQual2, NUD.IST, and ATLAS/ti. Those programs do more than coding alone, and there are others (some of which we mention in a later section) that are based on some notion of coding as well but add further analytic functions (see

Weitzman & Miles, 1995, pp. 148-203). The Ethnograph and NUD.IST are probably the most widely used and best known of the programs that are predicated on a coding strategy. That does not mean necessarily that they are the best—indeed, there is no single best software—but it reflects in part when they entered the market and the general level of acquaintance of the research community.

The computer-based approaches of this sort depend on procedures for coding the text (such as interview transcripts, fieldnotes, transcribed recordings, documents). This means marking the text in order to tag particular chunks or segments of that text. Code words are attached to discrete stretches of data. The purpose of the software is, at root, twofold. First, it facilitates the attachment of those codes to the strips of data. Second, it allows the researcher to retrieve all instances in the data that share a code. Such code-and-retrieve approaches are exemplified in programs such as The Ethnograph, one of the most widely disseminated and used applications.

The underlying logic of coding and searching for coded segments differs little, if at all, from that of manual techniques. There is no great conceptual advance over the indexing of typed or even manuscript notes and transcripts or of marking them physically with code words, colored inks, and the like. In practice, though, the computer can offer many advantages. The speed and comprehensiveness of searches is an undoubted benefit: The computer does not search the data files until it comes up with the first example that will "do" to illustrate an argument, nor will it stop after it has found only one or a few apposite quotes or vignettes. As we indicate later in the chapter, the capacity for comprehensive searching is often a valuable part of hypothesis testing in the course of data analysis. The software has additional merits that definitely mark advances on the practical value of manual coding and searching: It can cope with multiple and overlapping codes, and it can conduct multiple searches, using more than one code word simultaneously. Software such as The Ethnograph allows the analyst to combine code words in order to facilitate complex searches. In other words, the analyst can use the operators AND, OR, and NOT to combine code words in complex searches. The software can handle very large numbers of codings. In purely mechanical terms, therefore, the computer can help implement more comprehensive and more complex searching tasks than can be performed by manual techniques.

Many software packages allow the researcher to do more than code data. Software such as The Ethnograph, Kwalitan, and NUD.IST permits the user to do things such as attaching analytic or other memoranda to specific points in the text. The aim is to incorporate many of the key tasks of grounded theory strategies (as discussed in Chapter 6) within the software applications. Throughout the process of analyzing data and reflecting on fieldwork, the researcher needs to maintain analytic, methodological, and other memoranda. There is, therefore, every advantage in incorporating such memo writing within the use of computing software.

There is, therefore, a close relationship between the processes of coding and the use of computers. It should be evident that coding data for use with computing programs and the retrieval of coded segments of text is not, in our view, analysis. At root, it is a way of organizing data in order to search them. It is a useful part of the research process. Anyone now embarking on a sustained piece of qualitative research should seriously consider the potential value of computer-aided storage and retrieval. Such a strategy of data organization should be thought about at an early stage in the research planning, not tacked on at the end of the data collection phase of fieldwork. Qualitative research is not enhanced if researchers decide they will take their data and "put it through the computer," as if that substituted for the intellectual work of analysis.

Language, Meaning, and Narrative

Contemporary uses of computer software do not follow precisely the analytic perspectives we outlined in Chapters 3 and 4. Nevertheless, there are software applications that can readily facilitate the detailed exploration of language, even of narrative structures. The former are mostly general programs for the analysis of text rather than specific ones to qualitative research, as are the code-and-retrieve applications previously outlined.

As we have indicated, it is one of the strengths of computer-assisted analysis that it facilitates the rapid and comprehensive scrutiny of large volumes of textual data. Such searching capacities are characteristic of programs that can be used to investigate aspects of language and meaning. Generic software types have been developed and widely implemented for the systematic searching of textual data sets. Their practical uses are various, including indexing large volumes of documentary sources, searching them for particular terms (such as proper names), or locating specific sequences of words and characters. Such programs, called text retrievers, are described thus by Weitzman and Miles (1995, p. 17):

> They specialize in finding all the instances of words, phrases (or other character strings), and combinations of these you are interested in locating, in one or several files. They can often do interesting operations with what they find, like marking or sorting the found text into new files, or linking annotations and memos to the original data, or launching new processes or other software packages to work on the data.

It is often useful to use such software to search extensively within a data set of interview transcripts, fieldnotes, transcribed interactions, or documentary sources. A comparison with coding may help to point out the value of this approach. When we code data, we tag segments of data with terms that represent analytic themes. We may find ourselves using as code words shorthand terms that stand for broad sociological or anthropological concepts. There is no necessary relationship between those analytic concepts and the terms used by the original social actors. In the anthropology data, we might, for example, code many segments of interview data as being about *isolation*. That code might cover expressions of personal and intellectual isolation as part of the experience of the research student. It goes without saying that the interview respondents will not all have described their own experiences and those of others only in terms of the word "isolation." They will have used a wide variety of words and phrases to capture the range of emotions and actions that may be captured by the category *isolation* (such as loneliness, alone, isolation, nobody to turn to). There are many good reasons to explore the kinds of terms—the vocabularies and folk terms—that informants actually use. Unless one is going to treat every word as a code word and undertake the laborious work of replicating them as codes in a program such as The Ethnograph, then a text retriever of some sort can be a very useful tool.

It is possible to construct a comprehensive thesaurus (a word list or dictionary) for the entire data set, from which can be identified items of vocabulary for further, more detailed, examination. In addition, words can be sorted into concordances, that is, retrieved and displayed in their immediate context. Words can be counted and sorted into relative frequencies. In themselves, these types of textual searching are not conceptually powerful or illuminating. They can be used for elementary types of content analysis, and programs of this sort have been recommended for such work. They are, however, more usefully thought of in terms of potential aids in more imaginative and creative kinds of analytic activity. As Weaver and Atkinson (1994, p. 77) write about the general approach, these programs

> enable researchers to explore their data directly, by searching for lexical items and analysing the lexical content of fieldnotes, interview transcripts, and any other documents of interest. By prompting the program to produce a vocabulary list, we can examine the vocabularies displayed by respondents, and thereby gain insights into how people articulate phenomena, or through language make sense of their everyday lives. Similarly, we may find that a certain word dominates interviews with a certain person, or certain social encounters, which may be analytically significant. Also, these programs enable us to conduct searches not only on particular words, but also combinations of words. In these searches, researchers can specify conditions for text to be retrieved, regarding the proximity of one word to another, by using a variety of Boolean operators in a search string.

In other words, complex searches can be performed (as in code-and-retrieve operations) by combining terms with combinations of AND, OR, and NOT (the "Boolean operators" referred to above) to develop, for example, synonym lists.

Programs often help in the exploration of texts by allowing "wild card" characters. A search may be undertaken using the root of the word plus the wild card character, thus capturing all the forms of the term in question. To give a concrete example, in searching the data about PhD students and their advisers, we might well find ourselves searching out all the instances where students had mentioned their supervisor, the process of supervision, or related terms, such as supervising. We could find every instance matching the sequence SUPERVIS*.

In the same way, we saw in Chapter 4 how we might start to build up an analysis of a domain such as *the field*. Given the importance of fieldwork to PhD research in anthropology, we would expect to have a code for it, using The Ethnograph or a similar program. That would not guarantee finding every reference to the field or its equivalent. We could search the entire corpus of interviews for FIELD*, which would find every instance of field, fieldwork, fieldnotes, and so on. A comprehensive and systematic search of that sort could well be a valuable preliminary to the thorough examination of anthropologists' own folk terminologies. By examining the *contexts* in which such terms are used, we would start to examine the range of connotations associated with such key terms, the kinds of imagery and metaphors associated with them, and the distribution of such terms among the informants. The capacity of software to retrieve selected words or strings of words in context is a vital function in performing such analytic work. Again, one must emphasize that the real analytic work is created by the analyst, using the output of such a search as the raw materials. Software will not itself complete a domain analysis, but it can be an enormously useful tool in doing the groundwork for such a task. Tesch (1990, p. 182) highlighted the value of such lexical searching:

> Even researchers who normally deal with interpretational analysis, in which they handle meaningful chunks of text rather than words, could find some of these programs' options helpful. For instance, a researcher may notice that a certain concept is alluded to in his/her data. As a validity check s/he could create a list of synonyms and phrases that capture that concept, and explore whether, and how frequently, it was directly addressed by the participants in his/her research.

Weaver and Atkinson (1994) are in no doubt that text-retrieval, or lexical-searching, strategies are an important element in the research process. They suggest that these are especially useful tools during early, exploratory scrutiny of the data. They also suggest that the results of such examination of the data can yield unpredictable results when compared with coding strategies, because codings reflect the analyst's own decisions, while lexical searching can be much more open ended. Text-retrieval strategies are not dependent on the kind of labor-intensive work involved in adding codes, so they can be used for more speculative, freewheeling kinds of exploration at low cost. There are many programs that perform elements of text retrieval and can be used productively for qualitative data analysis. Weitzman and Miles (1995) review Meta-morph, Orbis, Sonar Professional, The Text Collector, Word Cruncher, and ZyINDEX. Weaver and Atkinson (1994) based their analysis on FYI3000 Plus, an older program.

There are very few programs that will help directly with the analysis of narrative structures. The software generally is more valuable for the organization and retrieval of content than the discovery of form or structure. One should pay attention, however, to one especially interesting program, developed by Heise, called ETHNO. This program helps in the conduct of narrative analysis. The actual use of the program is not always easy to follow, but it holds out intriguing possibilities for the formal analyses of narrative. The analytic approach is not identical to that advocated by Labov or Cortazzi (see our discussion in Chapter 3). ETHNO is a particularly interesting program that differs in style and purpose from many that are more familiar to the community of qualitative researchers. It is designed primarily to deal with "verbally defined events," including narratives (written or spoken). The analyst must define the events to be analyzed from within the narrative. The software is then used to construct a model of the relationship among those narrated events.

The analyst must first identify the events manually. They are then entered into the computer, and the program generates a diagram of the events and their arrangement. The analysis is based on four principles: (a) events have prerequisites, (b) an event cannot occur until all of its prerequisites have occurred, (c) the occurrence of an event uses up its prerequisites, and (d) an event is not repeated until the conditions it created are used up by some consequences (Corsaro & Heise, 1990; Mangabeira, 1995). The software uses these logical principles to construct the diagram of events and their interrelationships. The analyst enters the first narrated event on screen, then enters subsequent events in turn. At each new event, ETHNO requires the user to respond to simple prompts in order to specify the logical relationship between the two events. The researcher goes on entering events and responding to the program's prompts. The program thus progressively builds up a diagram of the relationships implied within the narrative of events. As the structure is built up, the software draws on previously entered information and infers relationships that already have been established.

Heise (1988) demonstrated the use of ETHNO in an analysis of the story of Little Red Riding Hood. It clearly can be used to construct models of a wide variety of narratives. Comparison of the models of different narratives may reveal not only different events or narrative elements but also different relationships among the constituent parts. ETHNO establishes, as we have indicated, *logical* structures from narrated events and is not used to construct formal structures such as those we described in Chapter 3. Nevertheless, in conjunction with those kinds of analytic models, ETHNO can be a useful tool for the representation of narrative structures and for analysis of logical properties of the narrated reconstructions of events. For that reason, the analyst may construct his or her own reconstruction of events (such as rituals) and use ETHNO to tease out and compare structures of sequences of action that have been observed (cf. Corsaro & Heise, 1990).

ETHNO also has functions relevant to domain analysis through general semantics. It permits the analyst (or indeed, an individual informant) to construct taxonomies of terms through a series of structured questions. This can be an extremely useful heuristic device. If the researcher chooses to use the program to undertake a domain analysis, then ETHNO can help to make explicit the knowledge that is being represented and the relationships among the elements in the domain or taxonomy. It is by no means necessary to subscribe to a strong version of semantic or semiotic analysis in order to recognize the general heuristic value of such an approach.

Theory Building and Hypothesis Testing

The kind of representation that is generated by ETHNO's taxonomic analysis is facilitated, on a different scale, by several code-based programs, among others. Programs such as NUD.IST and ATLAS/ti are explicitly designed to encourage the researcher to do more than undertake the coding and fragmentation of the data. They encourage the analyst to build up systematic relationships among the code categories. They are often referred to as having theory-building functions, although one should be careful not to imply that "theory" can be constructed mechanistically through the aggregation of codes or categories. Together with other, similar, programs (such as Kwalitan), software such as NUD.IST is claimed to support the generation of grounded theory. As Richards and Richards (1990, pp. 9-10) argue,

> NUD.IST supports "grounded theory" research . . . a method that has little
> to do with coding and retrieval of text segments, but a lot to do with catching
> and interrogating meanings emergent from data. "Coding" in that method
> refers to a very different process from the labelling of lines of text for retrieval.
> Rather it is about construction and exploration of new categories *and* points
> of view in the data, linking these to text.

At the heart of the theory-building procedures in NUD.IST is the fact that all codes are arranged into hierarchically structured trees. In contrast to the simplest systems of coding, therefore, NUD.IST arranges codes in relation to one another, with orders of generality or specificity. In working with the data, adding or modifying codes and coding schemes, one is therefore simultaneously modifying the structure of interrelated codes. The product of coding (in NUD.IST terminology, indexing) the data is not simply a mechanism for searching and retrieving chunks of data; it is also the conceptual framework indicated by the index system itself. The arrangements of codes into hierarchical relationships is not automatic: The analyst must initially specify the relationship with other codes.

It is this approach to the conceptual structure implicit in many analyses, and rendered explicit in NUD.IST, that makes this software attractive to many actual or potential users. It is not, however, the only software product that encourages the explication of such conceptual links and structures. ATLAS/ti and HyperRESEARCH, among others, support similar functions. ATLAS/ti, for example, has a number of functions that encourage the analyst to create explicit links among elements, such as codes. These and other analytic links (such as those linking passages in the original data) can be displayed graphically in ATLAS/ti. Using the network editor, these graphically represented relationships can be modified on screen. The analyst can use the editing function as a heuristic device in exploring relationships among categories or concepts; they can, for example, be arranged into hierarchical relationships. In addition to having powerful and revealing ways of searching text, therefore, ATLAS/ti is an especially useful tool for the analyst who wishes to explicate and to visualize emergent patterns of concepts and the links among them. In effect, as we indicate below, it can be argued that the ordered set of codes and the relationships among them constitutes the researcher's knowledge base. In other words, the emergent framework of concepts and ideas is an ordered set of relationships that parallels the database of the original texts.

It is, of course, not necessary to base the representation of concepts and relationships on coding strategies. There are several generic programs that help one to develop and display conceptual schemes, semantic networks, and the like. In other words, one can take the ideas derived from other kinds of strategies—such as possible elements for a domain analysis—and use network-mapping software to build and display those semantic relationships. We have not used any of the relevant programs at Cardiff, and we do not comment on them any further here. Several are described in detail by Weitzman and Miles (1995, pp. 266-309), who also summarize their general characteristics:

> You can see your variables shown as nodes (typically rectangles or ellipses), linked to other nodes by lines or arrows representing specified relationships (such as "belongs to," "leads to," "is a kind of"). The networks are not just casually hand drawn, but are real "semantic networks" that develop from your data and your concepts (usually higher level codes), and the relationships you see among them. (Weitzman & Miles, 1995, p. 18)

Weitzman and Miles themselves review Inspiration, MECA, Meta Design, and SemNet as representatives of this software type. Such software clearly helps in the development of ideas, establishing links between ideas, mapping out possible organizing themes, and so on. One of the major strengths of software of this type is the strongly *visual* character of their representations. It is abundantly clear that qualitative data analysts often think most productively about their data through graphic displays of various sorts. In the study or the seminar room, one can draw on the chalkboard or doodle on scrap paper to create conceptual links and patterns. The computer now helps do similarly creative work with our data and our ideas.

There is no doubt that the strategic use of software can help in the crucial interactions between ideas and data. The important issue here is not simply the generation of analytic categories and concepts. There is usually a need to systematically check those ideas against the data. The shuttling process between ideas and data means that emergent concepts and hypotheses must always be checked, modified, abandoned, or developed. Formally, one may choose to think of such a process as one of hypothesis examination and verification (Kelle, Sibert, Shelly, Hesse-Biber, & Huber, 1995). As those authors put it,

> It is in this area of qualitative hypothesis examination and refinement where researchers can draw the greatest benefits from *computer aided methods* for the coding and retrieval of textual data. If qualitative data were not organized and structured, the search for evidence or counter-evidence would be a practically insurmountable task: every time a researcher examined a certain hypothesis he or she would have to re-read several hundred, or several thousand transcript pages. This would make it very difficult to withstand the temptation to "validate" theoretical concepts with some hastily gathered quotations, thereby neglecting negative evidence contained elsewhere in the data. On the contrary, the use of storage-and-retrieval methods can go a long way towards helping to avoid those dangers that are always prevalent in qualitative analysis due to the ever-present data overload. (p. 107)

Here it is claimed that the capacities of computer software to help organize and interrogate a large corpus of data exhaustively may contribute directly to the comprehensive testing and modification of hypotheses that are grounded in those data.

Some uses of qualitative analysis software may go further toward hypothesis generation and testing. Sibert and Shelly (1995), for example, describe the use of *logic programming* for the development and testing of hypotheses. Such programming involves use of computational methods to produce formal propositions about the researcher's knowledge base (as represented in the coding scheme). In a similar vein, Hesse-Biber and Dupuis (1995) commend the use of computer-aided techniques to test hypotheses. They describe an *automatic hypothesis tester* based on the identification of co-occurring codes. A search procedure using Boolean operators (AND, OR, and NOT) permits the researcher to build up complex and precise searches of the data.

Hesse-Biber and Dupuis base their discussion on their own development of the program HyperRESEARCH, although the functions they describe are by no means confined to that software alone. The hypothesis-testing element of the software, in addition to more basic code-and-retrieve aspects, is claimed to reside in the ability of the researcher to construct "if ... then" propositions and to test them by exploring the overlapping, nesting, or proximity of codes in the data. It must be born in mind—as the authors themselves acknowledge—that such an approach rests on the assumption that the co-occurrence or proximity of codes in the data set can be used to infer relationships of analytic significance.

Several programs allow the researcher to examine co-occurrences of codes, and the general strategy may often prove to be a valuable heuristic device. It is far less certain that it can be described strictly as a general means for hypothesis testing. Given the inherently unpredictable structure of qualitative data, co-occurrence or proximity does not necessarily imply an analytically significant relationship among categories. It is as shaky an assumption as one that assumes greater significance of commonly occurring codes. Analytic significance is not guaranteed by frequency, nor is a relationship guaranteed by proximity. Nevertheless, a general heuristic value may be found for such methods for checking out ideas and data, as part of the constant interplay between the two as the research process unfolds.

Hypertext and Hypermedia

We have tried to indicate in this chapter that computer programs can help the qualitative analyst to undertake important tasks of data management, retrieval, and analysis. Some of those computing strategies essentially recapitulate the logic and the procedures of manual data handling, as in the simplest code-and-retrieve functions. Other strategies build on those procedures but include functions that could not be accommodated under manual methods, such as use of Boolean operators in multiple-code searches. Others readily exploit features of general software that are less dependent on manual procedures of data sorting and more directly dependent on the special characteristics of computer software.

We turn now to one strategy of analysis and representation that is, arguably, the most thoroughly grounded in contemporary information technology. We venture to suggest that it provides the basis for an analytic and representational strategy that promises to make the most of contemporary information technology. It is potentially most faithful to the representational flexibility and diversity that best capture contemporary qualitative research (Weaver & Atkinson, 1994).

Hypertext is not an especially new idea, but it may prove to be one whose time has come. In essence, its underlying ideas are fairly simple.

They are predicated on the view that the reader's relationship with a given text (such as a literary work or a work of reference) should not necessarily be restructured to the linear reading of that text in a predetermined sequence. The hypertext approach is nonlinear, akin to browsing and following up cross-references. Hypertext software allows a reader to follow, and indeed to create, diverse pathways through a collection of textual materials. Hypertext applications thus support a much more interactive relationship between the text and its readers. Readers, in a sense, become authors of their own reading; they are not simply the passive recipients of a determinate textual form.

This approach has exciting possibilities for qualitative researchers. Many people working with qualitative data—whether they use field-notes, interviews, oral history, or documentary sources—feel frustrated by the necessity of imposing a single linear order on those materials. It is, after all, part of the *raison d'être* of ethnographic and similar approaches that the anthropologist, sociologist, historian, psychologist, or whoever recognizes the complexity of social interrelatedness. We recognize the overdetermination of culture, in that there are multiple, densely coded influences among and between different domains and institutions. It is part of the attraction of hypertext solutions that a sense of dense interconnectedness is preserved—enhanced, even—while linearity is discarded.

Dey (1995) commends the use of hypertext links, not least in the interests of reducing the fragmentation of qualitative data (cf. Atkinson, 1992a). Dey also suggests that "technology has been used to enhance rather than transform traditional methods" (1995, p. 69). His own program, Hypersoft, was developed to facilitate the establishment of "hyperlinks" between segments of data text. Dey (1995, p. 75) argues that "because we can link text segments, we can analyse data in ways not previously practicable. We can retain information about narrative and process." In other words, it is not necessary to recapitulate the physical disaggregation of the data that is characteristic of cut-and-paste approaches and elementary code-and-retrieve methods. Dey does not go on to draw out the full potential of a true hypertext environment: He does not discuss or illustrate the use of such a strategy for the writing and representation of qualitative analysis more generally. We suggest that one of the most exciting possibilities of hypertext software lies precisely in its capacities to support novel forms of representation.

The basic implementation of a hypertext application is fairly simple. It is based on the idea of the "button," which marks a point in the text (or other data) at which various functions can be performed. A *link button* allows the user to go to another point in the data to make a suitable cross-reference or to pick up another instance of "the same" occurrence or a conceptually related instance. Such links join "nodes." The analyst can create dense webs or networks of such links, which can then be "navigated" in various explorations of the data.

By contrast, an *expansion button* allows the analyst to attach additional text to the node. Activating a button can reveal, for example, an analytic memorandum about an actor or a given incident, or an explanation of a particular item of situated vocabulary. In working with his or her corpus of data, therefore, the analyst can use hypertext applications to create complicated linkages among different items and can attach all sorts of explanations and other helpful materials to them. In addition to explanatory material or memos, we might also attach additional materials, such as career details of individual respondents, their family trees, or details about their domestic lives.

In principle, the range of such information that can be linked to specific buttons is limitless. If we were using such an approach with our anthropology data, for example, our procedures might include the following operations. We would not have separate phases of data storage, retrieval, analysis, and writing up. Instead, we would prepare the data sets of interviews, documents, and other representations together with our sociological commentary in such a way as to allow the reader to navigate her or his unique pathways through them all. The reader (working at a multimedia workstation rather than reading a book or journal) therefore would not be constrained to inspect only those extracts from the data that we had chosen for illustrative purposes. By activating links across all the data files (created by us or by the reader, or both), readers become analysts in their own right. Furthermore, the full possibilities of hypertext and hypermedia mean that it is not too fanciful to think in the near future of hypertext-based ethnographies in which the reader can activate sound and visual playbacks, so that original documents can be inspected in the context of the ethnographic analysis. One may thus go beyond the purely textual by working in a *hypermedia* environment, so that still and moving images, sound, and other representations can be included. When an informant talks about field research, we might click a link button or an expansion button to bring in photographs or moving images of the field settings themselves, together with the voice of the informant describing his or her experiences. In the course of descriptions of academic departments, we could draw in graphic representations of their physical layout, lists of faculty members, genealogies of their leading lights over the generations, references to and extracts from key publications by our informants, and so on. These would all in practice create ethical problems, but we are concerned here with the analytic and representational possibilities that are on offer, not their precise application.

The work of analysis with a hypertext approach need never be complete. The analyst can go on creating links and adding information indefinitely. There will always be practical limitations, of course, and there are also limits placed by human cognitive capacities. There is, for example, the widely recognized possibility of becoming lost in "hyperspace" if the whole thing becomes too complicated and the user cannot get back to where he or she started, or cannot navigate to where she or he actually wants to be. It is apparent, however, that once the relevant linkages and expansions have been set up, with appropriate introductory material and commentary, the resulting hypertext *is* a form of analysis. It is not necessary to recast the whole thing into a conventional, linear, printed text. Hypertext applications are authoring systems, often used to develop and deliver instructional materials. The construction of a hypertext based on systematically ordered and suitably edited qualitative data thus collapses the processes of analysis and writing.

In other words, looked at from the other end of the process, a reader would not settle down with a book as "the ethnography" or "the history" but instead would interact with data and analytic commentary in a flexible and interactive way. Reading through introductory and explanatory text, for example, the reader—by clicking on a button—could choose to examine relevant data in some detail, go to other examples of the same phenomenon, or examine extracts from relevant literature (a far more user-friendly process than the average literature review!). He or she thus picks a path through a variegated collection of texts and cross-references. It is for this and similar reasons that it is sometimes claimed that hypertext approaches work with a postmodernist approach to texts. It is certainly the case that hypertext helps to preserve a sense of complexity, intertextuality, and nonlinearity.

In Chapter 5, we wrote briefly about the relevance of visual representations. In this chapter, we have referred to the use of computer software to generate visual displays as part of the heuristic exploration of data and in the development of theoretical ideas. Hypertext/hypermedia provides one powerful context for working with visual data generally. We have suggested that although many qualitative researchers think visually, they pay insufficient attention to visual materials as part of their data collection, analysis, and writing. Hypermedia software can provide an especially useful way to link textual and visual materials, in flexible ways, in the analysis and representation of social worlds, actors, and cultures.

It is possible, for example, to construct a hypermedia environment in which links are established not only between segments of text but also between text and data of many other sorts, including visual materials, such as video images and still photographs. The hypermedia approach means that such visual materials are not incorporated merely as illustrations to the main body of text; they are given full weight as part of the work of representation. The reader of the hypermedia ethnography, for example, could readily gain access to a large number of visual materials in a flexible manner. Consequently, the author/analyst can freely incorporate detailed commentary on such materials, together with the images themselves, into the ethnography. Hypermedia accounts of our anthropologists might, hypothetically, draw not only on volumes of textual data, such as interview transcripts, but also on visual evidence taken from the anthropologists' own fieldwork and their academic departments (always subject to access and ethical considerations). Informants' accounts of fieldwork experience could thus incorporate visual testimony.

Likewise, our investigations of material artifacts as memorabilia and self-presentational devices (a possibility referred to in Chapter 5) could incorporate visual representations of those artifacts directly. Our understanding of, for example, accounts and metaphors of "the field" thus could be paralleled and developed by a corresponding analysis of those concrete representations of the fields in question. We could thus compare directly the spoken accounts of fieldwork (always in the past or in the future, always elsewhere, always private) with the visual icons and memorabilia of field trips (present in time and space, bringing other cultures "home" to the academic setting, which is in turn rendered exotic). We could thus explore and re-present directly to the reader the multiple connotations of such concrete artifacts and their symbolic functions in the creation of a disciplinary and departmental collective identity. Iconography can thus be incorporated into textual materials (and vice versa) in a densely interlinked patterning of data and analysis.

The implementation of such an approach to analysis and dissemination is not easy. Data need to be edited—in order to preserve confidentiality and to render them comprehensible, for example. The nodes need to be identified and the relevant links and expansions put in place. Additional material must be entered into the database (and there may be copyright problems if extracts from the relevant literature are to be included). The opportunities are potentially wide, however, especially when we enter the world not only of hypertext but also of hypermedia. It is possible to incorporate not only textual materials but also information in other media. As we have suggested, the ethnographer may look forward to a time when a reader can choose to hear extracts from interviews or other spoken data, or to find video images when an expansion button is clicked on, or to have access to a wide array of graphic images. Given the extent to which ethnography proceeds through the concrete example and the actual type (cf. Atkinson, 1990; Edmondson, 1984) and to which it is grounded in the vivid reconstruction of everyday life, there is every likelihood of advances in ethnographic representation coming though such information technology. The ethnography itself might be published in hard copy, as a conventional book, but there might be another "ethnography," consisting of an array of information stored in different media, accessed via a computer and a CD-ROM through which the professional social scientist, the student, or the lay reader could navigate pathways and pick up information appropriate to respective interests and levels of sophistication.

The systems and software all exist now, and qualitative researchers are starting to exploit them. Predictions in this area are often doomed to failure, and one would be foolish to try to second guess how and to what extent possibilities will be exploited. There is no need to assume that all future ethnographers will become (or need to become) totally committed enthusiasts of information technology, any more than one need predict that fate for all literary critics, even though the same opportunities exist in the humanities. It will be a tragic irony, however, if ethnography ends up in the hands of the culturally and computationally illiterate because the majority of its practitioners insist on print technology for the presentation of their work.

Conclusion

In the course of this chapter, we introduced a number of computing strategies that parallel and complement the more general analytic approaches already outlined. There is no implication here that the qualitative researcher is bound to use any of the computer-aided strategies to which we refer. The important issue is that none of the computer programs will perform automatic data analysis. They all depend on researchers defining for themselves what analytic issues are to be explored, what ideas are important, and what modes of representation are most appropriate.

There is, as we have stressed repeatedly, a variety of analytic approaches that are perfectly proper. Many of them can be *aided* with computer software, and the computer can often help us perform data-handling tasks with speed and with comprehensive thoroughness. On the other hand, it would be wrong for qualitative researchers to allow the available software to drive their general research strategy. It is important to guard against the development of a single orthodoxy predicated on the assumptions and procedures built into contemporary software applications.

We have not attempted to provide a systematic review of the available software. Several of the volumes listed in the "Suggestions for Further Reading" should be consulted for technical specifications, hardware requirements, suppliers, prices, and so on. Our intent has been to follow the general logic of the rest of this book to show how contemporary software can be used to help achieve various analytic and representational tasks we have identified. Here, once more, we emphasize that the researcher should not try to seek out a single orthodoxy or think that there will be a single "best" software package. Such a solution is not in the nature of qualitative research. The student or researcher therefore should not regard this chapter or the other methodological literature we refer to as "consumer reports" on the software. It is important to bear in mind that software provides tools that can be used in various ways, and in various combinations, to realize a number of different analytic strategies.

Suggestions for Further Reading

Delany, P., & Landow, G. P. (Eds.). (1994). *Hypermedia and literary studies*. Cambridge: MIT Press.

A collection of essays that discuss the relevance of hypertext and hypermedia applications to the humanities, including reports of specific projects.

Fielding, N. G., & Lee, R. M. (Eds.). (1991). *Using computers in qualitative research*. London: Sage.

An important collection of papers, wide ranging in scope though far from comprehensive in their coverage of software types and specific programs.

Joyce, M. (1995). *Of two minds: Hypertext pedagogy and poetics*. Ann Arbor: University of Michigan Press.

A fascinating collection of essays exploring hypertext applications, by the author of the software called Storyspace.

Kelle, U. (Ed.). (1995). *Computer-aided qualitative data analysis*. London: Sage.

Contains an excellent series of papers, each dealing with an important aspect of the field. Especially useful are the chapters relating to theory building and hypothesis testing. Together, the chapters discuss a large number of programs.

Lee, R. M. (Ed.). (1995). *Information technology for the social scientist*. London: UCL Press.

An extremely useful collection of essays in the general area of information technology, applicable to a wider range of research approaches than qualitative methods alone.

Tesch, R. (1990). *Qualitative research: Analysis types and software tools*. London: Falmer.

In many ways an outstanding systematic and general introduction to computing strategies in the context of different analytic approaches. The specific software specifications are now rather dated.

Weaver, A., & Atkinson, P. (1994). *Microcomputing and qualitative data analysis*. Aldershot, UK: Avebury.

Differs from the main sourcebooks and edited collections in reporting results of using several complementary programs to analyze the same field data.

Weitzman, E. A., & Miles, M. B. (1995). *Computer programs for qualitative data analysis*. Thousand Oaks, CA: Sage.

A thorough review of a large number of programs, with systematic summaries and appraisals of their functions and uses. Includes practical information about program developers and distributors. The definitive sourcebook.

8

Coda

There is always a danger in writing books of this sort: Readers may readily assume a more prescriptive intent than actually motivated the authors. We do not have a strong prescriptive message about what methods—those we have discussed and others—should be used. We certainly do not wish to convey the message that researchers of the social world should use all the approaches we have discussed. The full range of qualitative methods is not merely a toolbox, from which methods of analysis can be picked up and put down at will. As we suggested in Chapter 1, it is important to recognize the variety of data types and the variety of appropriate analytic strategies that exist.

We have not advocated one particular type of analysis, one particular theory or way of writing. Principled choices of method reflect academic disciplines, theoretical perspectives, foreshadowed research problems, and individual intellectual styles. We would not wish to see all the possibilities of qualitative research being limited by the adoption of common paradigms. We are prescriptive, however, in another sense. We believe that there are some basic principles to be adhered to, whatever particular method is adopted. We summarize what we regard as the main prescriptive messages of this book in this short concluding section.

We started out in this book by remarking on and commending a variety of approaches. We try to resist the dominance of one or other orthodoxy. Different authors embrace different approaches to qualitative research. The intellectual style, the personal voice, and the research procedures of an author such as Wolcott (e.g., 1994) are very different from those of, say, Miles and Huberman (e.g., 1994). Denzin (e.g., 1989) is different again. A recognition of such diversity does not lessen the need to undertake research—in whatever style or tradition—in accordance with some general methodological precepts. Here, therefore, we indicate some general guidelines that have informed our discussions in the previous chapters.

Make Principled Choices. Nobody should adopt a particular approach toward research without making well-informed decisions and choices. It is certainly not good enough to fall in with one or another version of orthodoxy and follow it slavishly. There seem to be too many advocates of a paradigm mentality who believe that the qualitative researcher must buy into a particular approach and then stick with it obsessively. We do not think that such views are helpful, and they definitely are not necessary. There are many ways of approaching qualitative research, including a variety of strategies for data collection and analysis. We should be celebrating that variety and choice, not trying to stifle it. We want to exhort our students, our readers, and our colleagues to develop a well-informed and principled awareness of that methodological variety. We are conscious that "analysis" often is used to mean only one approach to handling qualitative data (though the precise approach that is celebrated or advocated differs from author to author). We want to assure our readers that there are plenty of ways to think about and to engage with one's data, whatever form the latter take.

Do the Research Methodically. Many of the precepts about methodology come down to the need to be methodical, so we are also prescriptive to the extent of insisting that qualitative data analysis needs to be conducted with rigor and care. Whatever approaches and strategies are tried and adopted, the analyst should always be reflexive and critical. Decisions and actions should be documented systematically and in detail. In the same way that there should be a constant dialogue between the researcher and the data, so should there be the internal dialogue of reflection on the part of the analyst (and dialogue of a more conventional sort within a research team). Analysis should not be viewed as something that is tagged on to data collection, given little time, attention, or critical reflection. Analytic strategies should be chosen in accordance with clear criteria for their relevance and executed with adequate time, care, and attention. Throughout the research process, analytic ideas and issues should be thought about, discussed, documented, and tested against the data.

Qualitative research is extremely hard work that demands a lot of the researcher. Not least is the requirement for comprehensive examinations of the data. Although we encourage speculation about the data, that does not give the researcher license to abandon criteria for rigor. In particular, the requirement to try ideas out through repeated interactions with the data means that those ideas must be tested rigorously with comprehensive examinations of the evidence. It is never enough to illustrate good ideas with supportive examples. The grounding of theory in empirical evidence requires comprehensive searching and systematic scrutiny.

Document Reflections and Decisions. We have suggested from time to time that we can understand the research process, metaphorically, as a series of dialogues: with the data, with ideas, with informants, with colleagues, and with oneself. All those interactions should lead to reflections and decisions. The qualitative research process unfolds and develops through those various transactions with and about the social world. At every stage of the process, those transactions and the ideas that emerge from them should be documented. The construction of analytic or methodological memoranda and working papers, and the consequent explication of working hypotheses, are of vital importance. It is important that the processes of exploration and abduction be documented and retrievable. Their documentation is part of the transformation of data from personal experience and intuition to public and accountable knowledge.

Use Data to Think With. Data are not inert. They are not a fixed corpus of materials on which procedures of analysis are performed. We should be using data to think with and think about. That means bringing to bear an active, creative approach. Although one should be careful not to build elaborate theoretical edifices on inadequate data or inadequate explorations of the data, one should be prepared to speculate about them. Ideas do not emerge from the data or from the imposition of analytic procedures, however helpful it may be to code the data or to map some of its formal features. No amount of routine analytic work will produce new theoretical insights without the application of disciplinary knowledge and creative imagination. Although one cannot legislate for all aspects of creative work, one can encourage success by having ideas early in the research process and being willing to explore them, modify them, and even abandon them in the light of further analysis.

Use Computer-Aided Software Appropriately. We have tried to show that computer-aided qualitative data analysis software can be used to support a variety of analytic and representational tasks. Among other things, it can help us to be systematic and rigorous in searching for and retrieving data. We believe, as has been shown by a number of authors, that the use of such software can enhance qualitative research. One must be aware, however, of the extent to which different programs inscribe particular versions of research and analysis. Investment in one software package should not be taken to imply total commitment to the accompanying methodological assumptions. The use of software should not be allowed to dictate all the ways in which a researcher interacts with his or her data. Software should always be subordinated to general analytic strategies and not allowed to dictate them.

Do Not Separate Analysis From Other Features of the Research Process. We have emphasized that although we have concentrated on analytic strategies in this book, that does not mean that they can be separated from all the other facets and phases of qualitative research. Analysis is not a separate set of tasks, and it is certainly not a self-contained phase of research. We see a clear danger in some contemporary treatments of methodology that qualitative analysis is being hived off from the overall strategy of research. We do not intend to conclude this book by conveying such an impression. On the contrary, analysis proceeds throughout the development of the qualitative research project. At a practical level, one should never allow the data to accumulate without analyzing them or without generating and applying ideas about appropriate analytic procedures. At a more general level, it is important to realize that the exploratory, developmental nature of much successful qualitative inquiry is entirely dependent on a constant interaction among research design, data collection, and data analysis.

Recognize the Importance of Representation. In the same way that data analysis is not a distinct aspect of the research process, neither are writing and representation. Variety makes imperative the conscious choice of methods and the choice of representations. There is no one way of writing about our research, and we should not adopt one style or another without adequate reflection. Because there is no neutral medium of written or visual representation, our writing is inescapably implicated in how we reconstruct the social worlds we have researched. Writing and representation cannot be divorced from analysis, therefore, and they should be thought of as analytic in their own right. We do not advocate experimentation for its own sake. We do seek to encourage the principled awareness of alternatives and their implications.

Do Not Confuse Research Methods With Theories or Disciplines. Although we are enthusiastic advocates and practitioners of qualitative research, we do not believe that it provides a surrogate academic discipline. We pursue research in the interests of developing disciplinary knowledge: sociological, anthropological, educational, geographical, and so on. The pursuit of qualitative research is not self-justifying, and we do not think that it is helpful to try to divorce it from the intellectual contexts that provide its rationale. It is important not to lose sight of those more general intellectual frameworks when undertaking research and analyzing data. They are means toward understanding and not ends in themselves.

In drawing out these simple precepts, we emphasize that we do not advocate a haphazard mishmash in bringing together different analytic strategies. Whatever methods of data collection, analysis, or writing one prefers, it is important that the research activity is performed in a rigorous and scholarly way. The types and forms of analysis may and should differ, but careful attention to detail, to scholarship, and to the rigorous execution of the research should always be paramount. Choice and experimentation are not synonymous with sloppy and poor-quality work. That is not to say that things will not go wrong or prove problematic: They probably will. Being reflexive about the research process and your place within it, however, will ensure that you add value to the scholarship and the research you pursue.

As should have been obvious, we are enthusiastic about the deployment of a range of qualitative approaches, but we do not advocate a sectarian spirit. We see no need to segregate qualitative methods into some exclusive and superior category of research, nor do we need to impose a spurious sense of internal coherence onto such a collection of methods. One may construct a series of family resemblances among particular methods and more general methodological assumptions. By and large, advocates of qualitative research subscribe to general perspectives on social life and its investigation: They tend to emphasize research issues of social action, meanings and their interpretation, processes of social interaction, and so on. In more formal terms, affinities are claimed with such theoretical and epistemological standpoints as phenomenology, symbolic interactionism, postmodernism, feminism. There are many differences among such perspectives, however, and it is wrong, in our view, to try to fit them all to one Procrustean bed of an undifferentiated interpretivist perspective, much less a qualitative paradigm.

Finally, therefore, in concluding this introduction to analytic strategies, we remain aware of the far greater variety of approaches that lie beyond the scope of this single volume. We have not explored the full range of approaches that are now characteristic of qualitative research in this "postmodern" moment. As Denzin and Lincoln (1994) remind us, contemporary research in this area is characterized by a multiplicity of voices and approaches. Now as never before, the student and practitioner of qualitative social research confronts an almost bewildering variety of epistemological and methodological perspectives. The consequences of such diversity include the urgent need for all researchers to exercise principled judgments and decisions in evaluating and using the strategies available. The contemporary popularity of qualitative research owes much to its flexibility and to the absence of methodological straitjackets. It would be a considerable threat to social research in general, however, were that popularity to flourish in an undisciplined, anything-goes atmosphere.

References

Acker, S. (1994). *Gendered education.* Buckingham, UK: Open University Press.

Atkinson, P. (1985). *Language, structure and reproduction: An introduction to the sociology of Basil Bernstein.* London: Methuen.

Atkinson, P. (1990). *The ethnographic imagination: Textual constructions of reality.* London: Routledge and Kegan Paul.

Atkinson, P. (1992a). The ethnography of a medical setting: Reading, writing and rhetoric. *Qualitative Health Research, 2*(4), 451-474.

Atkinson, P. (1992b). *Understanding ethnographic texts.* Newbury Park, CA: Sage.

Atkinson, P. (1995). Some perils of paradigms. *Qualitative Health Research, 5*(1), 117-124.

Ball, M. S., & Smith, G. W. H. (1992). *Analyzing visual data.* Newbury Park, CA: Sage.

Barley, N. (1986). *The innocent anthropologist: Notes from a mud hut.* Harmondsworth, UK: Penguin.

Barley, N. (1987). *A plague of caterpillars: A return to the African bush.* Harmondsworth, UK: Penguin.

Batchelor, C., Parsons, E., & Atkinson, P. (in press). The career of a medical discovery claim. *Qualitative Health Research.*

Bauman, R. (1986). *Story, performance and event: Contextual studies of oral narrative.* Cambridge, UK: Cambridge University Press.

Becker, H. S. (1967). Whose side are we on? *Social Problems, 14,* 239-248.

Becker, H. S. (Ed.). (1981). *Exploring society photographically.* Chicago: University of Chicago Press.

Becker, H. S. (1983). *Doing things together.* Evanston, IL: Northwestern University Press.

Bernstein, B. (1977). *Class, codes and control 3: Towards a theory of educational transmissions.* London: Routledge and Kegan Paul.

Bernstein, B. (1990). *Class, codes and control 4: The structuring of pedagogic discourse.* London: Routledge and Kegan Paul.

Bluebond-Langer, M. (1980). *The private worlds of dying children.* Princeton, NJ: Princeton University Press.

Blumer, H. (1954). What is wrong with social theory? *American Sociological Review, 19,* 3-10.

Bogdan, R., & Taylor, S. J. (1975). *Introduction to qualitative research methods.* New York: John Wiley.

Boon, J. A. (1983). Functionalists write too: Frazer, Malinowski and the semiotics of the monograph. *Semiotica, 46,* 131-149.

Bourdieu, P. (1988). *Homo academicus.* Cambridge, MA: Polity/Basil Blackwell.

Bowen, E. (1954). *Return to laughter.* London: Gollancz.

Burgess, R. G. (Ed.). (1982). *Field research: A source book and field manual.* London: Allen and Unwin.

Burgess, R. G. (1984). *In the field: An introduction to field research.* London: Allen and Unwin.

Burgess, R. G. (Ed.). (1994). *Postgraduate education and training in the social sciences: Processes and products.* London: Jessica Kingsley.

Casey, K. (1993). *I answer with my life: Life histories of women working for social change.* New York: Routledge and Kegan Paul.

Charmaz, K. (1983). The grounded theory method: An explication and interpretation. In R. Emerson (Ed.), *Contemporary field research* (pp. 109-126). Boston: Little, Brown.

Clifford, J., & Marcus, G. E. (Eds.). (1986). *Writing culture: The poetics and politics of ethnography.* Berkeley: University of California Press.

Clough, P. T. (1992). *The end(s) of ethnography: From realism to social criticism.* Newbury Park, CA: Sage.

Collier, J., Jr., & Collier, M. (1986). *Visual anthropology: Photography as a research method.* Albuquerque: University of New Mexico Press.

Corsaro, W., & Heise, D. (1990). Event structure models from ethnographic data. In C. Clifford (Ed.), *Sociological methodology* (pp. 1-57). Washington, DC: ASA.

Cortazzi, M. (1991). *Primary teaching, how it is—A narrative account.* London: David Fulton.

Cortazzi, M. (1993). *Narrative analysis.* London: Falmer.

Crocker, J. C. (1977). The social functions of rhetorical forms. In J. D. Sapir & J. C. Crocker (Eds.), *The social use of metaphor: Essays on the anthropology of rhetoric* (pp. 33-66). Philadelphia: University of Pennsylvania Press.

Davis, F. (1974). Stories and sociology. *Urban Life and Culture, 3,* 310-316.

Davis, W. (1986). *The serpent and the rainbow.* London: Collins.

Delamont, S. (1989). The nun in the toilet: Urban legends and educational research. *International Journal of Qualitative Studies in Education, 2*(3), 191-202.

Delamont, S. (1990). *Sex roles and the school* (2nd ed). London: Routledge and Kegan Paul.

Delamont, S. (1992). *Fieldwork in educational settings: Methods, pitfalls and perspectives.* London: Falmer.

Delamont, S., & Atkinson, P. (1995). *Fighting familiarity: Essays on education and ethnography.* Cresskill, NJ: Hampton.

Delany, P., & Landow, G. P. (Eds.). (1994). *Hypermedia and literary studies.* Cambridge: MIT Press.

DeNora, T. (1995). *Beethoven: The social construction of genius.* Berkeley: University of California Press.

Denzin, N. K. (1987). On semiotics and symbolic interactionism. *Symbolic Interaction,* *10*(1), 1-19.

Denzin, N. K. (1989). *Interpretive interactionism.* Newbury Park, CA: Sage.

Denzin, N. K. (1992). *Symbolic interactionism and cultural studies.* Oxford, UK: Blackwell.

Denzin, N. K. (1994). The art and politics of interpretation. In N. K. Denzin & Y. S. Lincoln (Eds.), *Handbook of qualitative research* (pp. 500-515). Thousand Oaks, CA: Sage.

Denzin, N. K., & Lincoln, Y. S. (Eds.). (1994). *Handbook of qualitative research.* Thousand Oaks, CA: Sage.

Dey, I. (1993). *Qualitative data analysis: A user friendly guide for social scientists.* London: Routledge and Kegan Paul.

Dey, I. (1995). Reducing fragmentation in qualitative research. In U. Kelle (Ed.), *Computer-aided qualitative data analysis: Theory, methods and practice* (pp. 69-79). London: Sage.

Dingwall, R. (1977). Atrocity stories and professional relationships. *Sociology of Work and Occupations, 4,* 371-396.

Donner, F. (1982). *Shabono.* London: Paladin.

Duneier, M. (1992). *Slim's table: Race, responsibility and masculinity.* Chicago: University of Chicago Press.

Edmondson, R. (1984). *Rhetoric in sociology.* London: Macmillan.

Ellis, C., & Bochner, A. P. (1992). Telling and performing personal stories: The constraints of choice in abortion. In C. Ellis & M. G. Flaherty (Eds.), *Investigating subjectivity: Research on lived experience* (pp. 79-101). Newbury Park, CA: Sage.

Emihovich, C. (1995). Distancing passion: Narratives in social science. *International Journal of Qualitative Studies in Education, 8,* 37-48.

Evans-Pritchard, E. (1940). *The Nuer.* Oxford, UK: Clarendon.

Evetts, J. (Ed.). (1994). *Women and career: Themes and issues in advanced industrial societies.* London: Longman.

Feldman, M. S. (1994). *Strategies for interpreting qualitative data.* Thousand Oaks, CA: Sage.

Fernandez, J. W. (Ed.). (1991). *Beyond metaphor: The theory of tropes in anthropology.* Stanford, CA: Stanford University Press.

Fielding, N. G., & Fielding, J. L. (1986). *Linking data.* Beverly Hills, CA: Sage.

Fielding, N. G., & Lee, R. M. (Eds.). (1991). *Using computers in qualitative research.* London: Sage.

Fisher, M. (1995). Desktop tools for the social scientist. In R. M. Lee (Ed.), *Information technology for the social scientist* (pp. 14-32). London: UCL Press.

Fleck, L. (1979). *Genesis and development of a scientific fact.* Chicago: University of Chicago Press. (Originally published 1935)

Geertz, C. (1973). *The interpretation of cultures: Selected essays.* New York: Basic Books.

Geertz, C. (1983). *Local knowledge: Further essays in interpretive anthropology.* New York: Basic Books.

Gilbert, G. N., & Mulkay, M. (1980). *Opening Pandora's box: A sociological analysis of scientists' discourse.* Cambridge, UK: Cambridge University Press.

Glaser, B. G. (1978). *Theoretical sensitivity.* Mill Valley, CA: Sociology Press.

Glaser, B. G. (1992). *Emergence vs. forcing: Basics of grounded theory analysis.* Mill Valley, CA: Sociology Press.

Glaser, B. G., & Strauss, A. L. (1967). *The discovery of grounded theory: Strategies for qualitative research.* Chicago: Aldine.

Goetz, J. P., & LeCompte, M. D. (1984). *Ethnography and qualitative design in educational research.* New York: Academic Press.

Goffman, E. (1961). *Asylums.* Harmondsworth, UK: Penguin.

Goodson, I. (1992). *Studying teachers' lives.* London: Routledge and Kegan Paul.

Goodson, I. (1995). The story so far: Personal knowledge and the political. *International Journal of Qualitative Studies in Education, 8,* 89-98.

Guba, E. G., & Lincoln, Y. S. (1981). *Effective evaluation.* San Francisco, CA: Jossey-Bass.

Guba, E. G., & Lincoln, Y. S. (1994). Competing paradigms in qualitative research. In N. K. Denzin & Y. S. Lincoln (Eds.), *Handbook of qualitative research* (pp. 105-117). Thousand Oaks, CA: Sage.

Gubrium, J. (1988). *Analyzing field reality.* Newbury Park, CA: Sage.

Hammersley, M. (1989). *The dilemma of qualitative method: Herbert Blumer and the Chicago tradition.* London: Routledge and Kegan Paul.

Hammersley, M. (1991). *Reading ethnographic research: A critical guide.* London: Longmans.

Hammersley, M., & Atkinson, P. (1983). *Ethnography: Principles in practice.* London: Tavistock.

Hammersley, M., & Atkinson, P. (1995). *Ethnography: Principles in practice* (2nd ed.). London: Routledge.

Hargreaves, A. (1981). Contrastive rhetoric and extremist talk: Teachers, hegemony and the educationist context. In L. Barton & S. Walker (Eds.), *Schools, teachers and teaching* (pp. 303-329). Lewes, UK: Falmer.

Hargreaves, A. (1984). Contrastive rhetoric and extremist talk. In A. Hargreaves & P. Woods (Eds.), *Classrooms and staffrooms: The sociology of teachers and teaching* (pp. 215-231). Milton Keynes, UK: Open University Press.

Heise, D. (1988). Computer analysis of cultural structures. *Social Science Computer Review, 6,* 183-196.

Hesse-Biber, S., & Dupuis, P. (1995). Hypothesis testing in computer-aided qualitative data analysis. In U. Kelle (Ed.), *Computer-aided qualitative data analysis: Theory, methods and practice* (pp. 129-135). London: Sage.

Heyl, B. (1979). *The madam as entrepreneur: Career management in house prostitution.* New Brunswick, NJ: Transaction Books.

Hill, M. R. (1993). *Archival strategies and techniques.* Newbury Park, CA: Sage.

Huberman, A. M., & Miles, M. B. (1994). Data management and analysis methods. In N. K. Denzin & Y. S. Lincoln (Eds.), *Handbook of qualitative research* (pp. 428-444). Thousand Oaks, CA: Sage.

Iser, W. (1978). *The act of reading.* London: Routledge and Kegan Paul.

Joyce, M. (1995). *Of two minds: Hypertext, pedagogy and poetics.* Ann Arbor: University of Michigan Press.

Kelle, U. (Ed.). (1995a). *Computer-aided qualitative data analysis: Theory, methods and practice.* London: Sage.

Kelle, U. (1995b). Theories as heuristic tools in qualitative research. In I. Maso, P. Atkinson, S. Delamont, & J. C. Verhoeven (Eds.), *Openness in research: The tension between self and other* (pp. 33-50). Assen, The Netherlands: Van Gorcum.

Kelle, U., Sibert, E., Shelly, A., Hesse-Biber, S., & Huber, G. (1995). Hypothesis examination in qualitative research. In U. Kelle (Ed.), *Computer-aided qualitative data analysis: Theory, methods and practice* (pp. 105-112). London: Sage.

Kleinman, A. (1988). *The illness narrative: Suffering, healing and the human condition.* New York: Basic Books.

Krieger, S. (1979). Research and the construction of a text. In N. K. Denzin (Ed.), *Studies in symbolic interaction 2* (pp. 167-187). Greenwich, CT: JAI.

Krieger, S. (1983). *The mirror dance: Identity in a women's community.* Philadelphia: Temple University Press.

Krieger, S. (1984). Fiction and social science. In N. K. Denzin (Ed.), *Studies in symbolic interaction 5* (pp. 269-286). Greenwich, CT: JAI.

Krippendorf, K. (1980). *Content analysis: An introduction to its methodology.* Beverly Hills, CA: Sage.

Labov, W. (Ed.). (1972). *Language in the inner city.* Philadelphia: University of Pennsylvania Press.

Labov, W. (1982). Speech actions and reactions in personal narratives. In D. Tannen (Ed.), *Analyzing discourse: Text and talk* (pp. 219-247). Washington, DC: Georgetown University Press.

Lakoff, G., & Johnson, M. (1980). *Metaphors we live by.* Chicago: University of Chicago Press.

Lather, P. (1991). *Getting smart: Feminist research and pedagogy with/in the postmodern.* New York: Routledge and Kegan Paul.

Lave, J., & Wenger, E. (1991). *Situated learning: Legitimate peripheral participation.* Cambridge, UK: Cambridge University Press.

LeCompte, M. D., & Preissle, J., with Tesch, R. (1993). *Ethnography and qualitative design in educational research* (2nd ed.). New York: Academic Press.

Lee, R. M. (Ed.). (1995). *Information technology for the social scientist.* London: UCL Press.

Lodge, D. (1977). *The modes of modern writing.* London: Edward Arnold.

Lofland, J., & Lofland, L. H. (1984). *Analyzing social settings* (2nd ed.). Belmont, CA: Wadsworth.

Lonkila, M. (1995). Grounded theory as an emerging paradigm for computer-assisted qualitative data analysis. In U. Kelle (Ed.), *Computer-aided qualitative data analysis: Theory, methods and practice* (pp. 41-51). London: Sage.

Lutz, C. A., & Collins, J. L. (1993). *Reading National Geographic.* Chicago: University of Chicago Press.

Lyman, S. M., & Scott, M. B. (1970). *A sociology of the absurd.* New York: Appleton-Century-Crofts.

Lynch, M., & Edgerton, S. Y. (1988). Aesthetics and digital image processing: Representational craft in contemporary astronomy. In G. Fyfe & J. Law (Eds.), *Picturing power: Visual depiction and social relations* (pp. 184-220). London: Routledge and Kegan Paul.

Mangabeira, W. (1995). Computer assistance, qualitative analysis and model building. In R. M. Lee (Ed.), *Information technology for the social scientist* (pp. 129-146). London: UCL Press.

Manning, P. K. (1987). *Semiotics and fieldwork.* Newbury Park, CA: Sage.

Manning, P. K., & Cullum-Swan, B. (1994). Narrative, content and semiotic analysis. In N. K. Denzin & Y. S. Lincoln (Eds.), *Handbook of qualitative research* (pp. 463-479). Thousand Oaks, CA: Sage.

Marton, F. (1986). Phenomenology—A research approach to investigating different understandings of reality. *Journal of Thought, 21*(3), 28-48.

Mascia-Lees, F. E., Sharpe, P., & Cohen, C. B. (1989). The postmodernist turn in anthropology: Cautions from a feminist perspective. *Signs, 15,* 7-33.

Measor, L., & Woods, P. (1984). *Changing schools.* Milton Keynes, UK: Open University Press.

Mienczakowski, J. E. (1994). Reading and writing research: Ethnographic theatre. *National Association for Drama in Education (Australia), 18,* 45-54.

Mienczakowski, J. E. (1995). The theatre of ethnography: The reconstruction of ethnography into theatre with emancipatory potential. *Qualitative Inquiry, 1,* 360-375.

Mienczakowski, J. E., Morgan, S., & Rolfe, A. (1993). Ethnography or drama? *National Association for Drama in Education (Australia), 17,* 8-15.

Miles, M. B., & Huberman, A. M. (1994). *Qualitative data analysis: An expanded sourcebook* (2nd ed.). Thousand Oaks, CA: Sage.

Miller, W. L., & Crabtree, B. F. (1994). Clinical research. In N. K. Denzin & Y. S. Lincoln (Eds.), *Handbook of qualitative research* (pp. 340-352). Thousand Oaks, CA: Sage.

Mills, C. W. (1940). Situated actions and vocabularies of motive. *American Sociological Review, 5*(6), 439-452.

Mishler, E. G. (1986). *Research interviewing: Context and narrative.* Cambridge, MA: Harvard University Press.

Mulkay, M. J. (1985). *The word and the world: Explorations in the form of sociological analysis.* London: George Allen and Unwin.

Myerhoff, B. (1978). *Number our days.* New York: Simon and Schuster.

Noblit, G. W., & Hare, R. D. (1988). *Meta-ethnography: Synthesizing qualitative studies.* Newbury Park, CA: Sage.

Olesen, V. (1994). Feminisms and models of qualitative research. In N. K. Denzin & Y. S. Lincoln (Eds.), *Handbook of qualitative research* (pp. 158-174). Thousand Oaks, CA: Sage.

Paget, M. (1990). Performing the text. *Journal of Contemporary Ethnography, 19,* 136-155.

Parry, O., Atkinson, P., & Delamont, S. (1994). Disciplinary identities and doctoral work. In R. G. Burgess (Ed.), *Postgraduate education and training in the social sciences* (pp. 34-52). London: Jessica Kingsley.

Passerini, L. (1987). *Fascism in popular memory: The cultural experience of the Turin working class.* Cambridge, UK: Cambridge University Press.

Peirce, C. S. (1979). *Collected papers.* Cambridge, MA: Belknap.

Pfohl, S. (1992). *Death at the Parasite Cafe: Social science (fictions) and the postmodern.* London: Macmillan.

Plummer, K. (1983). *Documents of life: An introduction to the literature of a humanistic method.* London: Allen and Unwin.

Plummer, K. (1995). *Telling sexual stories: Power, change and social worlds.* London: Routledge and Kegan Paul.

Polkinghorne, D. E. (1988). *Narrative knowing and the human sciences.* Albany: State University of New York Press.

Potter, J., & Wetherell, M. (1987). *Discourse and social psychology.* London: Sage.

Preston, R. J. (1978). *Cree narrative: Expressing the personal meanings of events.* Ottawa: Canadian Ethnology Service.

Propp, V. (1968). *The morphology of the folktale* (2nd rev. ed.). Austin: University of Texas Press.

Psathas, G. (1994). *Conversation analysis.* Thousand Oaks, CA: Sage.

Richards, T. J., & Richards, L. (1990). *NUD.IST 2.3 reference manual.* Melbourne: Replee/PL.

Richards, T. J., & Richards, L. (1994). Using computers in qualitative research. In N. K. Denzin & Y. S. Lincoln (Eds.), *Handbook of qualitative research* (pp. 445-462). Thousand Oaks, CA: Sage.

Richardson, L. (1990). *Writing strategies: Reaching diverse audiences.* Newbury Park, CA: Sage.

Richardson, L. (1992). The consequences of poetic representation: Writing the other, writing the self. In C. Ellis & M. G. Flaherty (Eds.), *Investigating subjectivity: Research on lived experience* (pp. 125-137). Newbury Park, CA: Sage.

Richardson, L. (1994). Writing: A method of inquiry. In N. K. Denzin & Y. S. Lincoln (Eds.), *Handbook of qualitative research* (pp. 516-529). Thousand Oaks, CA: Sage.

Richardson, L., & Lockridge, E. (1991). The sea monster: An "ethnographic drama." *Symbolic Interaction, 13,* 77-83.

Riessman, C. K. (1990). *Divorce talk: Women and men make sense of personal relationships.* New Brunswick, NJ: Rutgers University Press.

Riessman, C. K. (1993). *Narrative analysis.* Newbury Park, CA: Sage.

Sapir, J. D. (1977). The anatomy of metaphor. In J. D. Sapir & J. C. Crocker (Eds.), *The social use of metaphor: Essays on the anthropology of rhetoric* (pp. 3-32). Philadelphia: University of Pennsylvania Press.

Schön, D. A. (1983). *The reflective practitioner: How professionals think and act.* New York: Basic Books.

Seidel, J., & Kelle, U. (1995). Different functions of coding in the analysis of textual data. In U. Kelle (Ed.), *Computer-aided qualitative data analysis: Theory, methods and practice* (pp. 52-61). London: Sage.

Sharrock, W. W., & Anderson, D. (1979). Directional hospital signs as sociological data. *Information Design Journal, 1*(2), 81-94.

Sibert, E., & Shelly, A. (1995). Using logic programming for hypothesis generation and refinement. In U. Kelle (Ed.), *Computer-aided qualitative data analysis: Theory, methods and practice* (pp. 113-128). London: Sage.

Silverman, D. (1993). *Interpreting qualitative data: Methods for analysing talk, text and interaction.* London: Sage.

Sparkes, A. C. (1994). Self, silence and invisibility as a beginning teacher: A life history of lesbian experience. *British Journal of Sociology of Education, 15*(1), 93-118.

Sparkes, A. C. (1995). Writing people: Reflections on the dual crises of representation and legitimation in qualitative inquiry. *Quest, 47,* 158-195.

Spradley, J. P. (1970). *You owe yourself a drunk: An ethnography of urban nomads.* Boston: Little, Brown.

Spradley, J. P. (1979). *The ethnographic interview.* New York: Holt, Rinehart and Winston.

Spradley, J. P. (1980). *Participant observation.* New York: Holt, Rinehart and Winston.

Stanley, L., & Temple, B. (1996). Doing the business: Using qualitative software packages in the analysis of qualitative datasets. In R. G. Burgess (Ed.), *Using computers in qualitative research* (pp. 169-193). Greenwich, CT: JAI.

Stanley, L., & Wise, S. (1993). *Breaking out again: Feminist ontology and epistemology.* London: Routledge and Kegan Paul.

Strauss, A. L. (1987). *Qualitative analysis for social scientists.* Cambridge, UK: Cambridge University Press.

Strauss, A. L. (1995). Notes on the nature and development of general theories. *Qualitative Inquiry, 1*(1), 7-18.

Strauss, A. L., & Corbin, J. (1990). *Basics of qualitative research: Grounded theory, procedures and techniques.* Newbury Park, CA: Sage.

Strauss, A. L., & Corbin, J. (1994). Grounded theory methodology: An overview. In N. K. Denzin & Y. S. Lincoln (Eds.), *Handbook of qualitative research* (pp. 273-285). Thousand Oaks, CA: Sage.

Sykes, G. M., & Matza, D. (1957). Techniques of neutralization. *American Sociological Review, 22,* 667-669.

Tesch, R. (1990). *Qualitative research: Analysis types and software tools.* London: Falmer.

Thomas, J. (1993). *Doing critical ethnography.* Newbury Park, CA: Sage.

Tierney, W. (1993). The cedar closet. *International Journal of Qualitative Studies in Education, 6,* 303-314.

Toelken, J. B. (1969). The "pretty language" of Yellowman: Genre, mode and texture in Navajo Coyote narratives. *Genre, 2,* 211-235.

Toelken, J. B. (1975). Folklore, world view and communication. In D. Ben-Amos & K. S. Goldstein (Eds.), *Folklore, performance and communication* (pp. 265-286). The Hague: Mouton.

Traweek, S. (1988). *Beamtimes and lifetimes: The world of high energy physicists.* Cambridge, MA: Harvard University Press.

van Maanen, J. (1988). *Tales of the field.* Chicago: University of Chicago Press.

van Manen, M. (1990). *Researching the lived experience.* London: University of Western Ontario Press.

Voysey, M. (1975). *A constant burden.* London: Routledge and Kegan Paul.

Weaver, A., & Atkinson, P. (1994). *Microcomputing and qualitative data analysis.* Aldershot, UK: Avebury.

Weaver, A., & Atkinson, P. (1996). From coding to hypertext. In R. G. Burgess (Ed.), *Using computers in qualitative research* (pp. 141-168). Greenwich, CT: JAI.

Weitzman, E. A., & Miles, M. B. (1995). *Computer programs for qualitative data analysis.* Thousand Oaks, CA: Sage.

Werner, O., & Schoepfle, G. M. (1987). *Systematic fieldwork: Foundations of ethnography and interviewing.* Newbury Park, CA: Sage.

Wetherell, M., & Potter, J. (1989). Narrative characters and accounting for evidence. In J. Shotter & K. Gergen (Eds.), *Texts of identity* (pp. 206-219). London: Sage.

Witkin, R. (1995). *Art and social structure.* Oxford, UK: Polity.

Wolcott, H. (1990). *Writing up qualitative research.* Newbury Park, CA: Sage.

Wolcott, H. (1994). *Transforming qualitative data: Description, analysis, and interpretation.* Thousand Oaks, CA: Sage.

Wolf, M. (1992). *A thrice told tale: Feminism, postmodernism and ethnographic responsibility.* Stanford, CA: Stanford University Press.

Index

About the Authors

Amanda Coffey is Lecturer in Sociology in the School of Social and Administrative Studies, University of Wales, Cardiff. She took a BA in Social Policy from Exeter, an MSc in Gender and Social Policy from Bristol, and a PhD from Cardiff. Her doctoral research was an ethnography of the occupational socialization of graduate accountants that has been published in articles in *Sociology, Qualitative Studies in Education,* and elsewhere. With Paul Atkinson, she edited *Occupational Socialization and Working Lives* (1994). Her forthcoming publications include *Teachers and Their Teaching: Feminist Analyses of Teachers,* and *Teaching and the Teaching Profession* (with Sara Delamont). Her research interests include gender and teacher education, the sociology of expert knowledge, and qualitative methodology.

Paul Atkinson is Professor of Sociology in the School of Social and Administrative Studies, University of Wales, Cardiff. He took his BA in Social Anthropology from Cambridge and his PhD from Edinburgh. His books include *The Clinical Experience* (1981), *Ethnography: Principles in Practice* (with Martyn Hammersley, second edition, 1995), *Language, Structure and Reproduction* (1985), *The Ethnographic Imagination* (1990), *Understanding Ethnographic Texts* (1992), *Microcomputing and Qualitative Data Analysis* (with Anna Weaver, 1994), *Fighting Familiarity* (with Sara Delamont, 1995), and *Medical Talk and Medical Work* (1995).